Barbara Crossette

SO CLOSE TO HEAVEN

Barbara Crossette, who joined *The New York Times* in 1973, spent seven years as a correspondent in Asia, and is now UN bureau chief. She was a Fulbright Professor of Journalism in India and has taught at the Columbia University Graduate School of Journalism and at Princeton University. She won the 1991 George Polk Award for foreign reporting. She lives in New York City and Upper Black Eddy, Pennsylvania.

Books by BARBARA CROSSETTE

India Facing the Twentieth Century

So Close to Heaven

SO CLOSE TO HEAVEN

SO CLOSE TO HEAVEN

The Vanishing Buddhist
Kingdoms of the Himalayas

BARBARA

CROSSETTE

VINTAGE DEPARTURES
Vintage Books
A Division of Random House, Inc.
New York

Grateful acknowledgment is made to the following for permission
to reprint previously published material:
Kingdom of Bhutan Mission to the United Nations: "A Message for My
Parents Far Away" by Kuenga Wangmo from *Tongsa Junior High School
Magazine.* Reprinted by permission of Ugyen Tshering, Permanent
Representative of the Kingdom of Bhutan to the United Nations.
Oxford University Press: Hymn excerpts from *Tibet's Great Yogi Milarepa,*
edited by W. Y. Evans-Wentz (1928). Reprinted by permission of Oxford
University Press, Oxford, England.

The Library of Congress has cataloged the Knopf edition as follows:
Crossette, Barbara.
So close to heaven: the vanishing Buddhist kingdoms of the Himalayas /
Barbara Crossette.—1st ed.
p. cm.
Includes bibliographical references and index.
ISBN 0-679-48127-X
1. Buddhism—Himalaya Mountains Region. 2. Buddhism—Bhutan.
I. Title
BQ400.H542C76 1995
294.3'095496—dc20 94-38193 CIP
Vintage ISBN: 0-679-74363-4

Random House Web address: http://www.randomhouse.com/

Author photograph © Marianna Cook
Designed by Anthea Lingeman

Printed in the United States of America
10 9 8 7 6 5 4 3 2 1

TO ALL HIMALAYAN BUDDHISTS WHO
FEAR THE EXTINCTION OF THEIR CULTURE
MORE THAN DEATH

CONTENTS

PREFACE

IN THE MONASTERY courtyard, a red-robed monk was dancing. His movements were studied, trancelike. He dipped and turned, balancing on one foot and then on the other. His open arms moved in slow motion as his hands traced studied patterns in the air. He was barefoot; it was winter. He seemed oblivious to everything the senses might register except perhaps for the rhythmic *skishhhh, skishhhh, skishhhh* of the small cymbals played by a fellow monk a few yards away under the cloistered porch. Oblique rays of a golden afternoon sun threw a celestial spotlight into the corner where these holy men toiled at perfecting their performance of a classical Bhutanese Buddhist temple dance. They were preparing for the Tshechu, the most important festival of the year for a Bhutanese monastery and for all who live or roam within striking distance of its walls. I stopped for a few minutes, unnoticed, to watch from a window above them, across the small courtyard enclosed by galleries where novices chanted, judges pored over codes of royal and religious law, and robed administrators of sword-bearing rank held court in the name of king and country. Centuries blurred.

Nothing in the tableau at Tashigang Dzong, a monastery-fortress near the eastern edge of Bhutan, would have been out of place in ancient times, when an esoteric form of Buddhism took root and grew into a family of Buddhist realms scattered across the Himalayas and into Central Asia. Bhutan, until very recently one of the world's least accessible nations, is also the last of these independent Buddhist kingdoms. Thus this Tashigang monk and his ethereal dance were especially absorbing, because he was not merely a performer in a temple ritual but also an unself-conscious practitioner of an ancient Buddhist art that is part of a culture under intense pressures from within and without. Himalayan Buddhism as a civilization (more than a religion) is endangered where its roots are deepest, in its native mountains and stark plateaus, where heaven seems so near.

The story of how Buddhism in its most arcane Tantric form came to entrench itself across a landscape of frozen peaks, high windy flatlands, and deep verdant valleys may vary from one local mythology to another. But what has become of this shared mystical universe is no mystery; the evidence is laid out in modern Asian political history. One by one, all the Himalayan Buddhist kingdoms except Bhutan have been gobbled up by bigger powers, just as earlier Buddhist civilizations from Afghanistan to Mongolia were overrun or undermined. The most recent kingdom to disappear was Sikkim, in 1975. Tibet, the Himalayan Tantrics' spiritual and literary heartland, fell under the heel of the Chinese army in the 1950s; during the Cultural Revolution the monasteries, focal points of Himalayan Buddhism and repositories of its books and records, were sacked. Since then, the Han Chinese have concentrated on changing Tibet's ethnic composition and coopting its religious leadership.

The Tantric schools—what most Westerners call Tibetan Buddhism—can be considered collectively as the third and most vigorous form of a religion that began more than 2,500 years ago in northern India. The Hinayana, or Theravada, school was the earliest; it is now the dominant form of Buddhism in Southeast Asia, Burma, and Sri Lanka. The Mahayana school followed; it would take root in China, Vietnam, and East Asia. Tantrayana, replete with secret and often sexual rites, emerged from the Mahayana school and was embraced across mountainous inner Asia from the Hindu Kush to the Himalayas. With an intensity and drama that were a match for its environment, Tantric Buddhism offered adherents a shortcut to Nirvana.

"The Hinayana should be taken as knowledge. The Mahayana should be taken as attitude. Tantra means practice. Tantrayana is the quickest way to become Buddha—like a rocket going to the moon," said Dasho Rigzin Dorji, who as head of a unique Bhutanese civic treasure, the Special Commission on Cultural Affairs, was the man in charge of safeguarding the Bhutanese way of life in the face of encroachments from the outside world and tendencies toward cultural carelessness at home.

Tantric Buddhism, sharing physical and psychic space with a pantheon of local deities and countless temperamental spirits, rose to its highest philosophical and artistic levels on the trans-Himalayan Tibetan plateau, where it had settled firmly by the eighth century, building on or supplanting earlier Buddhist teachings from both China and the Indian subcontinent. Over the years, the great monasteries of Tibet, set in the geographical watershed from which flow some of Asia's mightiest rivers—the Indus, Brahmaputra, Salween, and Mekong—became fonts of Buddhist scholarship. The teachings and miracles of great lamas were known and studied in Ladakh, Mustang, Sikkim, Bhutan, and smaller pockets throughout the region where Tibetan monks also traveled. Worldwide, the central relationship of the teacher-lama and his student-adept came to define the Tibetan-Tantric Buddhist tradition.

The Tibetan plateau was once truly a place close to heaven. Legend says that until a careless king cut down a miraculous rope, there was a stairway to the immortals somewhere on this moonscape terrain. In Tibet and all along the Himalayas, the mountains whose name means "abode of the gods," there are peaks still regarded as sacred, Kailash, Khumbila, Sagarmatha, Kanchenjunga, and Jhomolhari among them. In their shadows, spirituality survives, even in poverty and dislocation.

The Himalayan and Central Asian Buddhist universe was probably better known to ancient travelers and chroniclers than its history or its surviving cultures are to us today. These lands were part of an inner Asian world of no special interest to maritime powers during the age of European exploration, from which we drew much of our early knowledge of the East as schoolchildren, Marco Polo notwithstanding. Yet long before the explorers of our Western history books embarked boldly or even foolishly on their long ocean voyages to India, China, and the South Seas to build commercial empires or find "new" lands, vibrant sophisticated societies were thriving in inner Asia's vast expanses, far away from the sea lanes. From the edge of ancient Persia and the Turkic world to the portals of China, from the Pamirs to the Hindu Kush and the Himalayas, Central Asia was for centuries before the Prophet Mohammed's birth, and for some time after, a world influenced by Buddhism. For a few hundred years, in the seventh and eighth centuries, a

Tibetan empire strong enough to box in the Tang dynasty of China on its western flank flourished in the landlocked heart of Asia. Tibetan armies advanced and retreated from bases on the Tibetan plateau; Himalayan monks and soldiers traded influences with Buddhists of other schools, reinforcing a cosmopolitan culture.

From the vantage point of our era, Tibet may appear to be a sad civilization long stripped of the glories it enjoyed and the power it wielded more than a thousand years ago. Tens of thousands of its most devout people are scattered in a diaspora, and its god-king Tenzin Gyatso, the fourteenth Dalai Lama, struggles in exile to keep alive the Tibetan spirit, knowing he has scant material hope to offer younger hotbloods who want guerrilla war. We who encounter Tibet at the end of the twentieth century thus marvel at even what little we can discover of its glorious medieval history. In general, the lands where Himalayan Buddhism survived longest, in and around Tibet, are territories where much historical material is still undiscovered or inaccessible, and there has been very little modern archaeological and archival research. When extant, ancient documents are often laced with myth and magic. We are asked to believe marvelous, fantastic stories because the people whose history these tales tell believe them, and that makes them real enough. A traveler through Himalayan Buddhism often must put aside rational argument while traversing lands where spirits and the reincarnates of real and mythological heroes have never stopped sharing the topography with human life, with both comic and tragic results. In these thrilling histories, lamas fly or conjure up hailstorms and saints may have half a dozen or more manifestations, beneficent or belligerent, depending on the need of the moment. What unadulterated pleasure the unscholarly can take here in the knowledge that even academic experts cannot always agree on what constitutes historical fact, much less interpretation. So why not believe that certain monks could levitate a foot above the ground while circumambulating a stupa?

The flow of life and commerce that linked the Himalayan world to Central Asia was disrupted by Islam's relentless march and by the imperial urges of Britain, China, Russia, and, for the brief moment history assigned it, the Soviet Union. For long years, pilgrimage and trade routes withered, monasteries were destroyed or abandoned. However, the future of inner Asia is suddenly full of possibility again. Artificial borders and barriers established by great powers are crumbling, new nations have emerged from the collapse of the Soviet system, and at least some of inner Asia's severed cultural and economic arteries may be rejoined, if ethnic peace prevails. Whether there is a future for Buddhism there is another matter.

If Himalayan Buddhism, reduced to one surviving independent monarchy, seems threatened by demographic and other pressures at home, it is not without hope worldwide. Interest in Tibetan Buddhism is growing in Europe, North America, and Asian nations farther to the east: in Thailand, among ethnic Chinese Malaysians, in Singapore, South Korea, Taiwan, and Japan. This attention is beginning to translate into support, psychological as well as financial, for a renewal of Buddhist studies in the Himalayas, especially in Nepal, a Hindu kingdom with a Buddhist heart. In unexpected places, monasteries and individual lamas are receiving generous (some monks would say corrupting) gifts from people continents away who have dipped into meditation, holistic medicine, or a monastic life and found something satisfying, something of value. This may not make all newcomers Buddhists, but it makes most of them sympathetic friends at a time when Himalayan Buddhism needs friends if it is to survive in the environment that gave it life.

This book is an excursion across one swath of the Himalayan Tantric Buddhist universe, the kingdoms strung along the southern exposure of Tibet. These small realms—in particular Ladakh, Sikkim, and Bhutan— were shaped and strengthened by Buddhism even as the religion was being swept from much of West, South, and Central Asia. In Ladakh and Sikkim, no longer independent states, degrees of melancholy infuse conversations about lost monarchies. And while Bhutan alone has avoided political assimilation into largely Hindu India, the Bhutanese are learning how perplexing, dangerous, and, most of all, lonely it is on the barricades. Yet virtually everywhere the tolerance, equanimity, good humor, and generosity of Himalayan Buddhist culture shine through. Though there may be outbursts of violence and splashes of greed among the believers, this is still one of the world's most appealing civilizations.

"Here there is an openness," an exiled Tibetan master, Chokyi Nyima Rinpoche, told me in Kathmandu between incoming calls on his cordless phone. "So while this is a very difficult philosophy, there is also common sense in it—and science, too. You could also say we understand the common needs. That means we all need love, we all need care. Buddha *dharma* teaches us a lot: how to respect each other, how to care."

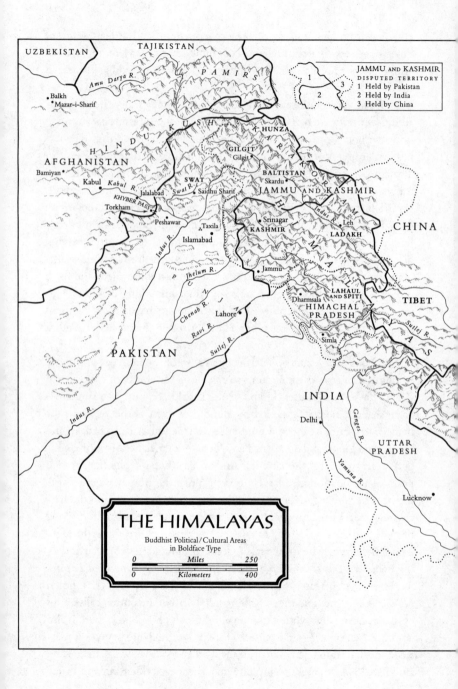

UZBEKISTAN
TAJIKISTAN

Amu Darya R.
PAMIRS

JAMMU and KASHMIR
DISPUTED TERRITORY
1 Held by Pakistan
2 Held by India
3 Held by China

HINDU KUSH
KARAKORAM

HUNZA
GILGIT
Gilgit
BALTISTAN
Skardu
JAMMU AND KASHMIR

AFGHANISTAN

Bamiyan
Kabul   Kabul R.   Jalalabad
SWAT
Swat R.   Saidhu Sharif
KHYBER PASS
Torkham
Peshawar   Taxila
Islamabad

Balkh
Mazar-i-Sharif

KASHMIR
Srinagar   Leh
LADAKH
CHINA

Indus R.

Indus R.

P   U   N   J   A   B

Jhelum R.
Jammu

HIMALAYAS

Chenab R.
Ravi R.
Lahore
Sutlej R.

LAHAUL
AND SPITI
Dharmsala
HIMACHAL
PRADESH
Simla

TIBET

Sutlej R.

PAKISTAN

Indus R.

INDIA

Delhi

Ganges R.

UTTAR
PRADESH

Yamuna R.

Lucknow

THE HIMALAYAS

Buddhist Political/Cultural Areas
in Boldface Type

0   Miles   250
0   Kilometers   400

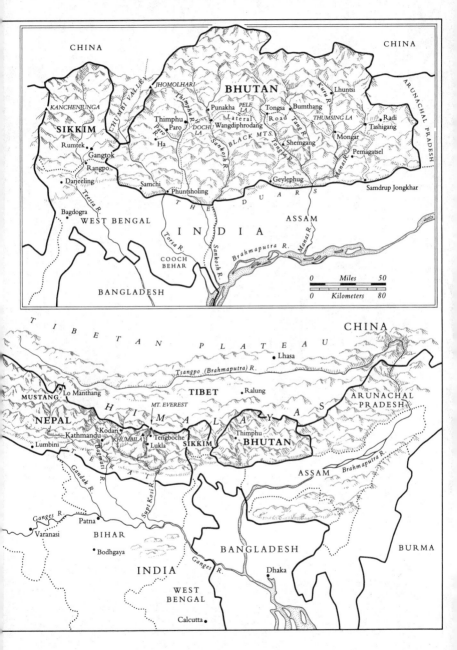

SO CLOSE TO HEAVEN

Chapter 1

AND THEN
THERE WAS
ONE

I AM HAUNTED by a particular front page of *Kuensel*, Bhutan's only newspaper. *Kuensel* is a weekly publication, and the date of this issue is April 10, 1993. The page is dominated by a large photograph of five young men in disheveled versions of the robelike garment, the *gho*, that Bhutanese men have worn for centuries. The shifty-eyed youth on the far right, on the edge of what is obviously an identity parade arranged by the police, looks uneasy and seems to be leaning out of this grisly group portrait. The one on the left appears slightly deformed or otherwise handicapped and has a hunted look. The three in the middle are fresh-faced, clean-cut lads who stare straight ahead, with little expression. In Bhutan, the last independent Himalayan Buddhist kingdom, a mountain paradise that only yesterday seemed untarnished by brutality or greed, the crime that this band of rural ruffians stands accused of is beyond atrocity: slitting the throat of an elderly monk (who had just given them food and a place to sleep) and smashing with a hammer and ax the heads of his two novices, in the hope of making off with a few treasures from the holy man's temple.

But that isn't all of the story. The gang failed to accomplish their goal of snatching the relics from Chimme Lhakhang, an isolated shrine, because they were interrupted by the screams of a village woman somewhere down the hill, and they fled. She was shouting, "Someone is being killed!" Unknown to the murderers in the temple, however, she wasn't exposing them. She was alerting her neighbors to her own situation. In a land where the avoidance of violence is a cultural assumption and women are strong, her husband was beating her to death.

The imagery is jarring. Isn't this supposed to be a Buddhist kingdom dedicated to the ideals of a nonviolent religion that sometimes seems more like an ethical system than a creed? Didn't I come here to see Buddhism as it is lived from day to day in a country that is the last of its line? Everywhere else in the Himalayan Buddhist world, people talked about how things used to be. Go to Bhutan, they said, where the universe is intact.

For decades, many Westerners repelled by materialism and a surfeit of industrial development have sought solace and reassurance in the Buddhist and Hindu East. In recent years, especially in India and Nepal, such sojourns have involved a certain measure of denial. Like writers looking for only those facts or quotes that will back a preconceived conclusion, spiritual tourists and other romantics who roam the Indian subcontinent and the Himalayas often bypass the worldly horrors around them: too many people, too little food, scant respect for nature, and a dearth of humane national policies to match professed beliefs and moral postures. To experience close-up the Eastern transcendence they extol from afar, outsiders must not look too closely at the commercialization of spirituality either—at the temple touts, the gold-plated gurus, the factory-wrapped loaves of sliced white bread left as offerings to the gods.

Denial, however, has never been demanded of visitors to Bhutan. In the increasingly choked and often turbulent regions of inner Asia, Bhutan—the nation known to its Buddhist majority as Druk Yul, the Kingdom of the Thunder Dragon—stood alone as a nation unsullied. It was a place where, despite a punishing terrain, life was (and mostly still is) lived at a different pace and with attractive values, among them a strong sense of individual self-reliance within supportive communities, an openness of spirit, and a large measure of self-respect that makes people look foreigners in the eye as equals. Bhutanese live in sturdy houses of mud walls and wooden half-timbering below gently pitched roofs finished with rough shingles held down by rocks. Woodwork and sometimes outer walls are decorated by village craftsmen in gently muted colors with designs drawn from Buddhist iconography and folklore. There are towns—I think of Mongar, Tongsa, or Tashigang—where clusters of painted, ornamented buildings could have materialized from illustrations in old fairy tales.

The land the Bhutanese inhabit, wedged between the world's two most populous countries, China and India, could also be drawn from the pages of a storybook. Spread over soaring icy mountains, black-dark gorges echoing with the roar of rushing water, emerald valleys silent under the sun, and forests rustling day and night with life of every kind, Bhutan is the size of Switzerland but has fewer than a million people, no cities as we know them, and no more than half a dozen paved roads of any significance. More people walk or travel by horseback than ride in motorized vehicles of any kind; topography ensures that this transportation pattern will endure indefinitely. The leg muscles of the Bhutanese, men and women, are magnificent. It takes strength and energy to live, as most Bhutanese do, at altitudes above five thousand feet, sometimes in villages so impossibly high above the valleys they farm that a lowlander can only stand and stare in disbelief at the precipitous passage between the warmth of home and the necessities and temptations provided by the outside world. And then urban life may be represented by no more than a ramshackle market stall at the side of the nearest (a relative term here) road. For the Bhutanese man or woman who leaves such an environment for a trip abroad, international travel is the easy part, or so Ugyen Dorji of the Jichu Drake Bakery told me with astonishing matter-of-factness as he described how he, a village boy, was shipped to Austria to be trained in pastrymaking under one of the more unusual national human resources policies. For him, the Austrian Alps were hardly worth writing home about.

Bhutan has had a modern capital (though mostly housed in a walled fortress) for less than half a century. In the rankings of world capitals, Thimphu has few competitors among the miniatures. Had it not just got its first traffic light, Thimphu and its mere hundreds of homes and wood-fronted shops arranged along a few short paved roads—only one of them connecting the town to anywhere else in the country—might have survived into the twenty-first century as the most bucolic seat of government on earth. With no airport or train station disgorging new-comers (just flocks of small buses, which, wisely, don't ply the narrow mountain roads at night), Thimphu has not had much of an opportunity to develop the ubiquitous landmarks that make so many cities inter-changeable, forcing the traveler to get out of town in order to see the country. Although it may not seem so to Bhutanese from the distant hills, Thimphu (with something like twenty thousand people; no one seems sure) *is* Bhutan from the moment of arrival. Mountains enclose it, monasteries and temples define its skyline, national building codes require that its homes and shops (there are no industries) hew to traditional architectural styles, strolling monks and farmers people its few pavements and numerous earthen byways, mingling with the modernized hustlers of a burgeoning middle class and the knots of idle young men caught somewhere between a subsistence past and a money economy.

At about seven thousand feet altitude, Thimphu and its environs along a willow-lined river are also much like the other high mountain valleys in which the majority of Bhutanese, and many other Himalayan people, live. Bhutan has four major climatological and topographical bands, but most of its towns and villages grew up historically in temperate regions stretching from east to west along the country's mountainous but fertile midsection from Thimphu to Tashigang. To the south of this strip there are a band of cooler broadleaf forests and then a subtropical zone. To the north there is alpine scrub, and the snow line that announces the high Himalayan peaks stretching along the frontier with Tibet.

Until relatively recently, Bhutanese Buddhists from the temperate valleys had no interest in the steamy southern lands along the Indian border, where the vegetation is subtropical and rain is heavy during monsoons, though there are no true rain forests. Heat, disease, pests, and soil inhospitable to the grain crops and vegetables preferred by many Bhutanese made the south unattractive. Spurning the south, however, meant leaving it open to influxes of immigrants, most of them Hindus from Nepal and India. Political and ethnic tensions followed.

Because Bhutan is underpopulated and has adopted a policy of conserving its natural resources, the country is a kind of living Himalayan natural park, full of the animals and plants that have disappeared in more crowded, less environmentally conscious countries in the region. In the south, where sal and other subtropical trees grow, there are deer, rhinos, monkeys, langurs, and elephants. The huge Manas game sanctuary is in this belt, which is more easily reached from India than from most Bhutanese towns, though there are one or two north-south feeder roads that invite detours from the main east-west road to Tashigang.

Above the subtropical belt, forests contain a mixture of deciduous and evergreen trees, dense shrubs, vines, and parasitic plants. Lush woodland floors, peppered with acorns and other edible nuts and seeds, support many animals, among them bears, squirrels, more monkeys, antelope, deer, leopards, wild boars, and an unbelievable aviary of birds. In the third band, the temperate zone, dominant along the east-west highway, there are cypress, blue pine, spruce, hemlock, fir, and juniper, along with oak, maple, larch, and giant rhododendron. There are also flowering fruit trees, peach and cherry, growing wild, and cultivated apple orchards. In the temperate zone the treeline occurs around eleven thousand feet, and yaks graze on windy grasslands dotted with scrub along the road as it climbs through that altitude to the mountain passes. Higher (and farther north) of this belt, animal and bird life would be alpine: the goatlike takin, some deer, owls, eagles, hawks, ravens. On the slopes up to the permanent snowfields at fifteen thousand feet or more, only stunted bushes, dwarf rhododendrons, and alpine flowers grow. No roads scar this pristine wilderness.

With a few notorious exceptions, the first outsiders to penetrate the self-imposed isolation of the Bhutanese were charmed and impressed by the country and its people. Explaining how Lieutenant Samuel Davis, a surveyor (and, fortunately for us, an artist) in imperial Britain's Bengal Army, came to produce as an eighteenth-century chronicler of Bhutan a very positive account of this land beyond the colonial pale, the historian Michael Aris wrote (with only a slight dig at the pretensions of the expatriate British): "The warm sympathy with which he accurately recorded the local scene was certainly inspired by the realization that here was a society *almost* as good as his own, enjoying a high state of civilization and surpassing natural beauty, inhabited by a people to whom he could truly relate."

A decade earlier, another Briton in colonial service, George Bogle—remembered for his methodical planting of potatoes everywhere he went in Bhutan, adding a new delicacy to the local diet—wrote in his journal: "The more I see of the Bhutanese, the more I am pleased with them." Apart from their trustworthiness and good humor, said Bogle, the Bhutanese were "the best-built race of men I ever saw." That is still stunningly true. In formal national attire, the men are dashing yet approachable, with sensitive Tibeto-Burman faces above strong bodies built of years on trails that would fell most trekkers. Poor farmers, old before their time and with their ghos well worn, have faces creased with humor and goodwill below towheads of snowy hair. Over and over, I saw men who would be called peasants elsewhere rise to full, self-possessed stature to welcome a guest or have a photograph taken in poses that effortlessly and probably unintentionally copy the stances and demeanors of a century of kings. Bhutanese women in the countryside, round-faced and hearty, display a Chaucerian mirth and sensibility; only their newly Westernized town cousins affect a demure or languid look.

For many years before and after Bogle and Davis, the Bhutanese, guided by a policy of wariness and aided by geography, shut out the world almost entirely. In the latter part of the twentieth century, as other once-closed Himalayan realms—Nepal, Ladakh, Sikkim, and Tibet—were opening to tourism, Bhutan held back, fearful of scarring its unspoiled terrain and turning its spontaneous, pervasive religiosity into a Buddhist performance for camcorders. When tourists finally began to arrive, limits were placed on their numbers.

But the Bhutanese are discovering that tourism may not be their most pressing problem. Some disturbing changes that threaten this unique Himalayan culture are springing from within the Bhutanese themselves as they proceed, through trial and error, toward integration into the wider world. What Bhutan is going through now should be of interest to all of us who worry about how an overcrowded planet increasingly headed toward a crisis of physical survival in the next century, especially in South Asia, will cope with the primal screams of small, endangered human cultures that get in the way of the scramble for farmland and living space.

But even among these threatened communities, the Bhutanese stand apart. Many of Asia's endangered societies are tribal—food-gatherers or pastoral nomads whose development stopped at a basic level of subsistence—and they attract the sympathy and support of anthropologists and good-hearted laypeople, particularly in Europe, who form paternalistic committees and organize demonstrations to look after their interests. The Bhutanese—proud, capable, lonely survivors of a developed ancient civilization of scholastic brilliance and considerable social achievement—are far removed in time and lifestyle from tribalism, by any definition. No charitable crusaders panting to save the world's naïfs reach out to them; in any case, they would disdain that kind of help. The few foreigners allowed to live in the Dragon Kingdom, ostensibly to help develop it, soon learn that the Bhutanese always do things their own way and in their own time. Down to the lowest farmer, they need to be convinced that something new being dangled before them is something they need and want. Then there's no stopping them.

In an electronic age, and at a time when people can move from place to place with relative ease, defying almost any nation's efforts to close its borders, the world beyond Bhutan intrudes with or without the catalyst of tourists or other visiting foreigners. The Bhutanese king's periodic orders banning satellite dishes become gestures sadly close to commanding the sea to hold back, because television receivers *are* permitted, and they connect to video players, bringing tales of casual violence to people barely out of an age of mythology. The five young men accused of killing the lama of Chimme Lhakhang and his two novices apparently told the police that they identified with the high-living gangsters they saw in cheap video films flooding the country from India, Hong Kong, and Bangkok. Or at least that's the way the police wanted the story to be told. "The motive for the murder was not village vendetta, revenge, or reprisal, but purely greed," the police told *Kuensel*. "Such cold-blooded murders are normally unheard of in this country."

If murder is still rare, theft from religious monuments is not, and this may sooner or later lead to the locking away of more temple treasures. Because icons and chortens, or shrines, are known to contain objects of value—if not pure silver and gold, certainly semiprecious stones—they are increasingly the targets of thieves no longer fearful of divine retribution for tampering with holy relics. Among the stones are corals, turquoise, and agates called zi, which many Himalayan Buddhists believe have been put in place by the gods themselves. Zi are small stones etched with white stripes in a process that has apparently been lost over the centuries, thus giving rise to the legend that the stones had miraculous origins. These old stones command very high prices from collectors. King Jigme Singye Wangchuck says that because of the lucrative market for relics from the last Himalayan Buddhist kingdom, there are hardly any chortens in Bhutan that have not been pilfered. Those in lonely spots along near-empty roads or on hilltops are most vulnerable; some have been sledgehammered to destruction in the search for booty.

Temple images are next, as the grisly murder of the lama of Chimme Lhakhang demonstrated. There are those thieves who are already more sophisticated and calculating than the brutal band who slit the lama's throat. Near Bumthang, a temple was robbed of a priceless image by a

Nepali-born con artist who represented himself to the abbot of the monastery as a would-be student. The thief pursued his religious studies long enough to become part of the community. Then one night he replaced the temple's most valuable image with a fake, and fled the country. The next day the old abbot immediately, almost instinctively, spotted the fraudulent image and spread the alarm. Remarkably, the thief was caught not long after in India trying to unload the treasure, and this story had a happy ending. But it was also a cautionary tale. Ominously, the robber later escaped while being moved from one Bhutanese jail to another. Such escapes often signal connivance.

In other South Asian nations, poverty and unemployment may be considered excuses for criminal behavior, but not in Bhutan. "We don't have beggars," said Rigzin Dorji, the scholar–civil servant who as head of the Special Commission on Cultural Affairs had the unique job of maintaining cultural standards and preserving what was called "the Bhutanese way." "Even a poor family will have a house, some chickens, maybe one or two cows, some pigs, and a little land for cultivation. The country is our mother; all the people are our children." Yet sophisticated international art thieves, on the prowl for booty from untouched monasteries and temples where literally priceless treasures are largely uncatalogued, clearly have ways of tempting even the offspring of this Himalayan Eden with windfall wealth and unusual excitement.

Bhutan has wandered without a map into that psychological territory where a magical innocence is lost and there are no signposts to what lies ahead. In Buddhist terms, the Bhutanese are collectively in some kind of *bardo,* the place between cycles of death and rebirth, waiting to see if they will enter the next life as a nation selectively modernized for the common good but otherwise unaltered, or as another small third-world country rent with social and ethnic divisions and vulnerable to corruption, violence, and political opportunism. One way or another, change is coming. This is not Brigadoon.

Until the 1960s, the Bhutanese lived a medieval existence. There were no roads, no postal service, no telephones, no national currency or money economy, no village schools, no hospitals, no airports, no towns of any size. Families in their brightly decorated half-timbered houses grew their own food, wove the cloth for their traditional garments, and bartered what they could for a few luxuries carried into their isolated mountain valleys on the backs of traders from Tibet or India. Travel by foot or horseback was a pageant, a procession of pilgrims, entertainers, farmers, or lords making their way through snowy passes and dense forests, stopping to eat, to rest, to sing, and sometimes to dance the gentle, repetitive, slow-motion folk dances of the hills. Temples and colossal monastery-fortresses, the *dzongs,* the capitals of feudal warlords and warring regions not united under one hereditary ruler until early in this century, were also the centers of spiritual, legal, and even medical sustenance for all Bhutanese who could reach them. In smaller communities, monks and lamas were the sources of wisdom and healing for soul, mind, and body.

Not all of this is history, and that is part of Bhutan's dilemma. People may be healthier and better educated and have a national airline to fly them away and roads to connect them to the Asian subcontinent. But many still travel on horseback, prostrate themselves in gloriously decorated temples, and ward off the curses of evil spirits with elaborately fashioned constructions of sticks and string placed outside the family home. Should this life be saved? And how?

International measures of per capita income and living standards based on the distribution of material objects—hospital beds or radios, for example—don't mean much in Bhutanese terms, when areas of the economy are still often based on barter, or are unmeasurable. Respiratory and intestinal diseases may persist, and as many as one in five village children under five dies because parents and lamas have not been taught hygiene or because the family lives too far from (or does not think of going to) a hospital. But food is abundant, babies get free inoculations against childhood diseases at village health centers or from mobile teams, homelessness is unheard of, education is free, and there are more jobs than citizens to do them.

"Many countries in the third world have to worry about poverty projects; this is not in our planning," Chenkyab Dorji, the planning minister, told me. "Joblessness is not there. Landless people are not there. There is no hunger here. We only wish to improve the living standard farther. In Bhutan people have their houses. They get their three square meals." His aims, ludicrous to contemplate in most other South Asian countries, are state-of-the-art communications systems, universal health coverage, and better roads. The Bhutanese adjust to technological change by planting prayer flags around satellite telephone relay stations and power generators.

Foreigners can still come to Bhutan and find a Buddhist peace untarnished by commercialism or artifice. An agnostic like me, climbing at dawn to an old, unkempt monastery, can be transported by the vigorous, insistent chanting of monks and the beat of drums and bells. A kind of peace and sense of well-being grow out of the rhythmic droning and the clang-clang-clang-clang of the percussion that punctuates it. Paradoxically, the experience recalls the inexplicable healing power and spiritual lift that can be drawn from the very different atmosphere of a silent Pennsylvania Quaker meeting, an empty European cathedral, or one of India's nearly deserted old synagogues, with only the ghosts of long-departed worshippers.

Maybe we on the outside are also drawn in because Buddhism, in almost every one of its many forms or rituals, is an individualistic (and never exclusive) faith. The mumbling of mantras while counting beads, the hypnotic spinning of prayer wheels—these are private devotions. Though all around a Bhutanese monastery there is activity—there are always pilgrims, layabouts, and hangers-on, and artisans at work creating or restoring something, sewing brocaded hangings, planing or carving fragrant wood, arranging trays of flower petals or spices, wrapping holy books in silk—essentially the act of worship is a personal tryst between any one of us rough-cut humans and a better heavenly world. The monks and abbots praying and reciting away the day in the inner sanctum are there to help when needed. The lore of monastic Tantric Buddhism is full of stories of great masters ordering, cajoling, or even tricking disciples into finding their own way to knowledge, religious or otherwise.

For most Bhutanese, life in the hidden Himalayan valleys that form the landlocked kingdom in the shadow of the earth's highest peaks is still simple and tranquil, if strenuous. Bhutanese Buddhists, inheritors of a phantasmagorical literature, see all around them the elaborate artistic representations of their gods, often in temples set in a natural environment of primeval beauty. To minimize disruption of this way of life, development under two enlightened kings has been very cautious since it began in the 1960s.

Alone among the generally overcrowded nations of the South Asian subcontinent, the Bhutanese enjoy an important quality of life that cannot be overvalued or underestimated: privacy. Though families may be large, virtually everyone has a home and therefore a sanctuary. The

Bhutanese are accustomed to solitude; many ride or walk alone for long hours, perhaps days, from high-altitude villages to market towns or schools and back again. But for an isolated people, they are unexpectedly cosmopolitan. A district administrator assigned to one of the remotest outposts ventured that maybe this had something to do with living on mountains, "where we can be far-seeing and maybe learn to take a broader look at life."

Samuel Davis thought that the Bhutanese were an intellectual match for any other nationality in the region. He wrote that they might need only secular teachers "to equal, if not surpass, their Indian neighbors, over whom they possess an advantage in an exemption from the restraint of caste, that insuperable bar to social improvements and national dignity." Furthermore, as Rigzin Dorji said, the people of Bhutan are spared the soul-destroying need to beg for anything: for food, for space, for shelter, for a moment of attention. They are never forced, as are the street people of Dhaka, Calcutta, or Bombay, to eat, sleep, wash, defecate, make love, and raise children in the crowded gutters of urban life. Their world smells of woodsmoke and pine needles, and resonates with birdsong and the splashing of waterfalls.

Into this setting creep the ugly tensions, deep and destructive, that threaten to wound and disfigure this extraordinary nation. As the outside world closes in, despite the Buddhist kingdom's best efforts to keep its distance from the corrupting influences and sins of others, challenges multiply. An open border with India and air links to Bangkok, Dhaka, Kathmandu, Delhi, and Calcutta not only have brought to Bhutan's doorstep high-stakes smuggling, including the illegal trade in temple treasures, gold, and endangered animal pelts, but also have exposed the Bhutanese to AIDS and other new diseases. A slowly expanding private tourism industry and soaring property values are creating a wealthy urban (by Bhutanese standards) middle class in the capital, Thimphu, where life grows more distant day by day from its medieval village roots. A few panhandlers and street children have moved in. Burglary is a new urban phenomenon; the lone hair dryer from Thimphu's first beauty shop was among the first objects to go. These crimes shock and could overwhelm a traditional system of justice experienced for the most part in resolving family quarrels.

What is lost? An atmosphere of trust. In late 1992, in Thimphu, a woman who owns a jewelry shop went out on an errand and left me alone with her entire stock, some of it extremely valuable antique corals and turquoise pieces. When I finally chose some earrings, and she hadn't yet returned, I left the money in the charge of an old lama who had dropped in for tea. He nodded and with a toothless smile indicated he approved of my choice. It never occurred to me that he might pocket the cash and leave. And it obviously didn't worry the shopkeeper that she had left me alone with her inventory in unlocked cases. A year or two later, I heard from one of the sophisticates who lunch at the Swiss Bakery that young hooligans had begun disguising themselves as monks in order to steal from trusting merchants like my jewelry seller as well as from temples. And what about the tourists? I asked, thinking of those well-heeled visitors who pried statues off their pedestals in the struggling stately homes of Rajasthan and packed them away as if they were souvenir ashtrays from a chain hotel. No trouble with them yet, most Bhutanese say. Once trust is broken and the magic is gone, however, everyone takes a piece of what's left.

There are other troubling changes, larger in scale than the criminal behavior of a few and more immediately dangerous to the integrity of the Bhutanese state. In southern Bhutan, along the unfenced border with India, available land and free education and health care continue to draw illegal immigrants, different in religion and ethnicity from the people of the central valleys and alien to the Buddhist culture that has defined national life for more than a thousand years. Immigrant Hindus of Nepali ancestry are part of a huge Nepali world outside Bhutan's borders. In the early 1990s, there were at least thirty million Nepalis in overpopulated (and environmentally devastated) Nepal and in India's Himalayan foothills, and fewer than three-quarters of a million Bhutanese citizens—Buddhist and Hindu together—in Bhutan. Only the small Indian state of Sikkim, where Nepali people long ago outnumbered the former kingdom's Tibetan and tribal stock, separates Bhutan from Nepal's teeming eastern border.

"The annual *increase* of the population of Nepal may be as much as the total population of Bhutan," King Jigme Singye Wangchuck told me in late 1992. "Their population increase per year is about five hundred thousand—half a million—people, and there is chronic unemployment. In Nepal they have destroyed and denuded all their forests, there is no land to be given to the landless people, and all the arable land can no longer be farmed because of environmental and ecological problems.

Where the water table has gone down, tremendous erosion is taking place. India today has about ten million Nepalese, and these ten million Nepalese have all come from Nepal. In Bhutan, the attractions were free education, free health, and easier availability of free land, and all this [immigrant influx] was done with the full support and cooperation of our southern Bhutanese people."

Faced with this threat to an already endangered Himalayan Buddhist culture, the kingdom's dominant Drukpa people and others in the Buddhist mainstream reacted initially in panic, setting the stage by 1990 for a rebellion among southerners who said that they were being culturally repressed and illegally evicted even when they were citizens. Their accounts were sometimes true, sometimes exaggerated. Undoubtedly there were outbursts of excessive zeal among the Drukpa administrators; that cannot be denied. A requirement that national dress be worn by all Bhutanese was enforced so rigorously that a Japanese scholar in Western clothes was roughed up trying to convince law enforcement officers that he wasn't Bhutanese at all.

National dress in Bhutan is defined as a kimono-like *gho* for men and boys and a somewhat different ankle-length robe called a *kira* for girls and women. Worn correctly and with knee-length socks and decent shoes, the gho, often in dark plaids or stripes (even pinstripes), is an elegant garment. Unfortunately, a lot of young Bhutanese, who are hit-or-miss about how they fold and fasten the ample robe and iconoclastic in their choice of what to wear with it (running shoes, athletic socks, and sweatpants are favorite accessories), make the national costume look unkempt if not ridiculous.

The gho has a bathrobe-like wide collar and buttonless front panels, one crossing over the other from left to right when the robe is put on. A gho is ankle-length in construction, but it is worn at knee level, hoisted up and secured by a woven belt, with the excess fabric bloused out at the top. At the back, the robe is folded from the waist down into two inverted vertical pleats that meet at the center, making the garment hug the body at the hips while having a roomy look at the top. In front, the pouch formed in the diagonal opening above the waist provides a generous pocket for carrying all kinds of useful items: a handkerchief, a traditional wood-and-silver bowl for drinking tea or homemade alcoholic brews, an appointment book, money, the shopping, or a supply of betel chews.

Under a gho, a Bhutanese man wears a white shirt with overlong sleeves, which are folded up over the outside of the robe at the wrists to form wide cuffs. Adding the *kabne,* a scarf that identifies one's rank, to this already taxing ensemble is a more complicated operation than one would guess, since the long piece of material has to be thrown over the shoulder and folded over itself at chest height before also being thrown over the left arm. The proportions of folded and free-flowing cloth have to be exact, so that the kabne falls with the correct drape and length.

The kira, for women, is slightly simpler. Basically a rectangular length of woven cloth (or more likely several pieces sewn together) about two and a half yards long and one and a half yards wide, it wraps around the body over a shawl-collared blouse, the *onju,* and is fastened at the shoulders with silver hooks—or sometimes safety pins and, lately, Velcro. A silver or cloth belt secures the kira at the waist. A short unbuttoned jacket, the *toego,* completes the outfit. The cloth chosen for a kira, traditionally handwoven in horizontal stripes (unfairly, since stripes for men are vertical), now varies in color and design with the whims of Bhutanese fashion.

Because many, though not all, southern Nepali-Bhutanese are Hindus with cultural links to fellow Nepalis all along the Himalayan foothills, most normally dress differently from the northerners of the high mountain valleys. If the Drukpas only grumble about wearing what is, after all, their traditional costume, the southerners, called officially Lhotsampas, see the enforcement of a national dress code based on a northern costume as a glaring violation of their civil rights and cultural customs. Southern Bhutanese favor either Western clothes or the Nepali jodhpurs, tunic, and multicolored *topi* (a kind of lopsided fez) for men or the sari for women, garments that set them apart from the northerners in their ghos and kiras. Efforts by some liberal local officials to ease the dress-code rules or mitigate their enforcement came late, but were real. On a hot, flat plain in the Samchi district, across the border from the Indian tea gardens of Cooch Behar, I saw farmers in Western-style trousers working their fields and a watchman at a Druk fruit-processing plant dressed in a "half gho," a kiltlike garment, with a sport shirt and Nepali topi. But by then, the damage had been done, and clothes had become a major civil rights issue.

At the same time that this ethnically based dress code was being imposed on the southern Bhutanese and other pressures were being applied to them to prove their legitimacy if not loyalty, some well-known politicians in Thimphu apparently took the opportunity to grab Nepali-Bhutanese property. Soon, government officials were forced, unarmed, into the theater of a shadowy guerrilla war notable even in violent South Asia for its senseless atrocities. In the village of Chiengmari, near Samchi, a Lepcha—whose people took no side in the Bhutanese dispute—was beheaded one afternoon and thrown, dismembered, by the side of the hamlet's one road to serve as a ritual sacrifice or a warning. Local people suspected the former, and told dark tales of Nepali blood rites. People of all ethnic groups lived in terror.

Yet the day after I heard this story, I watched in acute embarrassment as a local administrator, visiting an even smaller and more vulnerable border hamlet near Sibsoo, set out to humiliate (for the benefit of his audience) a headmaster who refused to live in the free house he had been given on the grounds of an isolated school repeatedly attacked by militants. The man had fled with his family to the security of a nearby village. Moral support was what he needed, but the government official, retelling the story in front of the hapless, crestfallen headmaster, suddenly turned on him and began to cluck—"Cawk! Cawk! Cawk! Cawk!"—like an enormous chicken. The painfully insecure headmaster had just served us all cookies and tea at a castoff table in his abandoned house, trying his best to show he was still in charge of the burned-out, stripped-down school. Across a vacant field, a few brave teachers huddled in the still-standing classrooms with groups of little children, most of them Bhutanese Nepalis so poor they had to be given their tiny regulation ghos and kiras by the government.

As all of these problems boil over at once, Bhutan's loyal friends fear not only for this imperiled society but also for the loss the world will incur if Druk Yul, the Kingdom of the Thunder Dragon, slides toward disintegration or extinction.

What to keep? What to give up? And how much time to make the choice? On such questions, there is no consensus in Bhutan. There is only a vague fear, spreading like an inkblot, that an era has ended and no one knows what the next age will bring. The future, unlike the past, holds no hope of fantasy, no expectation of miraculous intervention by deities in times of trouble. No magic dances or Tantric rituals can chase away the new demons that stalk the Bhutanese hills.

Trapped between India and China, two giant nations wary of each other; under relentless regional demographic pressures; and confused by their own uncertainties about how to deal with the secular outside world and its alien cultures, the Bhutanese are not optimistic. They have seen Ladakh, Tibet, and Sikkim vanish as independent Himalayan Buddhist realms, to be absorbed and altered by India or China. They derive only bleak hope from the knowledge that the Tibetan Buddhism that shaped their nation has found a new following in the West. Westerners take only what is relevant to them, usually the practice of meditation and aspects of traditional medicine. Himalayan Buddhism is much more than that; in Bhutan it is a rich stew of theology spiced by legend, superstition, astrological interpretation, and the worship of natural phenomena. Bhutanese Buddhism is Bhutanese Buddhism only in Bhutan.

At a time when the protection of minority rights and the spread of democracy have become high priorities worldwide, the Buddhists of Bhutan, followers of an arcane theology, are at a possibly fatal disadvantage. Nepali-Bhutanese rebels have set up shop in Kathmandu to spread the word that the panicked Drukpas—the Dragon People—are oppressors led by an evil king. In Thimphu, King Jigme Singye Wangchuck says ruefully that he knows how hard it is to defend monarchy at this point in history. One of his ministers was more direct: "If we were spotted owls, the world would care about us," he said. "Can't you see we are an endangered species, too?"

"The rich and splendorous culture of the Great Wheel of Buddhism, which once flourished in Sikkim, Tibet, Ladakh, Lahaul, and Spiti, is well on the path to extinction," Jigmi Thinley, a Bhutanese government official, told a 1993 conference of scholars at London University's School of Oriental and African Studies. "Today, Bhutan, the last bastion of this cultural heritage, is in a state of siege."

Chapter 2

THE DRUK GYALPO

THE PRECIOUS RULER of the Dragon People waits for visitors in his silk-lined lair at the top of a very steep flight of monastic ladder-steps in Tashichodzong, the fortress in Thimphu that houses the royal Bhutanese government and the head abbot of the Buddhist clergy, the *je khenpo*. Actually, there are several flights of punishing wooden steps from the austere stone gateway of the dzong to the upper reaches of the offices of the king, which are in a tower at the opposite corner of the long court-yard from the je khenpo's temple and, until recently, the hall set aside for meetings twice a year of the National Assembly, the Tshogdu. Even before being bedazzled by the splendor of the high-ceilinged royal audience hall and its gilded throne, the intruding outsider is rendered breathless from the exertion of getting there.

As courtiers part the curtains that cover the door to the large but dimly lit chamber, the king is standing just inside, ready with a brief, disarming smile. He leads his guest past brilliant *thangkas,* paintings on brocaded scrolls, and other richly colored hangings garnishing the saffron-colored walls whose remaining spaces are ornamented with religious symbols embossed in gold leaf. Benches and pillows covered with the skins of snow leopards define the corner where His Majesty settles himself for interviews and audiences. The scene is photographed often and pictured just about every week in *Kuensel:* the king with the Indian ambassador, the king with the resident representative of the United Nations Development Program, or, more recently (in the time of ethnic conflict), the king with leaders of Amnesty International, the king with a delegation from the International Committee of the Red Cross. Asked about the pelts of the endangered cats on which we sit, His Majesty disowns them, saying they were put there before his time, before Bhutan pledged to the world community to protect its animals and plants. "I had nothing to do with that," he answers quickly, with only a faint trace of impatience at being sidetracked by the upholstery. He has more urgent issues to discuss.

In appearance, the king exemplifies the arresting good looks and natural grace of many of the northern Bhutanese: black hair above a slightly tawny face with the high cheekbones and dark, almond-shaped eyes of the Tibeto-Burman people. Strong and well proportioned like most Bhutanese, the king is resplendent in a gho of handwoven silk in deep blue and gold stripes, the gold patterned lightly in red by adding an extra weft to the weave, a hallmark of the most highly treasured Bhutanese textiles. Over his left shoulder is draped a kabne of saffron-colored raw silk. Every Bhutanese man is required to possess a kabne in a color or design appropriate to his rank, whether exalted or lowly, and to wear it in dzongs and other government buildings. The saffron-gold shade is worn by only two men: the monarch and the je khenpo. His Majesty wears black knee socks and Western dress shoes instead of the traditional knee-high boots made of animal skin or felt, now seen mostly on ceremonial occasions. There is a winter chill in the audience hall, only slightly mitigated by the hot tea and fresh savory pastries. The king has a slight cold, and a bit of untraditional plaid flannel shirt escapes from beneath the collar of his gho as he reaches for a handkerchief now and then during a conversation on a dismal afternoon. He has a solemn, even superserious, demeanor and voices his thoughts in precise language, using his expressive eyes but almost no facial or hand gestures as he speaks—or as he listens with apparent interest to his guests. It is the common experience of those of us who have met him that at the end of your interview he begins his, asking very direct questions about international politics and soliciting opinions on Bhutanese affairs. His head is full of facts about Bhutanese development—he says he spends a lot of his time reading files—and he pleads his case for international understanding tirelessly and with a repertoire of well-rehearsed arguments, as delegations of foreigners who have heard about the trouble in the south come and go. Saving the last Himalayan Buddhist kingdom has become his full-time job.

Jigme Singye Wangchuck, born in 1954, is the fourth king of the hereditary dynasty established in 1907. Before his sagacious great-grand-father, Ugyen Wangchuck, adopted the royal title (with the blessing and encouragement of the British colonial government in India), Bhutan was at best a loosely united country with a three-hundred-year-old system of parallel religious and temporal leaders who left most local affairs in the hands of *penlops,* appointed regional governors. Early British chroniclers recorded how trips to the kingdom were often postponed or disrupted because of clashes between rival penlops, who had become feudal lords with bases in their respective widely scattered dzongs. From these for-tresses, with high walls and huge protective gates, they forayed out to war on one another much like medieval European kings and princes. By the turn of the twentieth century, power had concentrated in two pen-lops, in Paro and Tongsa.

Ugyen Wangchuck, whose family came from the Bumthang area in central Bhutan, was the penlop of Tongsa, a title kept alive today by Bhutanese crown princes. Penlop Ugyen Wangchuck had used both his military and his diplomatic skills to unite the country and best his chief rival, the Paro penlop. Ugyen Wangchuck's masterstroke internationally was to back (and join) a successful British expedition against Tibet in 1904, and then help draft the Anglo-Tibetan accord that followed. The British, rulers of neighboring India at the time, had immense power in the region, and they became his strong supporters.

Ugyen Wangchuck's decision to make common cause with imperial Britain, which had in the previous century snatched from his father, Jigme Namgyal, a large area of land along the Indian border claimed by the Bhutanese, could have been a difficult one. The Tibetans were virtu-ally kith and kin (barring about a century of aggression during and after the unification of Bhutan in the 1600s), and Tibet was the wellspring of Bhutanese Tantric Buddhist culture. On the other hand, Tibet's attitude did not seem entirely friendly at the turn of the twentieth century. Alu Dorji, a former Thimphu penlop and an old enemy of Ugyen Wang-chuck, had been in exile in Tibet plotting to draw Tibetans into a cam-paign to undermine the new strongman of Bhutan. Another of the

Tongsa penlop's rivals, the Paro penlop, had disapproved of the British march against Lhasa. His career paid the price.

Ugyen Wangchuck, on the other hand, went on to collect a British honor, the medal of a Knight Commander of the Indian Empire, and the crown of Bhutan, an unusual embroidered cap with a wide upturned brim all around. Ostentatious jewels have no place in Bhutan's crown or, for that matter, in royal Bhutanese court life. The crown, which photographs of Ugyen Wangchuck show him wearing several years before his formal coronation, is topped with the head of a raven. The raven is a manifestation of the preeminent local guardian deity, Gompo Jarodon-chen, a form of Mahakala, the black guardian god. The room or corner set aside for Mahakala in a monastery is barred to women, Bhutanese and foreign alike. The abbot at Tashigang Dzong—instinctively (if surprisingly) aware, as are most Bhutanese, that this kind of discrimination requires an explanation—made a great effort to explain the rationale to me.

"Especially the monks here have to emphasize celibacy throughout the life," he said through the regional administrator who had brought me into the monastery, causing the abbot a flicker of anxiety at the outset. "They have to refrain from the women," he went on, as we hovered at the door of Mahakala's temple, one of many shrines in the dzong. "Having contact with the women, they land up in human misery. And that particular deity is their deity. It's not that the deity is against women. But when we want to renounce the world, the first thing we give up is the women. This is the first reason. There are many other reasons." He rushed on to the next shrine without elaborating.

The enabling act that made possible the formal establishment of a hereditary monarchy in Bhutan came in a meeting of lay and religious leaders in 1907. They officially offered the crown to Ugyen Wangchuck and with it authority over both secular and some religious affairs. The first king's coronation took place in December of that year. It was a splendid affair, with "a dense throng of spectators, monks and laymen" crowding the great hall at Punakha Dzong, which was lit with countless butter lamps, according to John Claude White, the British political officer who attended the coronation as London's official representative. As a monastic band struck up the appropriate music, a crush of uninvited Bhutanese citizens tried to invade through the roof, where an opening had been made for light and air, and were "repeatedly driven off by the lamas," White wrote.

Ugyen Wangchuck was by most accounts a shrewd and generous ruler with an informed interest in the world outside Bhutan. White, based in Sikkim, remarked on his first official mission to Bhutan, in 1905, that "Sir Ugyen is the only Bhutanese I have come across who takes a real and intelligent interest in general subjects, both foreign and domestic, and he neither drinks nor indulges in other vices." The future king told White of his distress at losing many books from his large collection when a fire damaged the Dechen temple near Thimphu. "I held many long private conversations with the Tongsa," White wrote a little patronizingly in his journal, "and was deeply impressed with his sense of responsibility and genuine desire to improve the condition of his country and countrymen." The British political officer was moved by the penlop's confession that he had thrown himself into reading and scholarship in an effort to overcome his heartbreak over the death of a young wife to whom he was deeply attached. Noticing that Ugyen Wangchuck's eyesight was beginning to fail, White gave him a pair of his own reading glasses before taking leave of the penlop at the end of the mission.

White, an avid and skilled photographer, took pictures of the Tongsa penlop in 1905 after the British investiture ceremony and again in 1907 after his coronation as king. The 1905 portrait shows a stocky, barefoot man with a thin mustache and wispy beard wearing a gho that appears to be made of brocaded satin. White described it as "a handsome robe of dark blue Chinese silk, embroidered in gold with the Chinese character *fu,* the sign emblematical of good luck." Apart from his sword and raven crown, the Tongsa penlop sports the medal of the imperial British knighthood he has just been awarded. His bronzed round face is creased with a faint smile of self-assurance and pride. In 1907, the newly anointed king wore a robe of lighter blue brocade, his raven-headed crown, Western shoes, and long socks that disappeared beneath his gho. In the intervening years, he had made a trip to Calcutta, then the seat of the British colonial government of India. The shoes—various shoes— were seen more often, though not for the first time, after that trip. In 1911, Sir Ugyen also visited New Delhi to attend the glittering ceremonies celebrating the move of the British Indian government to the imposing new imperial capital. Official New Delhi, with its wide Raj Path boulevard and elegant government buildings, is still Asia's most impressive capital city.

Ugyen Wangchuck lived and ruled until 1926, when he was succeeded by his son Jigme Wangchuck. By the time Jigme Wangchuck died in 1952, Britain's South Asian empire had collapsed and four new nations had been created: India, Burma, Sri Lanka, and Pakistan, the last of which would again fracture in 1971, spawning independent Bangladesh. India's overwhelming size and the tendency of Indian political leaders to assume that they had inherited Britain's imperial legacy posed new problems for Bhutan, Sikkim, and Nepal, the three Himalayan kingdoms that had never been colonized. Another, Ladakh, was already part of India (as were the smaller domains of Lahaul and Spiti), and Tibet was being absorbed by China. The era of the third and fourth Bhutanese kings—Jigme Dorji Wangchuck, who ruled for twenty years, from the death of his father in 1952 until his own death of heart disease in 1972; and his son, Jigme Singye Wangchuck, who has ruled since—has been a time of unending tension across the southern approaches to the Himalayas.

When Jigme Singye Wangchuck became the Druk Gyalpo, the Precious Ruler of the Dragon People, in 1972, he was only seventeen. Although he had been to boarding schools in England as a boy and had inherited a warm personality and a reformist agenda from his respected father, the young monarch became a relatively reclusive figure—at least as far as journalists and most foreigners were concerned—until the early 1990s, when the propaganda successes of the rebellion by the Nepali-speaking Hindu minority in southern Bhutan made him realize what his ministers had missed: that an aloof and impenetrable nation can find itself without friends when it needs them most.

He told me this a little ruefully when we first met in March 1991. I had been trying unsuccessfully for more than two years to get a visa to visit Bhutan, part of the territory I was expected to cover from my base in New Delhi as a correspondent for *The New York Times*. It had never occurred to me to ask for an interview with His Majesty, who, like King Bhumibol Adulyadej of Thailand, another hardworking Buddhist monarch I had met a few years earlier, rarely travels abroad and has no interest in personal publicity. Both kings harbor a revulsion for the high-profile, jet-set potentate's existence, and would never be seen floating through the spas, casinos, and capitals of Europe, dressed by fashion designers and trailed by paparazzi. While I thought, of course, that it would be fascinating to meet the last reigning Himalayan Buddhist king, all I wanted from the Bhutanese government was the chance to report on ordinary daily life in the country, which had only recently, and with great reserve, opened its borders to tourists.

The Delhi press corps enjoyed a bizarre relationship with the Bhutanese in the 1980s. At the end of October 1988, for example, we were all invited to a Sunday-afternoon news conference in a large formal parlor at the Bhutanese embassy in the Indian capital to be told that His Majesty was getting married very soon to four sisters with whom he had been living for nearly a decade. The young women—Ashi Dorji Wangmo, Ashi Tshering Pem, Ashi Tshering Yandon, and Ashi Sangye Choden— had already borne him eight children collectively, including the boy the king now wanted to confirm publicly as crown prince, Jigme Gesar Namgyal Wangchuck. The date of the wedding and formal naming of the crown prince had been selected, we were told in the announcement delivered by Foreign Minister Dawa Tshering, to coincide with "an auspicious hour on the descending day of Lord Gautama Buddha from the Tushita Heaven on the twenty-second day of the ninth month of the Earth Dragon year."

Since journalists have no manners, we all clamored to go to the celebration, which was due to take place at the old royal capital of Punakha in the presence of hundreds of assembled monks and abbots. That would be out of the question, we were told by the minister, who must have found us faintly amusing. But we were treated to drinks, folk dancing, and a feast at the embassy instead. As we left the party through a path from the embassy gardens to the parking area, we were each given a weighty box wrapped in gift paper. It felt like a heavy piece of pottery, or possibly a stone sculpture. It turned out, however, to be a case of scotch, which my newspaper's rules dictated I return. I did so the next day—or rather my husband did, since I had gone on overnight to Sri Lanka. In a letter accompanying both my case of scotch and his, David, also a journalist, tried to explain to the uncomprehending Bhutanese how the mysterious Western press views the giving of gifts by news sources. In Delhi at that time it was nearly impossible to buy untainted or undiluted imported alcoholic beverages, except at extortionate prices from black marketeers with contacts in foreign embassies, duty-free

shops, or shipping companies. We must have seemed crassly ungrateful
for this windfall. In any case, my subsequent repeated pleas for visas went
unanswered. But then the journalists who kept the cases of Johnnie
Walker didn't get visas either.

In the spring of 1990, urged on by a friend in Nepal who was convinced I could join a tour group to Bhutan from Kathmandu without
attracting the Bhutanese government's attention, my husband and I did
just that. We went to Bhutan from Nepal as a trekking party of two; we
never knew what happened to the rest of the group to which we were
supposedly attached. Worried about being discovered and deported, we
memorized what we could on our daily sightseeing trips from Paro,
Thimphu, and Punakha, making notes at night for future articles. I could
not find one foreigner based in Thimphu on an international aid project
who would talk to me: a European volunteer looked up in outright
alarm when I cornered him in an office and explained who I was. The
foreign press had pariah status, and reporters could not help but wonder
what terrible secrets everyone was trying to hide.

We were assigned an owlish guide named Ugyen. All of them seemed
to be named Ugyen; the Bhutanese list of personal names is short. Françoise Pommaret, a French Tibetologist and writer on Bhutan, compiled
a nearly exhaustive list of about fifty, most of them used interchangeably
for boys and girls and in any combination, so that a child's name—
Sonam Wangdi, for example—may not relate to that of either parent.
Our Ugyen wanted to work with high-altitude trekkers and mountain
climbers, which we certainly were not. He was about to go to Austria for
training, and so he allowed himself a little room for complaint about the
country's recently instituted patriotic dress code, with its requirement
that he wear a gho at all times and don his kabne every time we approached an official building. He grumbled that if he violated the rules
he would be "put behind the bars."

Ugyen, who referred a little sardonically to his ruler as "our modest
little king," took us from one ornate, otherworldly institution to another: the National Library, the National Art School, the National Museum, several dzongs, and Thimphu's landmark Memorial Chorten.
Like so many others discovering this hidden kingdom for the first time,
we were amazed and enchanted by the Bhutanese and won over by their
repeated assertions that they were clinging to an endangered culture
which could survive only in controlled isolation. However, it was also

not hard to notice, in part through Ugyen's eyes, the underlying resentment of educated young Drukpas, children of the Buddhist majority, who had been forced into compulsory national dress just as they were discovering international fashion and foreign education. Inevitably, they would later lead a quiet campaign against the dress code, flaunting Western clothes as they dashed around in Japanese cars or hung out at new bistros opening around town. That behavior would in turn set off cries of "privilege!" from less affluent Bhutanese not only proud of their national costume but also unable to afford imported jeans. There were cases of official abuses, when the overzealous dress police would arrest or fine offenders on the spot in the north just as they did in rebellious southern Bhutan, sometimes for very small infractions. The king was beginning to question the value of forcing this kind of symbolic unity on the citizenry. In exasperation, he once told a visiting scholar that he didn't really care what people wore, so long as they didn't run round naked.

By this time the dress code had poisoned relations between ethnic groups and violence had begun to ignite in the Bhutanese south. The insurgency was initially sparked by a 1988 census that found thousands of illegal immigrants in the southern border districts. People who could not prove they had a right to citizenship historically or under the terms of a 1958 blanket grant of nationality to aliens faced expulsion, and the alarm was raised among fellow Nepalis in neighboring countries. The violence took an abrupt turn for the worse in the fall of 1990, when Nepali-speaking rebels with bases in India led demonstrations, marches, and attacks on Bhutanese government property. Backed by radical international student organizations and political parties in Nepal fresh from a triumphant democracy movement in Kathmandu, where the powers of the Nepali throne had been curbed in a new constitution, the southern Bhutanese launched their public relations campaign to have the royal government of King Jigme Singye Wangchuck branded internationally as a violator of human rights.

Cloaked in the language of a democratic, antimonarchical cause, press releases from the rebels charged Thimphu with the mass murder of protesters, including more than three hundred people shot in one incident near the Indian border in Samchi district in September 1990. The democracy campaign in Nepal had used the same tactic of inflating (in multiples as high as ten) the numbers of protesters killed or injured by soldiers or police in large demonstrations. The charges in both places were usually not true, as reasonably dispassionate investigations later proved. Only one young man was proved to have been killed in Samchi during the most widely publicized incident. A local administrator told me it had been the poor boy's unfortunate karma that he should be on top of a piece of earth-moving equipment when policemen fired into the air to dissuade a mob from crossing a bridge from the direction of India. I videotaped the impassioned official, a cast of one, energetically acting out the entire story of that fateful day by moving from one side of an imaginary battle line to the other.

But the initial accusations of hundreds dead lingered because they had been widely reported by gullible, unprofessional, or sympathetic news organizations in Nepal and India and picked up thirdhand by the international press. At a news conference in Delhi soon after the Samchi incident, an advocate for the Nepali-Bhutanese rebels who was in fact a representative of the Hong Kong–based Asia-Pacific Students Association acknowledged that he had never been to Bhutan and had no firsthand evidence of atrocities. But Thimphu was caught off guard and quickly forced into a hopelessly defensive position.

At that point, Bhutan began to reconsider its hostility to the press. In March 1991, while in Dhaka, I got a call from the Bhutanese embassy in Delhi, saying that a visa would be issued to me forthwith, and I could proceed to Thimphu from Bangladesh on the unspoken promise of an interview with the king, who had taken charge of the southern problem. The Bhutanese knew that I had gone to Bhutan the year before and written articles in contravention of the rules, but this was conveniently overlooked.

Forty-eight hours of comedy followed. Bangladesh was one of the hottest countries on earth at that time of year, and I was working in thin cotton Indian and Pakistani outfits of baggy trousers and loose-fitting shirts called *salwar-kamiz*. In Thimphu, a Himalayan winter was just tailing off into spring. Not only were tropical clothes unsuitable to the climate, but I was also determined to stick to my rule of looking appropriately presentable when meeting any official or other public figure in the third world, however small or unimportant the country. Often our Western reputation for arrogant behavior in poor countries is matched by a notoriety for sartorial casualness that, rightly or wrongly, can bespeak disrespect to locally important people and their institutions. And this was the king of a country I wanted to visit again.

I combed steamy Dhaka for warm clothes in something that would pass for an international style, and in a size bigger than any Bangladeshi woman would wear—if she wore Western dress, which very few did. I rounded up a knit skirt and sweater from a local designer who ran a boutique in a tourist hotel, then I had a morning left to tear through Dhaka's vast bazaars in search of any shoes that weren't sandals and something resembling warm tights or long socks that would at least clear my knees; mercifully, the skirt was longish. In Dhaka, they sold mostly imported (or maybe smuggled) tights made for doll-sized Thai women under five feet tall. I found some warm ones, but walking in them was a new experience, since they reached about two-thirds of the way up my legs. A day later, arriving in Bhutan wrapped in a shawl, I made my first project a visit to a handicraft store to buy a jacket made of *yatra,* a rainbow-colored rough woolen cloth, homespun and handwoven, that struggled catastrophically for compatibility with my slightly frumpy Dhaka designer ensemble. (After the interview, I threw all of this away except the jacket; hotel chambermaids tried to return only the shoes, uncertain why they were in the wastebasket.)

Altogether, I think I looked fairly absurd as I was driven to an afternoon audience with the king in a Foreign Ministry Mercedes-Benz. But the sitcom didn't end there. The protocol officer assigned to me reacted in horror as I proceeded to get out of the car carrying a tape recorder and camera. Those are not permitted, he announced. I objected. We argued. He relented on the tape recorder; this was, after all, an interview on the record. But he held out, almost to the point of tears, over the camera. I gave in. When I later asked His Majesty if it might be possible to have a picture taken during the interview by a court photographer, the king asked me in return, "Didn't you bring a camera?"

He summoned a royal photographer, who stood trembling halfway across the audience hall and took a few useless shots, while I told His Majesty that I had been asked to leave the camera in the car. He muttered something about how civil servants in Bhutan have a lot to learn about public relations.

The Druk Gyalpo was troubled but confident in that first interview. (A year later he would sound less optimistic about the future of Bhutan.)

"We have no choice but to preserve our culture," he said. "Being a small country, we do not have economic power. We do not have military muscle. We cannot play a dominant international role because of our small size and population, and because we are a landlocked country. The only factor we can fall back on, the only factor which can strengthen Bhutan's sovereignty and our different identity, is the unique culture we have. I have always stressed the great importance of developing our tradition because it has everything to do with strengthening our security and sovereignty and determining the future survival of the Bhutanese people and our religion.

"But we are not an orthodox race of people," he continued. "In fact, we are very liberal-minded. We want to modernize the country and develop our country as quickly as possible. A lot of journalists in different parts of the world have given a very unfair and wrong impression that we want to remain a feudal state. No country in the world today wants to go back in time, and certainly this is not the case with Bhutan."

King Jigme Singye Wangchuck is head of both state and government, serving as his own prime minister. His cabinet, still dominated in the early 1990s by middle-aged men older than he, drawn from the Bhutanese elite, is supposed to be helping to decentralize Bhutan, giving more power to district administrators and encouraging more local representation in lawmaking and development. When there is foot-dragging, the king loses his temper, a minister told me, describing a cabinet session that turned into a tirade. "He really tore into us," he said. "What a lecture we got!" Most Bhutanese seem to accept the king as a committed and disinterested advocate of national development, though they are critical of some royal relatives and in-laws who appear to see openings to the newly freed private business sector as invitations to corner markets and reap huge financial rewards.

When not in his royal offices, on the road meeting his subjects, or at one of the four separate palaces of his four spectacularly beautiful wives, the youthful king lives in what appears (from a distant allowable vantage point) to be a reasonably small mountain lodge tucked into a steep side valley away from the main population concentrations along the Thimphu Chhu, the river that runs through the Bhutanese capital. When he travels, he makes a point of repeating, in even the poorest of crowds, the symbolic gesture of serving tea to his people. The understated lifestyle and demonstrations of humility seem to have paid off. The king said that when he got a copy of an antimonarchical tract being circulated by southern Bhutanese dissidents, he was surprised by its limited scope. "After they wrote that I had four wives, they couldn't think of anything else bad to say," he recalled.

The king's style drives his enemies wild. "He is *so* charming, *too* charming, our lovely king," a southern Bhutanese student in self-imposed exile in the United States remarked acidly as he tried to convince me in New York that all foreigners are too easily taken in by this earnest young man who is the sole survivor of a lost brotherhood of Himalayan Buddhist kings. The theme of foreigners being hoodwinked by an articulate and elegant ruler runs through all Nepali-Bhutanese exile publications emanating from Kathmandu. There is no denying that as long as the king stays in control of policy in the south, and is the international face of Bhutanese Buddhism, rebels will have a difficult time winning a long-term propaganda war. Only a few years into the insurgency, by which time the king had pardoned more than fifteen hundred southern rebels, dissidents were already focusing their wrath and their news releases on a few government officials, usually the foreign minister, Lyonpo Dawa Tshering, or the home minister, Dago Tshering (who are not related: Tshering is another common Bhutanese name, first or last). Both men, incidentally, seem to have a veto power over decisions on admitting writers and scholars to the country, and that power has been used irrationally or at least inexplicably on some occasions, given the critical importance of getting a hearing for Bhutan abroad.

King Jigme Singye Wangchuck says he believes that the most important qualities of character a king or any other leader should have are fairness, honesty, and common sense. "Of course, any other human qualities, as many as possible, are good," he added. The crown prince, who was born in 1980, is being raised in the same spirit, the king said. "I am very strict with him. I'm not strict with all of my children, but I'm very strict with him, because I don't want him to be spoiled. I want him to lead a normal life, and I want him to understand the Bhutanese people and the way we feel." The crown prince is now also a regular in the pages of *Kuensel,* as he takes on more ceremonial tasks.

The king used to play basketball nearly every day—a court was installed in Thimphu's largest public park—but his preoccupation with the southern rebellion, and with the toll it is taking on the country's development, has sapped both his energy and his hopes, he said, speaking in an English colored lightly by British and Anglo-Indian accents. I asked him if it was a lonely and tormented life at the top, especially in such difficult times. He replied, veering off into more generalized introspection: "I don't find it a very difficult problem because of the fact that I don't have any personal ambitions for myself. I don't do what is best for the king, or for the monarchy. I have found in the last thirty years, what is good for yourself is ninety-nine percent of the time bad for the country, and what is good for the country ninety-nine percent of the time is not good for yourself." He wants to be remembered more than anything as a pacifier and developer of Bhutan, building on the example of his father.

"Real development only started in Bhutan in 1961, and in the first ten years we spent all our time constructing roads, building schools, building even office facilities for our government departments and staff, for our different ministries. So in the true sense, development programs started in the last twenty-one years," he said. "What is important for outside countries to know, as well as our own neighbors in the region, is that we today, after thirty-one years of very rapid development, have achieved primary health coverage of ninety percent and primary education coverage of sixty-seven percent, child immunization of eighty-four percent. Our literacy level has increased from twenty-five percent to fifty-four percent, and our per capita income is right now around four hundred and twenty-five dollars." The figure was higher than that of India, as are the Bhutanese literacy rate and the level of primary school attendance. But all the achievements, confirmed by international organizations that see Bhutan as something of a model for development, are threatened by the rebels the king calls "antinationals."

"We were very confident in 1990 that before the year 2000 Bhutan would be the first South Asian country that would be able to provide universal free primary education as well as primary health coverage, as well as one hundred percent child immunization, to all our people. But the problems we are facing in southern Bhutan have had a very, very negative impact. We feel that unless peace and normalcy returns in Bhutan this objective, which we could have easily achieved before the year 2000, now today seems a very remote objective to fulfill. The problem has had a very, very serious effect on the well-being and also on the future prosperity and development of our people, not only in the south, but in all parts of Bhutan."

By the turn of the twentieth century, it had already become clear to Bhutanese leaders and foreign visitors that the influx of Nepali-speaking settlers in southern Bhutan would someday be a problem. After Indian independence in 1947, before King Jigme Singye Wangchuck was born, tensions rose and finally a minor revolt erupted, sparked by a new Nepali-led Bhutanese Congress Party. It taxed the early years of his father's reign.

"As a child I wasn't very aware of these complexities and problems," he said. "In 1953, when we had that uprising, the main reason was because India was flush from independence, it had democracy, and the main political party in India was the Congress Party. So the Nepalese felt that if you called their party the same as the Congress Party you would automatically get the support and sympathy and cooperation from the Indian Congress Party.

"Nevertheless, my father was a very forgiving man," the king said. "By 1958, he gave Bhutanese citizenship to all nationals who were residing in Bhutan at that time. But it is no secret, everyone knew that sooner or later we were going to have a problem in southern Bhutan because of the large influx of illegal immigrants, and also because our southern Bhutanese people, who are Bhutanese citizens, were going all out to try and bring as many nationals from outside as possible to increase their demographic population. We have a very porous southern border of about seven hundred thirty kilometers. It is totally, completely impossible to close it."

Later, I drove along part of that open and ill-defined frontier, from Phuntsholing, a noisy market town on the only easily accessible road to India, westward to Sibsoo, a hamlet near the border of Sikkim. The great South Asian plain begins here as the Himalayan foothills drop abruptly, sending mountain streams meandering crazily as if in confusion onto flatland. Forests give way to jungle scrub, enough to hide guerrillas—in one place long enough to dig a trench almost under the nose of an administrative center. Bhutan has no road of its own here, and my car weaved in and out of Indian territory all along the route.

On a morning walk around Phuntsholing, I could see schoolchildren crossing into Bhutan to take advantage of not only free but also more exciting schools with curricula designed to reflect the geography and life of the area. No one checked their identities at the border, or the identities of traders moving back and forth, some in Indian dress and some in

Bhutanese ghos and kiras. India demands the right of free access for its citizens; not surprisingly, they dominate cross-border commerce in this landlocked kingdom.

The king speaks bitterly of how the very high levels of recent development in the southern districts acted paradoxically as a catalyst to further migration, pulling in more illegal immigrants to what he called "a paradise on earth." Meanwhile, the efforts to raise living standards in the south—where much of the country's new small industries such as cement-making and fruit-processing were built to be more accessible to subcontinental roads and ports—had brought him into sharp confrontation with conservative northern Bhutanese who wanted all assistance to the ungrateful region halted.

All the while, rebels were bent on destroying the factories, schools, and clinics the government had built in the south, often depriving their own people and poor laborers from the Indian tea plantations across the border in the Cooch Behar area of West Bengal of the free health and education services they used in Bhutan. The king said that 60 percent of the patients who came to free Bhutanese hospitals along the border were Indian citizens. At one clinic I visited in Samchi, medical charts and files confirmed that there was a high proportion of foreign patients. On a bench in the sweltering courtyard, a family from India waited to have a sick child examined.

"We felt that for all bona fide southern Bhutanese citizens we must do everything possible to bring them into the Bhutanese mainstream politically, economically, socially, by giving them much more than what we give to the northern Bhutanese people," the king said. "I'd always hoped that if we could increase their per capita income, if we could give them more land, if we tax them less—and we did so—if most of our industries were established in the south, then a lot of employment would be generated for our people in the southern districts. I felt that this would be a tremendous incentive for them to want to be a Bhutanese national, and not want to be a Nepalese national or Indian national, because the economic conditions and social conditions and political conditions across the border were much worse. But unfortunately, this policy was not successful."

In the fall of 1992, the king told me that he had just faced the most turbulent National Assembly session of his reign. Many northerners and some Sharchopas, people from eastern Bhutan, who had rejected overtures to join a crusade against the Drukpa monarchy, wanted a get-tough policy and the public swearing of loyalty oaths to the king. Some threatened to take action against the rebels themselves. "Buddhists may be nonviolent," an administrator in the south told me. "But you can't push a Buddhist too far. Never poison the mind of a Buddhist or the Buddhist will go out of control. Cambodia was a peaceful land, but remember the Khmer Rouge." And the militant monks of Sri Lanka, I thought to myself.

The king tells the nation at every opportunity that he is committed to as humane a policy as possible in the south. If it fails, he is prepared to abdicate, he says. "What can I lose when what is at stake is the future of the Bhutanese people?" Recognizing that monarchy is not a very popular form of government at the end of the twentieth century, he says that ultimately the Bhutanese must be free to choose whatever system they want. He is doubtful about democracy, however, saying that a society needs to achieve some kind of "perfection" before it will work. He noted that the expansion of voting in Bhutan in 1992 had almost instantly produced a political bribery case, the country's first.

He greatly admires the king of Thailand's devotion to the development of his country. The Thai monarch has made himself an expert on, among other arcana, urban sewage treatment, what to do with the water hyacinth that clogs the canals, and the dangers of planting too many eucalyptus trees, while also very skillfully using his immense moral and mystical authority to support democracy in times of crisis. "His Majesty in Thailand is one of the few monarchs who is keeping the flag flying for a dying race of kings," King Jigme Singye Wangchuck says with a touch of sadness. Aware of the Thai king's immense popularity and power of persuasion over the Thai people, the Bhutanese king is more deeply hurt by the personalization of the southern rebellion. Stricken by the image, he describes almost mournfully how southerners hang pictures on their walls of the king and queen of Nepal. "In their minds and hearts," he says, "they feel they are Nepalis."

Increasingly disheartened and even desperate, King Jigme Singye Wangchuck takes his message to the south, from village to village where citizens have applied to leave to join refugees in Nepal. His ministers and family fear for his safety. Since he has pledged his throne to the cause of peace in that turbulent region, he says he has no option but to go, again and again.

"I have no hatred for southern Bhutanese people," the king said. "I don't have any hatred or anger against antinationals who have perpetrated a tremendous amount of violence and bloodshed in southern Bhutan. Our hope was that if we could develop the south, this would go a long way toward winning the hearts and minds of our people. I had hoped that they would realize the benefits of remaining Bhutanese citizens, and I explained to them that if you emigrate, or if you abscond, or if you go to Nepal or to India, your future will be bleak. There is chronic unemployment in India, there's chronic unemployment in Nepal. I cannot understand how they could possibly have a better livelihood outside the country.

"But the dissident groups who are outside want to make very sure that the development plan fails, because only in the atmosphere of discontent and only in a situation where there is a lot of suffering and unhappiness and disgruntlement in the south can they be successful in getting the support of the local people. So their objective and our objective are at opposite poles."

As if the disruption of a southern rebellion cloaked in a democracy movement weren't enough to keep a monarch busy, the king of Bhutan also feels pressure from various factions within his own Buddhist community. The new middle class, allowed in the early 1990s to privatize the previously government-run tourism industry, now wants to expand it to make investments—in hotels, restaurants, trekking and camping equipment, and imported vans and cars—pay off more expeditiously. With only a few thousand tourists (not counting Indians, over whom Bhutan has virtually no control) allowed to enter the country every year, profits are not large. Furthermore, dozens of small enterprises jumped into action when government ownership of tourism as well as national bus routes ended and services were sold into private hands. If tourist numbers remain small, there is bound to be a shakeout of unviable businesses, some of them operating more or less from the backseats of battered jeeps. When the consolidation comes, the already rich (who took to tourism with alacrity) will be richer and the poor entrepreneurs will be in another line of work—and resentful.

The infant tourism industry also wants more of Bhutan's temples and monasteries opened to foreigners. That request provokes sharp counter-reactions from the religious leadership and monastic orders. Monks wield considerable power in Bhutanese society. They not only resist the further intrusion of tourists—saying that temple treasures will disappear and the sanctity of holy places will be irrevocably disturbed—but also quietly defy efforts to modernize monastic life and put thousands of state-supported monks into some form of public service.

"We have always had very close affinity, very close respect and cooperation and deep faith, with the clergy," the king said. "There has always been total and complete harmony. One of the reasons is because the religious institutions in Bhutan do not interfere in the political aspects of the country, and the king does not interfere with religious affairs. In fact, I have emphasized to the government as well as to the religious community of Bhutan that it is important to give them more and more powers as far as religion is concerned. But even within Buddhism, changes have to take place, whereby the monks can no longer like in the past live in the four corners of the dzongs. They will have to go out and do social work. We would like them to be doctors, be health workers, help the farmers, help the poor people. I think that in this day and age, the Buddhist institutions in Bhutan will have to reach out to the people."

Where the king and religious leaders seem to be in agreement is in their opposition to the creation of an urbanized plutocracy with only the thinnest of ties to traditional Bhutanese civilization. This, the king says, is why he has turned his attention to satellite dishes, which he has banned twice.

"In Bhutan, we don't want several classes of people," the king said, "a small number of people who are affluent, who are rich, who are prosperous, and a majority of our people who are poor and live on subsistence farming. A lot of journalists from outside incorrectly criticized us for not permitting satellite dishes to be installed by the rich and very affluent few. They didn't bother to say that there were only twenty-nine satellite dishes, and eighty percent of them belonged to members of the royal family or rich business people. I don't see why any individual should spend seventy or eighty thousand ngultrum [about $2,700–$3,100] to have a satellite dish installed for his or her personal entertainment when the majority of the people do not have safe drinking water, when they don't have any proper sanitation facilities, when they have to walk days to get to their villages, when they don't have the opportunity to see even one movie in a year."

King Jigme Singye Wangchuck and his late father have, at some risk to the monarchy itself, given the Bhutanese one tool that makes the outside world truly accessible: a command of the English language, now the medium of instruction in all the country's schools. "This is a decision that was made a long time back," the king said. "If the government and the kings of Bhutan had wanted to keep Bhutan on a feudal basis, we would never have given priority to mass education—and certainly not in English." The introduction of English as a medium of instruction minimizes clashes over the use of Dzongkha, Nepali, or any other regional language, and also shortens the route to high-quality education and vocational training. Bhutan does not have the resources to waste money sending students abroad on government scholarships if they are unable to work in an international language.

"Bhutan is a very small country and we need all the successes we can get," the king says. "We cannot afford any failure at all. We want our people to be educated and highly productive. We want them to be professionals in every field they take up. If you are a sweeper, we want you to be a professional sweeper. If he is a mechanic, we want him to be the best mechanic he can be. This is why we have opened over two hundred schools in Bhutan, and one hundred fifty-eight health facilities."

The policy of aiming high in human development explains how Ugyen Dorji, the village lad from faraway Lhuntsi district, found himself in Bregenz, Austria, apprenticed to a pastry chef a decade ago. He tells the story as we sit over coffee in his Thimphu café, a sideline to the most popular bakery in town. He calls the bakeshop the Jichu Drake in honor of a sacred Bhutanese mountain. In the kitchen, burly men in clunky shoes, flour-splattered ghos, and sheepish looks were furiously stirring batter and dough, chocolate in one vat, white éclair paste in another. The ambience may have been small-town Bhutanese, with babies playing around the pastry counter, but the cream horns and vol-au-vents Ugyen Dorji produces are European in both inspiration and quality. They are served in all the best homes, in government offices, and at all kinds of parties. Business is good. Last time I saw the chef, he tooted as he passed by in a new imported car as I was walking back from a tour of the general hospital. Next time I came to town, he was off in India (or was it Bangkok or Singapore?) buying more kitchen equipment.

Ugyen Dorji began his education in the mountains of eastern Bhutan by trekking for several days to a distant school at the beginning of each term, a sack of rice on his back. The rice was all his widowed mother could afford to give him for the food he would need as a boarder. She had pleaded with local officials not to take her son away to school; they were insistent that he had ability and would benefit from education. From time to time, Ugyen Dorji said, she would take precious time to walk to his school to visit him and replenish his small stock of food. After completing a basic education, he drifted to Thimphu, where he eventually found a job in a government hotel, the Motithang. His knack with food got him noticed. The apprenticeship followed. He spent five years in Bregenz, and he returned a master, this mountain boy. But his mother, still living in a Lhuntsi village, has yet to make the trip to Thimphu to see her successful son at work. And he can't spare the time very often for days of walking to his hometown.

There are other Ugyen Dorjis now, young men with scrubbed knees and new shoes or what are obviously their first pair of Western trousers, waiting at the Paro airport for a flight into the modern world to become engineers, doctors, business leaders, or maybe sanitation experts. Europeans welcome them as good investments in scholarship aid. They don't seem to get homesick. They work hard. And when they come home, they make a difference, just as King Jigme Singye Wangchuck expects they always will. He takes a paternalistic pride in every Bhutanese achievement because they were born of royal policy, not public pressure—at least in the past.

"What most people don't understand is that this development in Bhutan has not been asked for by the people; it was not thrust upon us," he said of the monarchy. "We have done it because we believe that this will go a long way in educating our people in becoming more politically conscious, and at the same time to be able to actively participate in the decision-making process in all forms of development programs, both in their districts as well as nationally. If democracy in essence means that the government has to be supported by the people, decision-making has to be shared by the people, then I feel that in essence we have a far more democratic system than practically all the developing countries and some of the developed countries.

"We want to develop as rapidly as possible, but nevertheless what is important to us is that the pace of development and the ability of Bhutanese people to stay abreast of that pace—the gap between our own ability to do development programs and the pace of development that we implement—should not be so wide that it can never be bridged," he said. "We also at the same time do not believe that more money means more development. We don't believe that unless the infrastructure is there it is not feasible for any developing country to achieve overnight economic prosperity and bring overnight changes, economically, socially, and politically."

Though he wants more political participation, he returns repeatedly to his reservations about democracy. "In Bhutan, I myself feel disillusioned both about the democratic system of government as well as monarchy, because both have very serious flaws," he said. "Like democracy, for instance, only works when you have a perfect society. You have to have a society which is highly literate, politically very conscious, and also enjoy a very high level of economic well-being and prosperity. Then at the same time, when it comes to monarchy, if you have a good king, he can do a lot of good. And if you don't have a very good king, then he can do a lot of harm. The flaw with monarchy is that too much depends on one individual, and in Bhutan we cannot hope that for all time to come we will have a wise and good king.

"The king does not have a monopoly over what system of government we should have," he said. Nor, he added, should anyone be making commitments about the future, when new generations may have different ideas. "Whatever changes we bring about in Bhutan, so long as it is in the best interest of the country, the final decision lies with the Bhutanese people. And that is how it should be."

A few hours after the interview, when night had fallen over Thimphu's small central square and I was back in the modest Druk Hotel, a car from the palace arrived and two men soon appeared at the door of my room bearing gifts: a thangka in brilliant embroidered silk, a ferocious ritual mask like those used in classical temple dances, and a tiny box made by Bhutanese silversmiths. I decided not to send them back. They live with me still, reminders of a culture on the edge.

"Everywhere else dramatic changes have taken place," the king had said that day. "What is at stake here is the survival of the Bhutanese people and our religion. We are really the last bastion of Himalayan Buddhism."

Chapter 3

BECOMING BUDDHA

ON A DISMAL afternoon, when a Kathmandu spring had reverted without warning to wintry drizzle and dull gray skies, I went for a long walk up the hill behind the massive white stupa at Bodhnath, where one splendorous new monastery after another has risen to serve exiled Tibetans and all others seeking to study Buddhism since the Chinese began their assaults on religious life in Lhasa and other holy places. I was looking for Shechen, the temple and meditation center established by this century's most revered and beloved Bhutanese lama, the late Dilgo Khyentse Rinpoche. These few square miles above what everyone calls "Bodha" are becoming the world capital of Tibetan Buddhism, a place to start or finish or break a journey of discovery in the Himalayan kingdoms. Along the muddy lanes and footpaths, mostly rutted tracks too narrow for cars, that lead away from the dominating stupa, Tibetan women with roundish, leathery faces and cheerful smiles sell all the paraphernalia of the faith: prayer wheels to be spun with flicks of the wrist while walking, prayer beads, offering bowls, bells, the stylized double-diamond thunderbolts called *dorjis* (which look like ornate little barbells), Tibetan seals with sealing wax, and sometimes the brass spoons used to measure the ingredients in traditional medicine. Scattered among the stalls are open-fronted tailor shops where men stitch simple monastic garments or more elaborate temple hangings. Monks and novices of all ages and nationalities scurry along the unpaved footpaths or dawdle in groups to talk with acquaintances. I asked directions of a very earnest American woman, struggling up a grade in rubber sandals and a rather unorthodox set of maroon robes; other pilgrims were speaking French. As evening approached, the familiar drones of lessons being read and prayers said rose to the accompaniment of blasts from monotonal monastic trumpets and the rhythmic beat of drums.

So far, nothing would disturb the soothing vision of Buddhism that its impassioned advocates promote, except for the green-and-white Pakistan International Airlines Airbus nosing its way into the valley to land over the hill at Kathmandu's international airport. The problem is underfoot. The once-gentle mountain meadows on which these *gompas*—monasteries—stand are strewn with garbage, trash, and human waste. Pink and green plastic bags take the place of spring flowers among tufts of grass where scrawny dogs root for rotting scraps of food. At the approach to the Shechen monastery, the large welcoming sign painted on the main staircase tells us in a couple of languages not to urinate on the walls. (The monks doing so are around the side of the building out of sight of the sign.) Someone on orange roller skates zips across the main courtyard, a rectangular space, perhaps a city block long and half as wide, enclosed by monastery offices and the cells of monks. The monastery temple—an arresting gold-trimmed, deep red building several stories high—occupies the center of the courtyard, its triple-tiered pagoda roof rising above an ornate portico held up by slender pillars whose capitals are lavishly painted in religious motifs. The temple's stone steps are littered with plastic sandals and running shoes, not the soft velvet-thonged slippers of Burmese monks. Inside the monastic walls almost no vegetation has survived the human traffic. Is this a life of peace in natural harmony with the environment, which every Buddhist has a duty to protect? How far had I come from the monasteries of Bhutan?

To travel through the peaks and valleys of Himalayan Buddhism is to become a collector of fragmented images and a teasing array of sense impressions, many of them bound to counter the stereotypes of simplicity and serenity that we expect to define a Buddhist universe. At the end of the journey, the traveler assembles these sense fragments into an individualistic understanding of what has been seen and experienced. Maybe that's the way it should be, since Buddhism itself teaches us that each person must seek his own way to knowledge and enlightenment in this life or some other. Furthermore, in the Himalayan kingdoms, past and present, there has always been diversity of practice, if not belief. Local deities elbow into the theology of textbooks. Natural landmarks may be sacred only to those in their neighborhoods. Certain mythological characters or *bodhisattvas*—deferred Buddhas who play the role of saints—are more highly venerated in one place than another. In Buddhism, there is no Rome, no Mecca, no Jerusalem, no single book of rules for all. Even in the golden age of Tibetan monastic life, each gompa was likely to follow only one school, sect, or famous lama. In short, what we conveniently label Tibetan or Himalayan Buddhism is at grassroots level a riotous assortment of rituals and superstitions, icons and symbols, folklore and creed. In a few far corners of this earthy faith, animal sacrifice persists, lamas work magic, and drunken monks have been known to brawl. There is nothing Zen-like about this branch of Lord Buddha's clan.

Maybe geography has more than a little to do with the uncommon vitality of Himalayan Buddhism. To be born in this environment—where the body is strained to its limits while the soul is freed to soar above nature at its most magnificent—is to live a daily life of extremes. You awake in the morning more often than not cramped by the misty chill that comes with nighttime in the thin air of high altitudes. By midday, the sun brings sweat and somnolence. Long evenings are cheered by a fire and draughts of *chang,* a grain-based alcoholic drink, or some other powerful fermentation that loosens the tongue and sometimes the temper. Smiles crack weather-worn faces, and eyes that may seem expressionless by day flash and twinkle with recharged animation. Then, in the last warmth of the hearth, comes sleep. The darkness of night is complete, unique, beyond the reach of adjectives.

Physically, this is a universe of hamlets clinging to some flat fragment of land or least-precipitous slope along the foothills of snow-covered mountains that divide earth from heaven in an almost unbroken line from Pakistan across the arc of inner Asia to Burma. Inhabited hillsides, mere anthills when seen from the sky, are laced at ground level with spiderwebs of dirt footpaths from field to home, home to home, village to roadhead. Climbing and carrying, all paths seem to lead up, up, up. Men, women, and children spend hours bent over, eyes on the trail, as they trudge between home and points of commerce, a clear spring, or the ever-giving forest, carrying loads of sticks, water, harvested crops, or family provisions. When streams tumble down the rocky creases where one slope meets the next, women gather over laundry and talk as water-powered prayer wheels work feverishly if squeakily at sending petitions to the gods.

My images of the Buddhist hills are always populated, as if the people and terrain were eternally interrelated. I remember how Tamara Bhandari, the unforgettable host of a once-famous travelers' stop in the Indian city of Amritsar known only as Mrs. Bhandari's Guest House, sorted the valleys to the north of her by religion—Hindu, Muslim, or Buddhist—as if the land itself had taken on a faith and the choice had tempered the atmosphere. The Himalayas, humanly speaking, are both vast and intimate. If a veritable sea of exhilarating, ruthless mountains rises and falls from horizon to horizon, these same peaks shelter and often divide hundreds (maybe thousands) of social microcosms united only by their roughly shared Buddhist touchstones, their monks, and their legends.

In my visits to Buddhist regions of the Himalayas, the starting point was more often political than religious, but ultimately this led to many questions about Buddhism itself. Only the sense-dead can spend any time in the Buddhist hills without wanting to know more about the sustaining faith, its obvious egalitarianism, its rationality—demons and deities notwithstanding—and its inherent justice and fairness. In Ladakh, Sikkim, and Bhutan in particular, I wanted to understand how a Buddhist polity worked.

Historically, Buddhism grew and expanded its reach through the support of enlightened (or shrewd) emperors and kings. These realms, while feudal in organization, were not usually intolerant theocracies. Rulers—among them the early kings of Tibet and Nepal—saw in Buddhism not a philosophy with which to garb authority or cloak conquest but a force for civilizing and elevating their courts and the people they ruled. More recently, with the demise or dilution of the old kingdoms, Himalayan Buddhists have begun putting more emphasis on the political parameters of their religious communities, drawing lines in the sand to save their cultures. Tibetans, Ladakhis, and Bhutanese in recent decades have consciously made Buddhism the hallmark of their nationality and sometimes a banner for militancy or even violence that in some few places (at certain overheated moments) approaches religious fundamentalism. I wanted to know why these embattled Buddhists thought this system was worth fighting for.

After visits to Buddhist sites across the subcontinent, I returned again and again to Bhutan for the obvious reason that this was the sole remaining Himalayan Buddhist monarchy, the only laboratory left to us at the end of the twentieth century. And time seemed to be running out there also. In Bhutan now, it is impossible to avoid being drawn into the debate over religion and the state. This makes it a fascinating place to experience Buddhism in its Himalayan environment, and to learn how Buddhism shaped much of the Himalayan world that is no longer strictly Buddhist.

No other nation outside Bhutan has Tantric Buddhism as the state religion; its monastic institutions, for better or worse, are found there in their purest forms—in the sense that they have been least disturbed over centuries, not necessarily because they set universal standards. When I had the opportunity to spend time in monasteries, temples, and fortresses once closed to outsiders, I went eagerly and gratefully. The journey began in Thimphu.

THE FLAP-THWACK, flap-thwack of spirit flags snapped by the wind, the whirr of prayer wheels, and the clang of bells were the only sounds to be heard as a royal protocol officer and I climbed through the crisp morning air toward the Changgangkha Lhakhang, an ancient temple and monastic school in the hills above Thimphu. The temple is somewhere between five hundred and eight hundred years old, depending on which account of its history one chooses to accept or how much literal truth one sees in the mythological chronology that surrounds its founding. But there is no disagreement that the monastery stands on sacred ground, blessed by a sainted lama, Phajo Drugom Shigpo, who is credited with being the first Tibetan to bring the official Drukpa sect's teachings to Bhutan.

According to the delightful story told by the custodians of the temple, the elderly Phajo Drugom Shigpo won the love of a village girl of heavenly beauty who indeed turned out to be a celestial nymph. They eloped to a cave in a recess of the Thimphu Valley, where they were trailed by her mother, who had been made the object of ridicule by her neighbors because of the odd match her nubile daughter had made. Bursting into their hideaway, she caught them in the act of meditating. That didn't stop her from launching into a tirade of recrimination against their presumed carnal union. The saint paused before this whirlwind, then promptly turned himself into a manifestation of Avalokitesvara, the Bodhisattva of Compassion, a figure of intense veneration across the Hima-layas. This particular manifestation of the popular androgynous-looking bodhisattva is known as the "Avalokitesvara with a thousand arms and eleven heads." The nymph's earthly mother was overwhelmed by the miracle and retreated. In due course, the pious couple had seven sons (or descendants?), one of whom built the Changgangkha Lhakhang on land the lama Phajo Drugom Shigpo had earlier blessed. The temple's most important treasure, apart from a trove of precious manuscripts, is a statue of Avalokitesvara in a sitting position, as if still in meditation. Bhutanese religious authorities say that all other statues of the god in temples around the country are standing.

A nervous civil servant was leading me to Changgangkha Lhakhang under orders from King Jigme Singye Wangchuck, who was eager to demonstrate to a world lukewarm about monarchy that Bhutan had an extraordinary culture to save and that he was willing to wager his throne on preserving it.

"His Majesty wants you to know our culture, which is very dear to us," was the explanation I got from the young protocol officer as we reached the top of the path and walked into a panorama of medieval life still being lived around the monastic walls. To the right, just outside the monastery's narrow gate, a householder had erected an elaborate *doe,* a pre-Buddhist construction of wood, straw, and twigs that I would later learn was a home for malevolent spirits, designed to draw them away from the temptation of invading a human habitation. Or maybe it was an anticurse device, or a lure to attract the gods of wealth; one could never be sure of the exact function of one of these fanciful objects unless all the facts were available from the owner of the house and the holy man who designed the custom-made talisman. Sometimes these spindly inventions are tossed by the roadside amid the remains of flower and food offerings; these have been used to exorcise something evil pestering a household.

This particular doe at Changgangkha Lhakhang was perhaps five or six feet high, resting on four sloping stick legs, which nonetheless managed to prop up a sturdy pole that rose from their conjunction. At odd angles around the pole from its top to where it met the slanted legs, colored strings had been crisscrossed over thin sticks into cat's-cradle and geodesic patterns and festooned around small rimless wheels whose spokes gave them the look of eight-pointed Christmas-tree stars. Small cloth flags and straw braids hung here and there, in no apparent order—

though a rinpoche (in Himalayan Buddhism, a guru/scholar) told me later that there is never anything casual about these constructions.

Not far away from this elaborate doe was a small altar of murky spiritual origins set into a niche in the monastery wall. Someone had placed fresh cuttings of an aromatic plant in vases on a narrow shelf beside the ubiquitous brass bowls. To the left of the altar was a whitewashed stone fireplace for burning offerings to a local deity who seemed to guard the monastery gate. Fat gaudy chickens pecked the ground around this ecumenical collection of shrines. Add to the picture the woman mending clothes in the sun, two strolling men in conversation, and a boy and girl with a tin washbucket clowning by the water tap near the center of the courtyard, and the scene became a perfect illustration of Himalayan Buddhism's relaxed approach to religious sites. The fullness of life continued inside the walls, where a white-haired man with a wispy beard, who had just made the rounds of dozens of prayer wheels, sat on the warm stones and with arthritic hands spread out to dry what seemed to be lengths of coarse handwoven cloth.

Though there is activity around Buddhist temples and monasteries everywhere in the Himalayas, the difference in Bhutan—and to a large extent in Ladakh and Sikkim also—is the complete lack of the kind of frenzied commercialization that engulfs the great shrines of Bodhnath and Swayambhunath in Nepal or pilgrimage sites in northern India, where all kinds of trinkets and garments are laid out in colorful profusion, and touts nag at you to serve as guides. At Thimphu's Changgangkha monastery, all workaday activity dwindled as we moved around walls with dozens of niches for prayer wheels and along a walkway to the temple door, which was no more than an unprotected stone ledge atop a dizzying slope. Down the steep hillside, the copses of prayer flags flapped in frenzy, sending their block-printed petitions to the gods. Father William Mackey, a Canadian Jesuit who spent much of his adult life teaching in Bhutan, says he has idled away many hours watching prayer flags and has never seen one flap in a downward motion. "Always up, up, up to heaven!" he says. He's right. Of course, there has to be a scientific explanation, but in Bhutan you usually don't feel much of a compulsion to know what it is.

And then, after the last prayer wheel on the last wall is spun, the low, dull cacophony of monkish chants—old men and novices reciting or reading from the sacred books—takes over the senses. We lean forward to enter another small wooden door and plunge into darkness, an eerie void filled with a hundred voices and a hundred simultaneous but unorchestrated recitations. There is no other sound quite like this hum of a Himalayan Buddhist monastery as its inhabitants do their daily chores. The chanting of monks has both an unearthly pitch and intonation and a breathtaking hypnotic cadence. A lama told me that while the basic beliefs of Tibetan Buddhism were the same across the Himalayas, the Bhutanese had "different ways of playing the instruments and different tunes to chant the mantras." To an untutored ear, however, the effect of chanting monks can be the same in a monastery in the Nepali hills, Sikkim, or Dharamsala, the Dalai Lama's exile headquarters in northern India. Whether in the orderly recitations of an organized prayer service or the disorder of ritual or educative readings, the droning produces an unlikely clarity that seems to empty the atmosphere of distractions and expose the soul.

The sound ballooned in intensity as we neared its source: a corner chamber basking in pale yellow morning sunlight where rows of monks and their fidgety novices sat cross-legged on the floor, chanting from their hand-lettered, wood-bound sacred texts, each page a work of calligraphic art. The monks were working their way through a set of books at the request of a royal family member, someone said, explaining that the act of reading them aloud conferred blessings and protection on the patron. The sound filled the monastic hall, surged along stone corridors and into dark, airless, dungeonlike recesses packed with all the ingredients of busy sanctuaries. At each altar, cluttered with offerings and ritual objects, the air was hot and pungent from the flames of butter lamps. Massive images of the Buddha or one of his incarnates sat heavily and solidly in place.

Most sacred statues are hollow receptacles. I learned this in Bumthang, one of Bhutan's most sacred valleys, where artists were preparing and painting images in one of three temples at Kurjey, a place of great significance to Bhutanese history. A row of Buddhas-in-the-making sat facing a wall in the newest shrine, each with a neat rectangular hole in its back. The statues were waiting for the holy objects to be installed before they could be sealed and consecrated. By wonderful chance during that week, the monk-scholar Lopen Pemala, who was then director of Bhutan's National Library, was at work in a back room of the second Kurjey temple preparing the stuffings for the waiting Buddhas.

The room was no larger than ten feet wide and twenty feet long, and it was cluttered with the sacred inventory of the important task at hand, along with the worldly possessions of the elderly monks, on one of whose beds I sat. They worked on the floor, surrounded by ceiling-high stacks of boxes full of blessed treasure. Old books were piled on several shelves, one of which also held a decrepit electric clock. The only other modern artifact was a ballpoint pen, with which the monks checked off the items that were ready to be inserted into the waiting Buddhas and the chortens built to hold the remains of famous lamas or holy scriptures and objects often dedicated to their memory. There were forty statues and chortens left to fill in preparation for the funeral of Dilgo Khyentse Rinpoche, the towering figure of Himalayan Buddhism who would be cremated in Paro six months later, after his body had rested at a number of holy places in Bhutan and Nepal.

The ingredients to be placed in each Buddha image or chorten were specifically prescribed. There had to be Tibetan mantras written on sticks in gold ink. There had to be crushed pearls, turquoise, coral, gold, and silver. There had to be holy scriptures in Sanskrit penned on hand-made paper rolled "right side up," Lopen Pemala said. There had to be nine kinds of grains, and "everything else we can think of that we require in this earthly world has to be put in, at least symbolically." There had to be three types of mystical diagrams called mandalas, on yellow paper. When all was collected, the items had to be blessed and sprinkled with holy water by a high lama.

As he worked with his cheerful elderly monks as helpers, Lopen Pemala, with his impish face, a thin white beard, and accidental but appropriate tonsure of white hair around the edges of a balding head, spoke of the wonders and tragedies of the Tibetan Buddhist world that he had seen and experienced in more than half a century in holy orders. A Bhutanese by birth, he had been sent to Tibet as a boy to train in a harsh monastery, where he had been beaten with sticks by the resident disciplinarians. He laughs as he shows some vestigial scars on the back of his head. Since the Chinese invasion of Tibet in the 1950s, the catastrophic military response to an uprising in Lhasa in 1959, and the depredations of the Cultural Revolution, he has made long, frustrating pilgrimages to centers of Western learning to look for Tibetan holy books scattered abroad so that he could write a history of Bhutan and its links to the Tibetan monasteries. He found important Tibetan works in

Britain, France, Switzerland, and the United States, many in private hands and all priced out of the reach of the Bhutanese and thus more or less lost to Himalayan Buddhism. Lopen Pemala had also gone to Mongolia, the outer limit of the old Tantric world. Daydreaming that memory for a few moments, he noted almost as an afterthought that in Mongolia he had seen "texts written on pure silver in gold ink."

Like Lopen Pemala, other scholars of Tibetan Buddhism in Bhutan, Sikkim, Ladakh, and Nepal believe that the Tantric school they follow is the highest form of a unique world religion that began in northern India sometime in the sixth century B.C. The founder of the faith, Siddhartha Gautama, is believed to have been born in about 560 B.C. to a king of the Hindu warrior caste in Lumbini, in what is now the Terai region of Nepal. Most Westerners with even a passing knowledge of Asia know the outlines of his life, though very little of the story has been documented. Legend says he had a miraculous birth, entering his mother's body as a white elephant descended from the Tushita (the highest) Heaven, and exiting through her side in perfect human form. As a boy, he led a sheltered, even hermetic, existence in his father's palaces, and while still in his teens, married a surpassingly beautiful cousin, Yashodhara. Life couldn't have been better for this young scion of a princely family belonging to a regional people called Shakyas.

But the young man was restless, eager to see the world from which his father had sequestered him. With his servant Channa, Siddhartha made, according to one account, four possibly secret but certainly fateful forays outside his home; others say the four experiences were combined in one trip. In any case, he saw four disturbing new sights: an old man, a sick man, a corpse, and finally a holy man dressed in rags. If the first three visions shattered the complacency he may have had about his world, the last taught him that it might be possible to find a human goodness and perhaps a sorrow-free existence that bore no relation to a material environment. After his encounter with the beatific *sadhu,* the young man returned home in mental and spiritual torment. He soon made the decision to follow the holy man's example. He stole away at night to become a wandering ascetic, cutting his long hair and discarding his silk robes and jewelry. He wanted, we are told, to find spiritual solutions for the temporal sorrows he had seen.

Years of preaching and teaching followed. At times the young man lived as a hermit, punishing his body with thorny beds and starvation.

But this extreme asceticism was no more satisfying to his spirit than a life of luxury. Mercifully for millions of Buddhists, he survived harsh deprivation and found the Middle Way. John Snelling conjures up the scene this way in his *Buddhist Handbook:* "At a place nowadays called Bodh Gaya, in the modern Indian state of Bihar, Siddhartha made himself a cushion of grass beneath the spreading branches of the famous bodhi tree, a tree of the species *Ficus religiosa*. He determined to sit in meditation here until he found an answer to the problem of suffering—or died in the attempt." By most accounts, he sat there for more than a year— some say six years—fighting off his ego and the temptations dangled before him by the evil demon Mara. At dawn one morning in May, he achieved Enlightenment, and became Buddha, the Enlightened One.

For forty more years, the Buddha Shakyamuni—the sage of the Shakyas, or historical Buddha, because there are numerous Buddhas or Buddha manifestations before him and yet to come—lived as a mendicant philosopher, practitioner of meditation, and founder of monastic communities. The earliest scene of his teaching, the Deer Park at Varanasi, is remembered in the pairs of golden deer placed high above the temple doors of many Himalayan monasteries. Buddha Shakyamuni never sought to be a messiah or a god, nor did he claim descent from one. The Buddhist message, simply put, was compelling in the caste-ridden Hindu world inhabited by bloodthirsty deities: salvation and the end of suffering come only through the understanding of one's own mind. The path to heaven is an individualistic journey from sorrow and suffering to enlightenment. One's karma, the accumulation of past and present deeds and thoughts, exerts a powerful influence as a believer passes through a recurring process of birth, death, and rebirth. But acts of merit and a life rightly lived may mitigate karmic fate.

The Buddha taught Four Noble Truths: that existence is suffering, that the origin of suffering is desire and attachment to material goods, that suffering ceases when desire ceases, and that desire can be washed away by following the Noble Eightfold Path: right understanding, right thinking, right speech, right (temperate) action, right livelihood, right effort, right mindfulness, and right meditation, leading to bliss. Buddhists learn not to take the life of a living creature and never to appropriate something not freely given them. Ideally, they also strive not to drink intoxicants or take narcotics, not to lie or speak (or act) abusively, and not to be sexually promiscuous or irresponsible.

The Buddha Shakyamuni had a practical streak, or so we gather from stories told of his common sense, tales perhaps invented to humanize him. He had clever ways of putting down the egocentric or self-righteously pious. In one story, he turned on a disciple pushing for a clear statement on vegetarianism with the remark that he was more concerned with what came out of someone's mouth than what went into it. On another occasion, he was approached near a river by a puffed-up monk who said he had spent years learning to walk on water. Why do that, the Buddha asked, when there is a ferry nearby?

By the time Lord Buddha died, possibly of food poisoning or dysentery, he had urged his followers to form communities for meditation and study of the *dharma,* the laws and practices of the Buddhist universe. These communities became the *sangha.* Those who want to call themselves Buddhist make only one initial promise: to take refuge in the Buddha, the dharma, and the sangha. These are the Three Jewels. Though in some countries "sangha" is now a term applied almost entirely to monastic orders, the Buddha Shakyamuni intended it to mean the whole community of believers, which he divided into four groups of equal importance: monks, nuns, laymen, and laywomen. It is interesting to note that over the centuries, the role of nuns has never met the high expectations of Lord Buddha. In the Himalayas, the importance of nuns seems to have declined, in fact, despite the equality women often enjoy in secular life.

Since Lord Buddha's death, the religion that came to be known as Buddhism has developed numerous sects and schools. But the first major divisions of Asian Buddhism were two: the Hinayana, the "lesser wheel" or "smaller vehicle," and the Mahayana, or "greater wheel" (or vehicle). Tantric Buddhism—also called Vajrayana, the "diamond vehicle"—evolved from the Mahayana sometime between the third and the seventh centuries A.D., and there is a division of opinion over whether it is a separate school or simply an extension of the Mahayana tradition.

Hinayana Buddhism, known as Theravada by the Thais, Sri Lankans, Burmese, and others who follow it, consolidated the first of Buddhism's great theological systems, codifying the basic teachings. The Mahayana school followed a few centuries later. With considerable oversimplification, one may say that Mahayana gives greater emphasis to service to humanity and less to the self-centered search for individual perfection. The bodhisattvas, compassionate could-be buddhas who chose to stay and serve in the imperfect world rather than enter heaven, became important figures to be emulated and worshipped. Coincidental or not, this underlying social-service philosophy seems to be reflected in the absence in Himalayan towns of begging monks making their formal early-morning rounds through poor villages, as they do in Thailand or in other Theravada communities. Ordained Tantric Buddhist monks or lamas (masters who are not necessarily in holy orders) are always on hand to teach, counsel, cure, and pray over important milestones in a person's life. Traffic in and out of the monasteries by monks and laypeople is constant, not limited to ritual occasions. Some families with money and large homes may maintain a resident monk. That lamas and monks are often paid, sometimes lavishly, for their services does not, ideally, diminish their sense of vocation. ("The best wheel is the Greater Wheel," says a Bhutanese dashboard sticker.)

Alone in the Himalayas, the Buddhist Bhutanese government feels free to press monks into public service projects, and is urging state-supported monastic communities to take a more active part in health or sanitation drives and other village development. One of these projects, backed by UNICEF, would also help monks improve their own living quarters as a way of setting an example. They might well start at Punakha, the ancient capital and seat for half the year of Bhutan's chief abbot, the je khenpo. There the stench of latrines nearly made my aristocratic Bhutanese traveling companion vomit as we searched for an exit in a little-trafficked corner of the monastery. The three-sided cloister of monks' quarters was teeming with unkempt novices, who tossed refuse, spat, and generally sullied the piece of muddy ground below them, over which hung the pungent smell of urine and feces that emanated from an unseen corner. We had also encountered human waste in a dark corner of the dzong itself, along a passageway to the grandest of monastic assembly halls. Chaucer would have enjoyed this.

Himalayan Buddhism developed a complex theology of birth and rebirth to govern the fate of ordinary believers as well as the reincarnations of great lamas and monastic abbots. The rebirth of religious leaders as infant reincarnates known as *tulkus* became entrenched as a system by the fourteenth or fifteenth century and persists into the present day, modified only by the fact that some reincarnates are now born abroad, as far afield as Europe or the Americas. A lot of politics and fund-raising considerations have crept into the otherwise miraculous appearance of incarnates, as monasteries look for well-connected tulkus as insurance against powerlessness or penury.

Sometimes, international geopolitics complicates the issue. Years of wrangling between rival claimants to the leadership of the Kagyupa Karmapa, a sect of the Kagyupa order based at Sikkim's Rumtek monastery, aroused such passion that Indian troops were called in at one point to break up rioting. The schism, during which charges of Chinese influence were traded liberally, led to the investitures of two Karmapa abbots, one in Tibet and one in India. At the latter ceremony, in 1994, uniformed police carrying automatic weapons stood between the little tulku on his throne of peace and the unpredictable congregation, which everyone assumed was laced with spies and agents provocateurs and armed with rocks and bottles. Of course, scholars remind us that Buddhism is the religion that has proved it can be rendered schismatic over the drape of a robe, or whether it covers one shoulder or two.

Tantric Buddhists view the history of Buddhism as a progression leading upward to the highest, most complex, and most sophisticated form of the faith—theirs. "The Hinayana should be taken as basic knowledge," said Rigzin Dorji, the Bhutanese scholar. "The Mahayana should be taken as attitude. Tantra means practice. In the Western concept this is called mysticism. Tantra is risky. It's very difficult also because lamas do not teach immediately. A lama has to judge the student, whether he can uphold the vows or not. Without testing the student, he will not impart any teaching on tantra. He may simply say, why don't you study the basic Buddhist texts: the Hinayana, the Mahayana? The student, once accepted by a lama, must strictly follow all of his instructions. The student has to find a suitable teacher; the teacher must select a suitable student—but only after a few years, when they know each other very well, like father and son." Rigzin Dorji, who compared Tantra to "a rocket going to the moon," added that we must remember "there can be terrible accidents in space." This religion is not for the timorous or half-hearted. Its monks live, Rigzin Dorji said, by no fewer than 345 rules.

Most simply described, the perfection of Tantric practice is "like building a house," suggests Chogyam Trungpa, a reincarnation of a leading Tibetan lama who became a monastic abbot at the age of eighteen months. "First you put down the foundation, then you build the first story, then the second. Then you can put a gold roof on if you like." In other words, first the Hinayana, then the Mahayana, then the Tantra.

"Looked at in this way," he says in *The Dawn of Tantra,* "the whole of the practice of Buddhism can be regarded as tantra, although all Buddhists outside the historical tradition of tantra might not agree with this."

"The basic idea of tantra is, like any other teaching of Buddhism, the attainment of enlightenment," he wrote. "But in tantra, the approach to enlightenment is somewhat different. Rather than aiming at the attainment of the enlightened state, the Tantric approach is to see the continuity of the enlightened mind in all situations, as well as the discontinuity of it." The achievement of the Tantric ideal, he later says, requires a student to pass through increasingly difficult stages of study. In the end, the student "has related to his body, learned to slow down the speed of muscles, veins, emotions, blood." With everything in low gear, "the student is able to relate to the ultimate space through his relationship and union with the teacher." Slowing down or altering the mechanisms of the body probably explains the superhuman abilities of certain great lamas.

Across the Himalayan landscape, stories persist of lamas who have the power to transform themselves into wild creatures. "Some people believe these lamas can assume the forms of animals or birds," a well-educated government official told me in Tashigang. "As birds, they can fly away and return to caves in the northern mountains where they meditate." Most modern Buddhists treat such accounts with derision or, to be on the safe side, say that today's lamas and monks no longer possess these special powers enjoyed by earlier generations of holy men. Himalayan Buddhists have for centuries been asked to explain not only occult practices but also the ability of holy men and women to meditate without food or clothing in bitter winter weather in the shelter of caves or exposed rock formations, sometimes at altitudes high and inaccessible enough to defeat mountaineers.

Alexandra David-Neel, a remarkable French Tibetologist and a recognized lama, noted in her 1931 book *Magic and Mystery in Tibet* that the *lung-gom-pa* lamas—those trained in secret regimens of breathing and body control to move with extraordinary speed—could travel "as if carried on wings." David-Neel, a scholar but also a popular writer who died peacefully at the age of one hundred in the French Alps in 1969, reported seeing lamas in trancelike states demonstrating *lung-gom* techniques on several occasions during her journeys in Tibet. This was her first encounter:

"I could clearly see his perfectly calm impassive face and wide-open eyes with their gaze fixed on some invisible far-distant object situated somewhere high up in space. The man did not run. He seemed to lift himself from the ground, proceeding by leaps. It looked as if he had been endowed with the elasticity of a ball, and rebounded each time his feet touched the ground. His steps had the regularity of a pendulum. He wore the usual monastic robe and toga, both rather ragged. His left hand gripped a fold of the toga and was half hidden under the cloth. His right held a *phurba* [magic dagger]. His right arm moved slightly at each step as if leaning on a stick, just as though the *phurba,* whose pointed extremity was far above the ground, had touched it and were actually a support."

In Kathmandu, Purna Harsha Bajracharya, a Buddhist from the ancient Newar community of Nepal, told me a story about the power of Tantric law that had been passed down through his family. His father, Chitta Harsha Bajracharya, was Nepal's first recognized Tibetologist; he had catalogued all the Tibetan monasteries in the country for the National Archives. "One of our forefathers, a student of Tantra, was in Lhasa," Purna Harsha began. "He was respected very much by Tibetan lamas. Some of them invited him to tea in the Potala. When tea was poured, he just took what was in his cup and instead of swallowing it, spat it out the window. The lamas were disturbed. Again they poured the tea; again he spat it out the window. After three times, when he finally took the tea and did not spit it, then the lamas asked him: 'Was there something wrong with the tea? Why should you suspect it, when it was the same tea served to us?' Our forebear then told them: 'You see, I saw in my mind my house in Nepal and it was on fire. The people there were trying their level best to put it out, but not succeeding. Then, with the help of a mantra from Tantric law, I took the tea and spat it out of the window, willing it to put out that fire.'

"After two or three months he was informed that on that very day all of a sudden his house had caught fire. After many hours, clouds suddenly came and there was a very heavy rainfall. It doused the blaze. The Tibetan lamas, hearing this, went to him and wanted to keep him there in Lhasa. But with some difficulty he left and returned to his home in Nepal. People told the story everywhere afterward, believing how it proved the power of Tantric law."

Sangay Wangchuck—then the undersecretary of Bhutan's Central Monastic Secretariat and later director of the National Library—told me that there always had been and probably still are lamas whose mastery of higher disciplines had given them extrahuman powers. There are also plenty of Himalayan magicians and charlatans who appear to perform abnormal feats. The difference, he said, was that the lamas who had developed extraordinary powers were not in show business and would be very reluctant to make themselves known in any public way.

"A magician is not an enlightened person, though he can show a lot of things using a combination of material objects," he said. "But that's not really spiritual. It is another thing if that is achieved through meditation, practice. But if one monk or lama had the power to perform miracles, this is mostly kept quiet. They are not showing these things. Only if it is necessary do lamas show the miracle. If someone is a magician working with material things, then he always performs it. Such a person might be a lama, might be a monk, but we have to be very careful about this kind of miracle or supernatural power he seems to be performing."

True supernatural powers are not contrived, but spring naturally from higher levels of Tantric practice, said Sangay Wangchuck. "When you are learning Buddhism, the basic teaching, we are not studying these things. But when you come to a certain level, these practices come to you naturally. Step by step if you study and do whatever you have to do, you reach that level by yourself. But we Buddhists are never concerned much about this." At a time when monastic communities are fighting to retain their primacy in the life of Bhutan, a debate over lamas who can turn themselves into animals or birds ranks in importance with the argument over how many angels fit on the head of a pin.

Chapter 4

BEFORE
TIBET, THERE
WAS BON

I MET SANGAY WANGCHUCK because I had asked for help in identifying the objects that crowded the altars of Himalayan temples and drew the devotion of ordinary people whose shared treasures they were. Village shrines, whose old statues and bright, polished vessels amid an array of offerings—replicated in the prayer rooms of thousands of Bhutanese homes, large and small—are as much an integral part of daily life as the fields, clinics, homes, and schools. In many small hamlets, a rudimentary temple with only a lama or two, or maybe none, is the only focal point for the community. Most Bhutanese shrines and monastic chapels have not been forced by security concerns to pack away altar treasures or restrict the spontaneous use of them by worshippers. Furthermore, confounding the outsider, Himalayan Buddhist holy places tolerate deities and legendary beings who wander in from other faiths or the powerful local spirit world and who may be accorded shrines of their own under the roofs of more classic icons. I had seen bowls, chalices, pitchers, money, food, candle-powered revolving lamps, photographs in silver frames, peacock feathers, and once a Heineken can placed before images of Buddhas or saints in various forms, temperaments, or colorations.

Monastery compounds and the courtyards of dzongs are egalitarian places for people as well as spirits. The rich and poor, powerful and humble, cross paths on pilgrimages to the country's holiest places, not only in Bhutan but also in other Himalayan kingdoms, past and present. Though temples are often dark and palpably holy, they are not forbidding places. Peals of laughter float out of corners perfumed by butter lamps, where worshippers pay (I guess they would say they make a contribution) to have a monk roll a set of three dice in the hope of getting a lucky number, which may be interpreted as a sign to be read before an important undertaking or just as a bit of extra good fortune perhaps to sweeten life. If the first throw turns out badly, you can always try again and again until something better turns up, preferably an auspicious odd number. The monks enjoy the game too.

To strip this wildly abundant universe down to its textbook basics, Sangay Wangchuck and I went on a tour of two more austere and orthodox holy places, Thimphu's Memorial Chorten, built in honor of King Jigme Dorji Wangchuck, who died in 1972, and Simtokha Dzong, a seventeenth-century monastery-fortress that is now a school emphasizing Himalayan Buddhist culture—though here, too, a frightening likeness of the familiar protector Mahakala, a destructive god apparently borrowed from (or shared with) Hinduism, glowered over a corner of the inner sanctuary.

We started with the Memorial Chorten's votive butter lamps and the brass offering bowls, usually seven of them in a row, filled with fresh water every morning to symbolize all the material donations that the gods appreciate. There were, however, eight bowls on the altar before which we stood at the foot of a three-story, three-dimensional mandala representing one deity and his entourage. Sangay Wangchuck had just finished saying that the mandala followed the teachings of the Nyingmapa school, the oldest order of Tantric Buddhism, even though Bhutan's official Buddhist school is the Drukpa branch of the Kagyupa order, a younger school.

But the eight brass bowls where there should have been seven was not a sectarian matter. My instructor was adroit. Sangay Wangchuck explained what each water-filled brass bowl symbolized, first the seven standard ones, and then the mysterious eighth. "From here, this is the drinking water, this the washing-the-feet water, then the flower offering, then incense offering, then lamp offering—should be the lamp here; light offering actually—then this should be the perfume offering, this food offering. Then music offering there. This is one, two, three, four, five, six, seven, eight offerings." Music? But by then we were moving on to the *torma,* those sugary-looking, pastel-tinted constructions of flour and butter that soften the brass and silver of altars. It was much later that I heard from a Tibetan-born lama about "eight lucky offerings." Unfortunately, the same lama told me there were always seven symbolic offering bowls. Okay.

The Bhutanese, not alone among Asians, love numbered categories. Among my favorites are Buddhism's "five nonretentions" and the "eight conditions of nonleisure." These are described by Khetsun Sangpo Rinbochay in his *Tantric Practice in Nying-ma* (translated by the Buddhist scholar Jeffrey Hopkins). As I tried to grasp even the outlines of Himalayan Buddhism, I identified immediately with the nonretentions: retaining the words but not the meaning, retaining the meaning but not the words, retaining the meaning without identifying it, retaining the meaning but confusing the order, and retaining the wrong meaning. As for the eight conditions of nonleisure—birth as a hell-being, as a hungry ghost, as an animal, as a god of long life, in an uncultured area, as a person possessed of erroneous views, in a land where Buddha has not been, or as a stupid person—I found not just a couple that fit.

But despite the twos (or fours or fives) of this and the eights of that, there is a certain marvelous flexibility to the Bhutanese mind when it comes to the quantification of phenomena—brass bowls, kilometers, or whatever—and to the application of universally accepted ordinal or chronological concepts. The calendar is an example. At the start of a public ceremony in eastern Bhutan, the presiding official began with a statement of that day's date, according to Bhutanese reckoning. It was a wonderful poetic recitation that went something like "On this twenty-sixth day of the ninth month of the year of the Water Monkey . . ." Because I didn't have a pencil and paper and the ceremony was long, the exact wording was gone from my head by the end of the event, but I wanted to make a note of it. That was on a Thursday. Only three days later, on Sunday, I remembered to ask a local administrator to recall Thursday's date for me. He said he didn't know. I replied that I would settle for today's date on the Bhutanese calendar, and would work back to the one I had missed. He said that wasn't so easy. "Sometimes we add extra days if they are auspicious, or drop one if it isn't," he said. "These things are never the same." Fascinated, I asked other people in the small town where I was staying about the Bhutanese calendar. The question drew a lot of blank stares. Many people did not appear to know how to reckon months and days—although I have seen the Bhutanese calendar displayed in schools—or simply did not feel it was necessary to focus on what particular day it was, unless it was a festival date or other important event. Yet somehow it all comes together again early each year on Losar, the Himalayan Buddhist New Year, after which everyone is left to drift off again into his or her own time zone.

At the Memorial Chorten, Sangay Wangchuck and I were studying the sugary torma, which he said were of two kinds. The bigger elaborate ones, great sunbursts of overlapping colored petals radiating from a central circle, similar to some of those on display at the National Museum, were the work of monks, who had created them as acts of faith to be semipermanent altar ornaments. Nowhere in the Himalayas had I seen such exquisite constructions as those on the altars of Bhutan. These are both larger than average and far more elaborately and artistically formed than others. Smaller torma, some looking like crudely formed cookies, were offered by lay Bhutanese worshippers, who also brought modest gifts to leave under a nearby portrait of the late king. That day, the centerpiece among these gifts was a yellow plastic bucket with a few plastic flowers.

"The small torma is like a symbolic food offering," Sangay Wang-chuck was saying. "They make these traditional shapes themselves and bring. Or sweets they bring. Here is a dry flower, a special flower. It is traditional, but we can use any flower here." Whatever else the faithful bring, water is still the most popular and sensible form of offering, given with the purest of intentions, he said. In Buddhist thinking (as in Christian parables and stories), the ideal attitude is that the simplest gift can have the most value. "So usually, we did water offering only," Sangay Wangchuck said. "Easy. You don't have any greed with that. Right? Water is everywhere available, so you can offer it without greediness—materialism. Some offerings may be more valuable. So maybe sometimes you think, well, this is too valuable, you cannot give that. Maybe you spend a lot of money, so there will be attachment there. But water doesn't have any attachment, because you can offer as much as you can. So therefore maybe it is simple, but is accumulating a lot of merit, free of attachment. Anybody can do it. Anybody can offer it."

Getting a handle on the three-dimensional mandala in front of us— one of the chorten's three levels of monumental constructions of carved and painted images climbing toward a pinnacle crowned by a deity— was a lot more difficult than understanding the purity of spirit required for making a meaningful offering. Sangay Wangchuck, a tall, easygoing, but erudite man with a cosmopolitan frame of mind after stints as a monk in Sri Lanka and as an adviser to a Tibetan Buddhist temple in Woodstock, New York, spoke English in his own way but certainly meant to speak clearly. Yet here was what he considered a simple explanation of what we were looking at on the chorten's ground floor: "So this is the mandala of the Dorji Phurba. Its main feature, we call in Sanskrit *Vajrakila*. *Vajra* means thunderbolt, or indestructible symbol, and the *kila* means 'nail' something, symbolizing 'subdue all the negativities.' The *Vajrakila* has many retinues, mainly four. Each one has the other retinues. So they will be called the mandala. 'Mandala' means an assembly of that particular deity. Especially you find in the Buddhism they use 'mandala' for two things: one a symbol of that particular deity, one an offering. That mandala offering is a universal offering, offering to the object all the universe, that is mandala offering. If you say 'mandala,' that is an assembly of that particular deity. But then you can see the diagram, flat that is, that is actually their palace, or something like that."

After a few hours in Sangay Wangchuck's company, if much remained murky because of my ignorance, what actually became reasonably clear to me, never a student of Buddhism, was that many of the terms we understand to represent only one object or aspect of a multifaceted religion like this may have many meanings and usages. I had raised the definition of the term "mandala" with him because in my mind the word had always meant a two-dimensional mystical graphic of circles and squares—whether schematic "paintings" in colored sand or the floor plan of the stupendous Javanese temple at Borobudur. Here in Thimphu I faced a larger-than-life jumbled pyramid of earth beings (some with animal faces) and demigods scrambling or struggling or getting tramped underfoot ("pressing out the negatives," Sangay Wangchuck volunteered) as they groped upward toward the commanding visage of their deity in the upper reaches of their world. At the top, the deity was locked in sexual embrace with his consort, an erotic pose that Himalayan Buddhists are taught is the interaction of compassion and wisdom, or means and wisdom, with wisdom represented by the female form. Some of the powerful faces on the way up the mandala were terrifying. Sangay Wangchuck explained that this was because the more intractable negatives didn't respond to a placid Buddha, and so there had to be "semiwrathful or very wrathful emanations."

Those who are tempted to dabble in Tibetan Buddhism are repeatedly reminded that such a quest is not a part-time occupation satisfied by occasional bouts of concentration. Among Tantric communities, the monks and scholars of the faith kindly but firmly deflected all but the most basic of questions about a very complex and often secretive religion with sexual rituals and intimations of the supernatural they could not or would not describe in detail. I acquiesced willingly because I was not seeking instruction or enlightenment, though it was frustrating to know that there would be much I would never comprehend. "You have to go through the practice," a Bhutanese monk told me. "Then you will understand." I came to learn that even in quests for what seemed like basic information, it was necessary to be patient and let knowledge come in its own time.

But on the ground in Bhutan, as elsewhere in these mountain realms, Himalayan Buddhism seems a much less esoteric way of life than its sophisticated theology would suggest. Early in the morning in Thimphu, I would sometimes go to the Memorial Chorten to watch the faithful at prayer from the distance of a park bench. It was a scene repeated with variations at temples as diverse as the high-tech (by Tibetan standards), Western-financed Rumtek monastery in Sikkim or at numerous small shrines in offtrack Buddhist enclaves in Nepal. In Thimphu, old women and men, well-dressed young professionals—probably civil servants or the vanguard of the new business class—and schoolchildren in uniform all turned up at the chorten before the workday began to spin the prayer wheels near the gate and take in a few circumambulations, clockwise walks around the shrine, while chanting mantras with the help of prayer beads and now and then pausing before images placed in niches on the four outer walls.

One morning, about two dozen people, alone or in small groups, were walking around the base of the chorten. There were old men and women in worn clothing and young executives in smartly tailored ghos in understated stripes or plaids, worn with silken knee socks, the best Western-style leather loafers or shoes, and sometimes stylish briefcases, which they put down on the grass to free both hands for worship. Most carried prayer beads. One elderly gentleman with a gigantic goiter and decrepit basketball shoes shuffled along alone, chanting, *"Om mani padme hum"*—"Hail to the jewel in the lotus"—the mantra of the mountains. The air was cool. Most people seemed to stop to pray before one niche bathed by warm sun. Each clasped two hands above the head, then before the face and again at chest level, all the movements in quick succession. This signifies mind-speech-body. Some then dropped to the ground and prostrated themselves. Others resumed walking.

The circumambulation routine seems to combine a morning constitutional with an act of devotion. People are ready then to face the day physically and spiritually refreshed. After an hour, as people came and went, several monks joined the procession, one leading a stately and very old woman in Tibetan dress. All gave the large prayer wheels near the gate the obligatory spin that rings a bell. At one point there was a constant clang of bells even when no one was entering the courtyard; an urchin had wandered in from the street and was spinning the prayer wheels for fun. He seemed to be Nepali or Indian, not Bhutanese, but no one chased him away. Another little boy arrived, ragged and piggybacking a baby. He stood and watched as luckier boys headed for school burst into the courtyard in a noisy pack, chewing bubble gum, to follow the daybreak ritual with about as much reverence as British schoolboys attacking compulsory morning prayers. The children's school uniforms, boys' and girls', had been tailored into small versions of the national costume.

A young couple came to share breakfast on the grass. Their clothes said they were not Bhutanese, but possibly Indian or Nepali laborers from one of the construction projects; these laborers live in hovels on the edge of town. She carried a tiffin box and a thermos, and served him rice, lentils, and tea, waiting until he finished before she ate. They did not circumambulate or pray. No doubt they were Hindus. Hindus find peace here, too.

There is a good deal of unseen ritual attached to the ubiquitous prayer beads carried around the chorten and everywhere else a pious Buddhist goes, said the Rinpoche Mynar Trilku, a Tibetan scholar who is also curator of Bhutan's National Museum. The beads are part of a good Buddhist's basic kit, along with a prayer book and an amulet containing a holy relic or religious writing. "Normally in olden days when you traveled, you had an amulet," he said. "Lamas have a bigger one, laymen a smaller one. Then maybe if the layman is a religious person who reads, he has his prayer book and his rosary. Other laymen, they have just the rosary. When you're traveling and you sleep, you keep it normally above your head. You hang the rosary, prayer book, and amulet on the head of the bed." To be effective, however, the amulet and beads must first be ritually prepared, the rinpoche said.

"Normally when a rosary you take, first you go to the lama to get the authorization, because in Buddhism the most important is you know how to read a mantra," he explained. "Unless you have authorization from a lama, the effect is nil, or not much. So normally, they go to the lama to get the authorization for a particular mantra. It may be just syllables. Then once the authorization is done, they give the rosary to the lama to bless. So the lama takes the rosary, he may chant a few mantras on the rosary, and then he gives it back. And then they do their mantras on it." A string of prayer beads may be custom-made to coincide in number with the syllables of an assigned mantra, though this is done less and less nowadays, the rinpoche said.

"Normally now the rosary has one hundred eleven or maybe one hundred eight beads. If somebody's really religious, then they have got other beads, ten each, which are side-hangings to keep count." The idea is to recite a mantra in multiples of one hundred; the extra eleven (or eight) beads on the main string are there for insurance. "We believe that when you do a mantra, you may make a mistake by finger or by mouth," the rinpoche said. "So we give ten percent extra beads. The one hundred eleven or one hundred eight is counted as one hundred." Each round of recitations can then be ticked off, abacus-fashion, by pushing aside one of the optional counting beads, if you have them. "Once you go around once, then you take out one on the side; that means you've done a hundred—though you've really done one hundred eleven," the rinpoche said. Is this extra-bead insurance policy universal? When I got home I dug out a string of Burmese prayer beads from a pagoda in Mandalay. There were 109. Maybe the Burmese are slightly more attentive, but still not perfect.

When the worshipper has recited one hundred mantras ten times and used all appended scorekeeping beads, there may be additional counters in the shape of sacred symbols to move to next, each signifying a thousand prayer cycles. The repetition of acts of devotion is important to the Bhutanese. In several temples I was shown hollows in the polished floors where certain monks or abbots were reputed to have prostrated themselves so many times that they carved imprints of their feet on the wooden planks as they dug in their toes to raise and lower themselves again and again and again. Contemporary worshippers often choose to pray on those same spots, burnishing a continuity of grace and merit.

The obsession with repeated ritual worries some Bhutanese purists, among them Rigzin Dorji, the national culture czar who was in charge of safeguarding tradition as Bhutan was opening to the world. A sophisticated layman hip to the jargon of the international lending organizations that conservative Bhutan holds at arm's length, Rigzin Dorji said he looked at ritual as the spiritual equivalent of "sustainable development"—enough grace to keep one afloat in this life and maybe to bank a little merit for the next. "Buddha said, Don't accept me blindly," Rigzin Dorji said. "He said, Test my teachings as you test for gold. Test the validity of my truth. Teaching should suit the changing times. Analyze my teachings, the Buddha said. But not everybody can analyze. Simple people can't. So they do simple rituals. Ritual is just to make yourself okay. It has nothing to do with the salvation. For salvation, you have to perfect yourself, become yourself Buddha, because salvation lies in your own hand. Salvation doesn't lie in the hands of the gods or deities. So therefore, they can just help you in removing temporary badness. Your problems are connected with past karma, and nobody else can help that."

Bhutanese Buddhists take every opportunity to demonstrate their faith, especially on holy days, when circumambulators crowd the ground around sacred shrines and some other, unexpected places. Because Thimphu's National Library has so many holy books, people come there to walk around the building, chanting mantras, as they also do at the National Museum. Indeed, the aura of sanctity around the National Library complicated a recent silverfish crisis, I was told by the deputy librarian, Gyonpo Tshering. We were looking out a window of the magnificent library building toward an incongruous squat log cabin that had sprung up just outside. It was the home of a newfangled fumigation machine.

Like silverfish anywhere, those in Bhutan love books—not for their tough, handmade Bhutanese paper, but for their tasty ink, made of natural products such as charcoal dust, plant extracts, and animal blood. The volumes in Bhutan's National Library are not ordinary library books. They are a rare collection of priceless little bundles of calligraphy, some of them hundreds of years old; each unbound "volume" consists of pages collected between carved boards, wrapped in silk, and tied with a

silken ribbon. The classification system consists of tiny satin flaps in colors coded, more or less, to match subjects. The books, most of them
devoted to the Buddhist canon—there are also some Western-style
books on an upper floor—sit on open wooden shelves in dark, silent
rooms that exude the atmosphere of a temple. In fact, an imposing altar
with images of Bhutan's most sacred legendary-historical figures—the
Guru Rinpoche, Pema Lingpa, and the Shabdrung Ngawang Namgyal—dominates the second-floor stacks.

Perhaps because a Japanese scholar of Tibetan Buddhism, Yoshiro
Imaeda, had served as an adviser to the National Library for a number of
years, or perhaps because the Japanese have lately taken a passionate interest in preserving the wellsprings of all things Buddhist in the Himalayas and South Asia, Japan offered to help remove the thousands of
silverfish that had begun to romp cheekily through the priceless collection of books, boring holes in volume after volume. The answer, said the
experts, was a fumigator, a wonderful machine into which the books
would go, to emerge insect-free. They could then be placed in custom-
made metal boxes and returned to sandalwood shelves, not so beautifully
displayed but certainly better protected from the ravages of one of God's
least explicable creatures.

Gyonpo Tshering said that he had been assured that the fumigator
could be tucked into the basement of the library. Anywhere else would
have been offensive to the gods and spirits, not least of all because the
fumigator had no other function but to destroy many small sentient beings. "Fumigation is some kind of poison, and we don't want to disturb
the spirits with it," Gyonpo Tshering said. Apparently the librarians had
come to terms with the need to take the lives of insects—or did the
machine just chase them away?—in the interests of saving irreplaceable
books. When the mechanical savior arrived, however, it was too big for
the cellar door. Admitting it through an upper floor was simply unthink-
able. So it got its own temporary little house on the ground between the
main library building and its administration wing, while librarians went
looking for money to build it a permanent residence.

This unexpected crisis took time and energy away from the librarians'
main task of cataloguing and preserving unknown thousands of books
stored indifferently in dzongs and temples all over Bhutan. I had seen
some of them tossed carelessly into wooden chests or on shelves gathering dust—and no doubt silverfish—in shrines far away from Thimphu.

Some get eaten by rats or made into shredded nests by other vermin. The librarians, then led by Lopen Pemala, wanted these scattered collections to stay in place, but with better care. The fear in Thimphu was that if word of the great fumigator got around, people would be arriving with fragile treasures in market sacks, wanting to put them through the machine whether they needed debugging or not.

Gyonpo Tshering said that there were untold numbers of old manuscripts stored in private temples and in monasteries, where lamas still produced books under distinctive imprints. "If you can keep them properly where they are, that's the best solution," he said, recounting the story of the Bumthang temple with books reputed to be in the handwriting of the saint Pema Lingpa, whose life is wrapped into the history of the place. "No one is allowed to see these, according to the monks," the librarian said. "But if the lama is not able to take care of these, they will be gone. We need a national literary survey. We need to reach illiterate people who may have these valuable things in private possession. We need funds. Then if people are interested to sell, we can buy. Or we can at least borrow these books for microfilming. Some people may be taking care of treasures. But human beings have their ups and downs."

Because books of holy writings are considered sacred in themselves, they are never to be abandoned as trash. They are burned instead— cremated, really. From this practice came the notion that all writing in Dzongkha, the Tibetan-based "language of the dzongs," is sacred, no matter what the subject. Modern Bhutanese label this a quaint myth no longer applicable in an age of textbooks and newspapers. Maybe. But it is still more than likely that if your purchases in a shop are not plunked into a plastic bag they will be wrapped in a castoff Indian newspaper, not the Bhutanese weekly *Kuensel,* in any of its three languages, Dzongkha, Nepali, or English.

In the minds of many rural Bhutanese, the concept of education outside monastic walls is recent, and learning is associated primarily with the world of lamas and monks. Even in the schools that are now changing the lives of a new generation, the day begins with a Buddhist hymn, linking the schoolroom to the heavens in the minds of tots. But if an outsider has to suspend a preference for the separation of church and state in order to experience the seamlessness of the overlap of spiritual and mundane in Buddhist regions of Bhutan, the visitor also comes to realize that a lot of what seems to be associated with Buddhism is in reality based on something far deeper and older in the traditions of this country and others across the Himalayas and the Tibetan plateau.

At the most basic level, there is secular superstition, probably linked to the fear of bad magic. Superstition is woven deeply into daily life in Bhutan, to judge from many small rituals. When it is time to make decisions, in rural villages and among the sophisticated, Western-educated elite of Thimphu alike, the adherence to superstitious acts or astrological advice varies only in degree. A poor farmer may put off a new venture if he is warned against starting it on a given day. His middle-class town-dwelling counterpart may try to trick the spirits instead. "If we want to go on a trip Thursday but the day is not auspicious," a businesswoman explained, "we pack the car on Wednesday and pretend to drive away but go along the road only for a short while to fool the spirits. Then we come back and leave the next day the way we planned all along." A family in Thimphu found a novel way to avoid a wedding curse. Monks given a prospective bride's and groom's horoscopes to scan had warned against an impending marriage, finding dissonance between the two charts. To circumvent trouble, the family of the bride dressed a female relative in the wedding dress and ostentatiously conducted a mock ceremony. When the meddling spirits had departed, apparently believing that the wedding was over, the real marriage took place. Everybody enjoyed a good laugh, and a sigh of relief.

The Himalayas host a cosmos of spirits, malicious or mischievous but always in possession of their own bit of terrain. Standing on the ramparts of Bhutan's Tashigang Dzong one afternoon, listening to the *dzongda,* a district administrator akin to governor, Rinzin Gyetsen, talk about creeping deforestation on nearby mountainsides, I noticed a small shrine a little way down the hill from our commanding height on a narrow ridge. "That is the home of the protective deity," the dzongda interrupted himself to explain. Somewhere in the dark depths of legend-history, that spirit had reached an agreement with civil authority to look after this critical fortress in return for a proper respect from the warriors on the ridge. It was a story repeated, with variations, everywhere I went.

In homes and villages in Bhutan and parts of Nepal and Ladakh, garden gods are propitiated by the burning of offerings in constructions that look like backyard fireplaces. Where rooftops are flat, families light incense fires in bowls placed on the parapets of their homes. It used to be popularly believed that all such rituals had their origins in a shamanistic ancient religion loosely described as Bon. Some guidebooks still leave the impression that Bon (whose followers are called Bonpos) is no more than the worship of spirits and natural objects that thrived for centuries around these mountains and valleys, springs and rushing rivers.

Western scholars and Bonpo religious leaders have now demonstrated that Bon is more likely an early form of Buddhism with local underpinnings and a distinct history. By their definition, Bon would be, in effect, a fifth order of Tibetan Buddhism, joining the classical four: Nyingmapa, Sakyapa, Kagyupa, and Gelugpa. Orthodox orders, experts say, have been the leading detractors of Bon, helping to perpetuate the notion that it is a primitive throwback to pre-Buddhist Tibet.

In Nepal, Tenzin Namdak Rinpoche, a Bonpo leader whose name is better known in Paris, Rome, Rio, or New York than in most Himalayan towns, takes exception to the notion that Bon is just another form of mainstream Buddhism, though he does acknowledge areas where his faith and at least one Buddhist school intersect. He is directing the building of the first Bonpo monastery in the Kathmandu Valley to train mainly novices from Tibet and western Nepal, where the faith has its deepest roots but a lack of scholarship and educated religious leadership has led to deterioration. The presence of a Bonpo gompa near Kathmandu, a thriving Buddhist center, may do a lot to bridge gaps in understanding and establish a more respected place for Bon in the Himalayas.

Tenzin Namdak has found considerable support in France and the United States, where this extraordinary religion is, surprisingly, gaining many adherents who prefer to see it more as an ethical system than a faith denigrated in the past as an outgrowth of black magic and the worship of rocks. If this reputation for shamanism is no longer relevant (or was always a misperception), this is only one of many points of debate about Bon among experts on Himalayan religions, who are still learning and refining their knowledge of early Tibetan worship. It is obvious that not only Bon but also the mainline Buddhist schools have accepted if not incorporated a good deal of pre-Buddhist belief and ritual. The stories of deals struck with local spirits by the Guru Rinpoche, Himalayan Buddhism's founding saint, are important symbols of this.

Tenzin Namdak's monastery climbs a vertical hill facing a sea of rice fields that was blanketed in spring green when I went to visit him. Across the fields, on another hill, looms the ancient Buddhist shrine of Swayambhutnath. The rinpoche says the isolated spot is full of spirituality and natural beauty, where Bonpos from everywhere can feel at peace. As we climbed the stairs to his sanctuary, we passed a group of cheerful monks happily making *momos,* the small Tibetan dumplings filled with vegetables or meat that sustain pilgrims and travelers across the Himalayas.

The Tibetan-born Tenzin Namdak, who escaped a Chinese prison in 1961, had for nearly two decades been in charge of a Bonpo monastery-school he founded in the Indian state of Himachal. But there, he said, there was no hope of a truly permanent home. "Most of the students coming to India from Tibet and Dolpo in western Nepal are in monasteries right in the center of Hindu villages. There are no holy places for them nearby, nothing. This place will be bigger. It is also very beautiful. People should look after it well."

We sat down for tea in a small classroom dominated by an altar over which hung a thangka, a religious painting on a silk scroll, bearing the blue-white likeness of Samantabhadra, the preeminent Bon god. Tenzin Namdak, wearing dark maroon monastic robes not unlike those of Buddhist abbots, explained that while his order accepted the existence of the Buddha Shakyamuni it did not take his teaching as the basis of their beliefs, insisting that Bon had other origins, albeit within the same Buddhist universe. As for Padmasambhava, another name for the Guru Rinpoche, his divinity is also denied, though it is said that he may have been the son of a Bonpo sage. Bonpos venerate instead a founder whom they call Shenrap, who seems to approximate closely the position of the Buddha Shakyamuni in orthodox Buddhism. Shenrap (or Shenrab) and Shakyamuni are competing manifestations of this era's version of the universal Buddha, who has past, present, and future forms symbolized by the Buddha Dipankara, the Buddha Shakyamuni, and the Buddha Maitreya, respectively.

Bonpos believe that their faith has roots in West Asia: "Kashmir in olden times, the Swat Valley, Gilgit, and Persia—we say Tazig; this we call the source of our religion," the rinpoche said. The teachings blossomed in Shang-Shung (or Zhang-Zhung), an independent ancient realm that is now western Tibet. Bon entered the Tibetan mainstream when Tibet became a unified kingdom, Tenzin Namdak said. This raises the intriguing possibility that what the Bonpos saw as a distinctive import from another part of Asia was really early Buddhism coming back via Central Asia (i.e., Tazig = Tajik) and areas of what are now Pakistan and Afghanistan, where it had spread soon after the Buddha Shakyamuni's enlightenment. No one knows for sure; in any case, Tenzin Namdak doesn't put much credence in that hypothesis of Buddhism come full circle. For him, Bon stands alone, historically. "We have a very rich culture, so we don't have to take from any other source."

"Long before there was Tibet as a kingdom, there was Bon and it was what the people believed there," the rinpoche said. "It became a national religion." Bon has its own set of texts that, in centuries of philosophical development, grew closer to old Buddhist canon, shedding a shamanistic image, he said. "If you are looking at an outside picture of us, we are very much similar as the Nyingmapas, Buddhist Nyingmapas." There are a few practical differences, which he called "details." Apart from the unfamiliar image of Samantabhadra at the altar, there is the counterclockwise circumambulation of holy sites. Where Buddhists pass or walk around a shrine keeping it to the right, Bonpos go the other way, with the object of veneration to the left.

Tenzin Namdak, an internationally recognized and published scholar as well as a teacher of Bon who has done much to universalize its appeal, says he practices neither old Bon nor new Bon, but a third stream called Swastika Bon, which has historically been dedicated to education. The swastika, an ancient Indian symbol of eternity or good luck, is common to both Hinduism and Buddhism. His choice of spiritual path is partly explained by his upbringing. Until he went to study at the famous fifteenth-century Menri monastery in central Tibet, he lived in a household where his father's side followed old Bon, the religion associated with magic and nature worship, and his mother's family were new or reformed Bonpos. But he does not reject all the old spirituality and pantheism of ancient Bon, or whatever worship may have predated it and later got its name.

"In the first Bon, whether in Bhutan or in Nepal or in Tibet, so many gods they are worshipping—the mountain gods, the water gods, the fire gods," he said, as we sat at the classroom seminar table over tea served by a novice. "That is part of the Bon tradition. It is also part of the tradition of Tibet generally, even among the Nyingmapas and other Buddhists, for many centuries." The rinpoche said that the Dalai Lama had recognized Bon as an integral part of Tibetan culture. Although Tenzin Namdak does not accept the older worship as part of modern Bon teaching, he said that in the countryside he is often asked to visit a spot where there is a natural spirit to be honored in prayer, and he goes there out of understanding for the people to whom this matters. He added that he still hears occasionally, though very rarely, of blood sacrifice among Bonpos and Buddhists, who share occult rites in remote communities, often to appease a demanding natural deity. "Goats or sometimes, I heard, yaks are sacrificed," he said. "This is very rare, but they do."

On the positive side, the lingering preoccupation with nature and the spirits living in the elements of earth, fire, and water can form a base for teaching about respect for the environment, Tenzin Namdak said. "This is a very large part of the culture in Bon. Fire, rocks, water, trees, everything—each of them we must preserve. We believe that these natural things are like relations." He thought this emphasis might be part of Bon's contemporary international appeal, despite the efforts of Tibetan Buddhist scholars to discredit the Bonpos' formal canon. He also believes that the popularity of Bon and various forms of Tibetan Buddhism almost inevitably followed the Tibetan diaspora into the West and East Asia.

"Myself, I'm thinking that there is much more knowledge about Tibetan culture than before," he said. "People can see us and what we are doing here. Otherwise in earlier time, they are just hearing stories about us from other people. Westerners clearly are taking interest in Bon. They are even practicing our highest teaching, zog-chen. These people are not scholars. Very often they are people who find they need some religion. You may want to prepare for the next life. Meanwhile you can have peace and calm and quiet and gentle life now. Obviously if you practice this you can do good for your country."

Tenzin Namdak led me higher up the hillside to the imposing new temple he is building above the monastic school and monks' quarters. At the back of the high-ceilinged, airy room, several artists were at work constructing an altar with a Buddha image seven or eight feet high. Where had he found the artists?

"They are Bhutanese," he said. "I asked around for people who could do this, and someone found them for me."

How fascinating is the evolution of the Buddhist world. Centuries after Bhutanese monastery builders sent for Nepali craftsmen, a Bon temple in the Kathmandu Valley, headed by a Tibetan-born teacher with an international following, has closed a Himalayan circle by going back to Bhutan for an authenticity and purity of craftsmanship not found in many other places outside the last of the vanishing kingdoms.

Chapter 5

THE ROAD FROM LUMBINI

THE JOURNEY of this ancient faith that seeped northward to settle comfortably in the cool Himalayan valleys and on the arid Tibetan plateau began in the steamy groves of Lumbini, where alpine Nepal flattens out to meet the great Gangetic plain of India. Sitting one torrid Nepali summer day under a bo tree, watching pilgrims from the mountains come to pray near the spot where millions believe that Queen Mahamaya gave birth to the Buddha Shakyamuni, I thought again about an ambitious fantasy I have been nurturing for years. A group of adventurers with months to spare would assemble here in the hot Terai region of southern Nepal, in a land still inhabited by the Shakya clan into whose royal family Prince Siddhartha was by legend born. From this sacred ground, now being developed by Buddhists from around the world as a center for meditation, study, and environmental conservation, we would turn quickly and directly westward to the edges of the old Hellenistic, Turkic, and Persian worlds, where Buddhism flourished early and with spectacular success in the centuries following Lord Buddha's enlightenment. That journey would take us first to Afghanistan, where we might pause to mourn not only a ruined past but also a tragic present. Central Asia, where Tibetan was once the language of diplomacy and Buddhism the culture of the trade routes, would be next. Southeastward, then, to Pakistan and India before turning north into the heart of the Himalayas to follow the still-warm trail of Tantric Buddhism across Ladakh, Nepal, and Sikkim to its last outpost in Bhutan. (There would have to be other excursions someday to the shrines of Buddhism's other schools, in Sri Lanka, Burma, Thailand, Indochina, Korea, and Japan.)

If we wanted to travel with a ghost or, more likely, a still-living spirit, since his reincarnations are apparently unlimited, we could choose no better companion than Padmasambhava, the Guru Rinpoche, that almost universal spiritual ancestor of Himalayan Buddhists. Sooner or later, we would find him everywhere, recognizable by his distinctive attire. He wears a peaked red helmet, sometimes with upturned flaps or a wide brim in the shape of a crown, and cradles a magic staff topped with two miniature Buddha heads and a skull. His pierced earlobes hang heavy with rings of precious metals or luminous jewels set in gold. His bold eyes stare out of a smooth, squarish face marked by a wispy, curled mustache and the hint of a goatee. Padmasambhava—"the lotus-born"—did not appear until more than a thousand years after the Buddha Shakyamuni's life on earth, but he brought Tantric Buddhism to the mountains and plateaus, where as the Guru Rinpoche his visage flutters from prayer flags and peers from dim recesses of old shrines. When the scholar David Snellgrove went on a seven-month trek through uncharted Buddhist territory in Nepal in the 1950s, he saw the Guru everywhere. Once, when all that could be discerned on a rock carving in the middle of nowhere was the shape of Padmasambhava's hat, Snellgrove was moved to remark that "one is led to reflect once more on the ubiquity of this wonder-working master of religion, who is supposed to have passed along almost every route that connects Tibet with India."

From peak to peak and valley to valley, there are crackling tales of the Guru Rinpoche's show-stopping miracles to tell on snowbound nights, and fading paintings to admire by the dim glow of candles in dark monastery chapels. His legend is at home here. The Guru was a master of long meditations, often performed in caves, of which there are many in the mountainous terrain. So such stories about holy men in their hermitages come easily to the tongue and ear. His mythological exploits drew supporting casts from a familiar animal world. In one of his eight manifestations, as Dorje Drolo, the Guru Rinpoche rode a tiger, we are told. Tigers figure in many heroic legends hereabouts, and so it is only proper that he should have one at his disposal.

Like other stars in the Tibetan galaxy, he bears a legend far larger than life, and some secular scholars question whether any human could possibly have existed in such stupendous glory. His story is too good, too seamless, to be literally true, they say. But that isn't really the issue. The important thing is that the Guru Rinpoche becomes a comforting, familiar face as one travels among the countless gods, goddesses, reincarnations, and manifestations in Himalayan Buddhism. We can pick up his thread, his trail, and more or less follow it across countries and eras.

Historians debate, but may never know, whether he was a historical person, a politically useful composite of several saints, or perhaps the personification of myths that help root the origins of the Tantric Buddhist school in an earthly reality. Only the Bonpos, who claim a form of Buddhism that predates not only the Guru Rinpoche but also the Buddha Shakyamuni himself, reject his miraculous life, though not his existence. North Indians often claim him as one of theirs, but believers in the Himalayan kingdoms say he was native to the Swat Valley, in the shadow of the Hindu Kush in what is now northwestern Pakistan. Bonpos excepted, all agree he was a reincarnation of the Buddha himself. Bhutanese textbooks inform us that the kingdom of Swat was then called Ugyen—other sources name it Uddiyana, a variation—and that the Guru was born there in a lotus in the middle of a lake, as prophesied by the Lord Buddha. The lotus, with its ability to produce a bloom of purity and beauty from a watery medium seemingly free of earthly constraints, was the favored birth environment of Buddhist saints. The Guru Rinpoche, as babe-in-arms, was adopted by the Ugyen king, Indrabutti, who was childless.

There are other versions of the tale, but the Swat story is a good one, because Swat's reputation as a cradle of Buddhist sainthood serves as a reminder that even before the Macedonian ruler Alexander the Great marched into the Indian subcontinent in the fourth century B.C. (about two centuries after Buddha's birth), the now-austere landscape of northern Pakistan and Afghanistan was familiar with Buddhist worship and learning. The era and the art this region produced are often described collectively though loosely as Gandhara for the domain of the Kushan dynasty, whose empire reached the height of its artistic and administrative achievements in the second century A.D. under a great Buddhist emperor, Kanishka. The winter capital of the Gandhara court was the frontier city of Purushapura, later named Peshawar, the subcontinent's last outpost before the Khyber Pass.

In summer, when Afghanistan's ferocious winter weather subsided, the Kushana rulers decamped across the pass to take up residence not far from Kabul. Incredible though it may seem now in the rough-and-ready towns of the Afghan-Pakistani border area, the serene and contemplative Buddhist world once stretched west from here to Persia and north into Central Asia. Some scholars believe that the first images of Buddha, sophisticated and finely wrought works, were created by religious artists in this wild region. Buddhism's most lifelike, least stylized art was produced by the Gandhara school; it has never been equaled.

In years of travel on the subcontinent, I knew Afghanistan only as a battlefield, its fertile valleys seeded with mines, its towns in ruin. At the Afghan end of the Khyber Pass, near Torkham, travelers were stopped and warned not to enter a country in turmoil. Poor Afghanistan. It seems to have had a reputation for danger for as long as pilgrims have known it. In the seventh century A.D. the Chinese monk Hsuan Tsang, who made a trek of unprecedented proportions through the Buddhist world and kept extraordinarily revealing records, was told not to attempt a foray into the lands beyond the Khyber because the terrain was thick with brigands. Nearly a millennium and a half later, I could look down from the windy hills at the end of the pass to the eerily empty plain below and try to make sense of the notion that not so far away in the battle zone of Jalalabad, where fierce Islamic militants and Soviet troops had slaughtered each other before different Afghan factions chose to continue the carnage as a civil war, the land had once been blessed by a wealth of Buddhist stupas, sculptures, sacred caves, and stores of ancient writings produced by innumerable monks and saints. Pilgrims like Hsuan Tsang came here from the eastern reaches of Asia to revel in the atmosphere of piety and grace. Farther to the northwest there was Bamiyan, which boasted the tallest statue of Buddha built anywhere in the ancient world. And north of that is Balkh, the major town in ancient Bactria (now roughly northern Afghanistan), commanding the crossroads of two important silk routes. A story has been told there for centuries of two brothers who trekked across India to take a gift of sweets to the still-living Buddha as he meditated in Bodhgaya, in northern India. They returned with hair from his head to be enshrined at Balkh, thus certifying its antiquity in the Buddhist world.

The Guru Rinpoche's Swat Valley, north of Peshawar, was an active part of this early West Asian Buddhist universe. Swat gloried in hundreds of Buddhist monasteries and temples, scattered among the steep hills and narrow gorges along the rushing Swat River, tumbling down from the

Hindu Kush. The monk-theologians of Swat, who are sometimes credited in legend with developing or perfecting the Tantric school and sending out its missionaries, also instilled in the valley a Buddhist influence that withstood centuries of Islamic onslaughts. Swat capitulated, finally, to the Moguls—eight centuries after Padmasambhava's storied mission to the Himalayas. Today, a titular Muslim king of Swat remains all that is left of the valley's long-lost independence of body and soul. Swat is Pakistani and Islamic, exemplified by the noisy bazaar in a town called Bahrain or the impressive new mosque in the mountain hamlet of Miandam. A local inkeeper there told me with pride that the people of Miandam, no more than a few dozen householders, had written away to Saudi Arabia for money to build their house of worship and were delighted to be showered with funds by a foundation eager to bolster the faith in this insignificant place.

"General Zia gave us the health center," the innkeeper said, as we stood at the edge of the inn's cliffside garden overlooking the village and talked about the legacy of Mohammad Zia-ul Haq, the military ruler of Pakistan who died in a mysterious plane crash in 1988 and who was thought of, more than a little erroneously, as primarily a champion of Islamic orthodoxy. "Zia also built a school," he said, "but it was the Saudis who helped Miandam with the mosque." Not even a memory of Tantric Buddhism remains here—certainly no hint of the brilliantly florid, extravagant style of image-making that would later define Buddhist temples in the Himalayas, where Chinese and Tibetan folk art influences were more powerful. Although the ruins of stupas and monasteries still draw pilgrims to the lower reaches of Swat, from the perspective of isolated towns like Miandam, in its own small tributary valley, the Buddhist era seems long ago and far away. Day to day, the people of Swat look south and west to the Arab world and Islam's holiest places, not east and north to the world of Himalayan Buddhism.

Some of the most extensive excavations of Buddhist civilization in Pakistan have been made farther east, around Taxila, a fifty-five-square-mile valley between the Muree and Margala Hills only about twenty miles from the Pakistani capital, Islamabad. Several ancient cities were founded in this area of culturally diverse history. The most famous (though not the first) of them, Sirkap, was built in the second century B.C. and then rebuilt several times by later Central Asian conquerors. Through years of extensive turbulence, Sirkap apparently kept Buddhist stupas intact, at least for a few centuries, augmenting them with a variety of temples to other religions. The stories of Sirkap and Taxila's other ruins have been well told for lay travelers by Hilary Adamson and Isobel Shaw in their 1981 *Traveller's Guide to Pakistan,* a little-known book with a handmade look (wobbly maps, wrinkly paste-it-yourself end-papers) that never got the circulation inside or outside Pakistan that it deserves. But then Pakistan does not get much attention either. That's a pity: there is an abundance of history crumbling or already buried along the Indus and on the windswept edge of what for a mere flicker of centuries later was British India. Contemporary India also has roots here. Ashoka, the Mauryan emperor who in the third century B.C. became disgusted with the excesses of his own militarism, converted to Buddhism, and propagated rules for a humane civil society, was, according to some accounts, assigned in his youth to service in the Taxila area, the widely recognized intellectual center of early Buddhism. Other accounts say that he promoted Buddhism here with a missionary zeal.

Adamson and Shaw warn us that those who revel in climbing around archaeological sites may be disappointed at first with the ruins at Taxila. The visitor must look beyond the "meaningless jumble" of stones and picture instead golden domes, colorfully robed monks, and camel caravans—the rich mixture of images conjured up by a place where trade routes from China, India, Europe, and Central Asia converged. Good advice, I thought, when I first climbed the steep hill to the Jaulian monastery, Taxila's most intriguing site. Crossing the irrigation canal at the foot of the hill, or looking down from its three-hundred-foot-high crest over miles of grazing land, sometimes enlivened by an encampment of nomadic herdsmen and their families, I was forced to consider Buddhism in a setting and society unlike any experienced in other Buddhist lands from Indochina to Thailand and Burma, Sri Lanka, or Bhutan. I remembered how as a young child I had similarly to confront some essential truths of the Christmas story, primarily that Jesus was born not amid a glistening blanket of snow with reindeer in the sky above, but in a little town in the arid Middle East without Christmas trees as we knew them. My father was a Christian by faith but a historian and geographer by avocation; romantic images of far-off places had to check out or be abandoned.

Jaulian was a thriving Buddhist "university" in the third century, about five hundred years before the Guru Rinpoche vanquished unruly

Himalayan deities and made them guardians of the Buddhist faith. Built in the second century and sacked a few hundred years later by conquerors from the north, Jaulian lay in ruins until the British archaeologist Sir John Marshall began to excavate the site just before World War I. He worked at Taxila for nearly twenty years, and he was followed by other archaeologists, the most recent from Pakistani institutions. Now cleared of debris and partially restored, Jaulian looms over terrain populated mostly by poor villagers, whose low-slung, walled farmhouse compounds reflect the rural Islamic life of Pakistan and Afghanistan. It is an introverted culture all but devoid of decorative arts (if you don't count the garish urns for sale to tourists along the roadside) and a society in which women are kept safely behind walls, unlike their free-spirited Buddhist contemporaries elsewhere. At the Jaulian monastery ruins, friendly but indifferent Pakistani men in their baggy *shalwar* trousers and long *kamiz* shirts (topped often with the distinctive woolen Pathan cap with rolled brim) guide the infrequent visitor around the artifacts of a civilization that was never theirs.

Despite the forewarnings that some imagination has to be called into play here, I have never been able to re-create on several tramps around Jaulian a satisfactorily vivid picture of daily life as it might have been lived around the now-bare ruins of monks' cells, domeless stupas, kitchens, stairwells, baths, and drains. The artifacts don't help much, though simple shelters protect the extant and often exquisite (if mutilated) statues of Buddha, boddhisattvas, and various animal images. Buddhism hums and drones and tinkles; here drums and chants and temple bells have been forever silenced. On the plains below, we who have scaled this small peak of history and returned thirsty sit on the ubiquitous charpoy and drink Coke to the blaring music of a South Asian film. Local hustlers accost us with fake coins and images, some of them so skillfully reproduced, however, that, bargained down to a bazaar price, they are fun to buy and own. The people who make and sell them are, oddly, one real link between this Pakistani world and Taxila as it was.

But even the artifacts and fakes aren't much compensation for the sense that the inspiration and soul of these Buddhist ruins have long departed, and they seem aloof and sterile. In part, this is because the Gandhara civilization is really twice removed from contemporary Pakistani life: neither the Hellenistic influence on its art—the drape of a robe or the occasional image of a Greek god—nor Buddhism itself has a place here. Pakistanis are not hostile to Buddhism; it is merely irrelevant to the all-encompassing Islamic society in which most of them live, a culture that does not separate religion and the state and only (and barely) tolerates minority beliefs. Contemporary life in the northern territory of Baltistan may be something of an exception; there descendants of Tibetan-speaking Buddhists maintain some old temples and are encouraged by foreigners trekking in the area to take more interest in their unusual history.

Many of the best examples of Gandhara Buddhist art and architecture are no longer where their creators placed them. Pieces have been lost or removed to museums. Fortunately, there are three good collections not far away. One is the Taxila museum itself, a lovely single-story gallery set in a park with flower gardens near the Bhir Mound, site of the first of three ancient cities in the Taxila Valley. Other collections are in museums in Lahore and Peshawar. The best-known of the Gandhara sculptures, the startling skin-and-bones image of the fasting Buddha, sits in illuminated glory in Lahore, Pakistan's cultural capital. This gaunt, riveting, disturbing figure is worlds removed from the self-possessed, plump Buddhas of East Asia or the fearsome manifestations of Himalayan Tantric iconography. Until I stood before the Gandhara Buddha I had no real sense of the diversity, and thus the universality, of Buddhism.

Chapter 6

LADAKH: ECLIPSED BY OTHER GODS

ONE OF SEVERAL long, once-busy trade routes leading away from ancient Taxila could—if war and politics had not intervened—bring today's Tantric pilgrim home from the source of his faith in the Swat Valley to the first outpost of the still-living Himalayan Buddhist world, Ladakh, and beyond it to the heartland of Himalayan Buddhism in Tibet. The journey eastward from Swat is a pilgrimage now largely encumbered or more often blocked altogether at heavily fortified mountain borders guarded zealously by India, Pakistan, and China. But there are accessible pockets and detours. For example, Gilgit and the already mentioned Baltistan, northern territories of Pakistan, were once part of a Tibetan Buddhist empire and they too are littered with ancient artifacts and resonant with tales of monks and magic. These areas are mentioned frequently by Tibetans as repositories of knowledge. A Tibetan empire once encompassed them.

The old caravan trail eastward into the Himalayas passed through Kashmir, a bastion of Buddhist art and scholarship that survived longer than most Buddhist centers of northern India. The road then branched into two main routes into Central Asia across high passes in the Karakoram Mountains. The more easterly route, through Srinagar, the Kashmiri summer capital and now a largely Muslim city, leads to Leh, Ladakh's main town, on the barren edge of the Tibetan plateau.

The land fate willed to Ladakh may be parched and the air painfully thin, but these hardships only add to the power of an uncommon natural setting that overwhelms the senses of even those who feel they have seen it all. Here, at 11,500 feet or more, the upper Indus winds across a rocky desert fringed in peaks under a crystal sky bejeweled after dark with a million extraordinarily brilliant stars. Even if insomnia is a warning of altitude sickness, a bout or two is worth having on a clear and cold Ladakhi night. My first night in Ladakh was in October. I lay awake in a country guesthouse, stuffed with aspirin and bottled water, wondering whether to worry about my inability to sleep. This is life above and beyond the craggy Himalayas; one can easily be enveloped in the disorienting sense of being on another earth. I pulled back the curtains to take in an acrylic-black Ladakhi sky. The jumbo stars seemed to pulsate and flare. The white moon shone on strange, empty mountains, pale intruders against a backdrop of nothingness. It was mesmerizing. In the utter silence, I fell asleep.

Missing here are the undulating pastures, the frequent sheltered valleys, and the dark, canopied, vine-wrapped groves of much of the rest of the Himalayan landscape. In a lot of Ladakh, you can see where you are headed, and where you've come from, for many unobstructed miles. Old monasteries and the remains of palaces often cling, sunbleached, to vertical rock faces, as if monks and kings plotted to make a harsh land yet tougher on frail humans condemned to trek and climb, trek and climb, without so much as a cooling stream, a grassy bank, or a spreading tree for respite.

"In the barren wilderness, nothing grows wild," wrote Helena Norberg-Hodge in a 1988 socioecological study of a land she had lived in for more than a decade. "Not the smallest shrub, hardly a blade of grass. Even time seems to stand still, suspended on the thin air. Yet here, in one of the highest, driest and coldest lands on earth, a people has for more than a thousand years not only made a living, but prospered. Channeling water down from snow-fed streams, they have formed oases in the desert, and established a remarkable culture."

Himalayan Buddhism is at home here, though the atmosphere is still laced with traces of Central Asia. The terrain lacks the lushness of Nepal, Bhutan, and Sikkim but shares the latitude and landscape of much of Tibet. Although Buddhism probably first reached Ladakh from India via Kashmir, and most likely in its Hinayana form, Mahayana schools prevailed as the region came under the influence of Tibetan migrants, monks, and conquerors. Ladakhi Buddhists say that the ninth and tenth centuries, following the introduction of Tantric Buddhism, were years of revitalization of the faith. Today, in houses, temples, and chortens, in language, art, and rituals, the Tibetan, Nepali, Sikkimese, or Bhutanese Buddhist would find familiarity and similarity.

What is gone, however, is the richness, the profusion of Buddhist art spilling into public life that marks, for example, the ambience of a Bhutanese dzong, which served as both fortress and monastic center, with civil administration thrown in for good measure. Ladakh once had dzongs, too, built on commanding hilltops, but they faced operational obstacles that may have doomed them even in what should have been their days of glory. In this dry region, according to Alexander Cunningham, a colonial British military engineer who surveyed Ladakh in the mid-nineteenth century, the inaccessible dzongs, most now in ruins, had no internal water supply. Water carriers struggling up steep tracks from springs, wells, or a river below could not meet the needs of any significant population; a community's growth was perforce constricted.

No glittering new temples and sturdy monasteries rise here nowadays as they still do in Bhutan, Sikkim, and Nepal. Surviving Ladakhi monasteries seem more spartan, even decrepit, when compared with the gompas of other Himalayan Buddhists. Where monastic communities remain, their populations seem thin and their temples and courtyards often lack the bustle and purposefulness of a Bhutanese dzong or a Tibetan-Nepali temple. Water is still a problem.

True, there are roadside chortens and many walls bearing the familiar incantation *Om mani padme hum.* Prayer wheels spin in the shadows of monasteries. Prayer flags flutter on garden poles and from corner to corner of flat rooftops, where small hearths for offerings to local guardian deities are also constructed. As in many other places in the Himalayas and the Tibetan plateau, such altars and the deities Ladakhis seek to appease antedate Buddhism but have been happily incorporated by it. In daily life there is often much more comfort to be derived from keeping the neighborhood spirits content than from contemplating the greater glories of Buddhism, which can wait for festival days. In Ladakhi homes, couch-beds are covered with Tibetan-style carpets and the furniture or woodwork may be painted with colorful designs incorporating one or more of the Eight Lucky Signs common in one form or another in all

Tantric Buddhist decorative art: the treasure vase, the endless knot, the victory banner, the wheel of law, the protective golden parasol, the omniscient golden fish, the conch shell, and the lotus.

Still, Buddhist life in Ladakh bears only a pallid resemblance to the Bhutanese cultural environment, though both were almost equally steeped in an all-embracing Buddhist civilization when they began to modernize in the 1960s and open to tourism in the 1970s. Sikkim, too, seems a livelier place, its active temples full of monks and boisterous novices. Ladakhis, convinced that their mounting religious and material losses are by-products of politics and geography—forces beyond their control—alternate between panic and grief as they confront the erosion. Now and then, anger explodes into rebellion.

Historically, the Ladakhi capital of Leh was not only an important town on the trade routes to Central Asia and old Cathay, but also the center of an independent Tibetan Buddhist nation under a king, called a *chogyal* in Tibetan, for about eight hundred years before falling to Hindu rulers, the Dogras, in the 1830s. A few decades later, Ladakh was folded into the princely state of Jammu and Kashmir by the British. When India won independence in 1947, New Delhi incorporated Ladakh along with part of Jammu and Kashmir; the rest is under Pakistani control after several inconclusive wars and India's repeated stubborn refusals to allow a plebiscite. The Kashmiri act of accession to India is still technically a matter of international dispute—the subject of unfulfilled United Nations resolutions—but in practical terms, Buddhist Ladakhis became a minority within a minority. Ladakh, with about 150,000 people and a slim Buddhist majority, fell under the jurisdiction of Muslim-majority Jammu and Kashmir, which in turn is part of Hindu-majority India.

Because a road links Leh to the Muslim Kashmir Valley, Ladakhis believe they are especially vulnerable to shrewd Kashmiri traders and hoteliers, who, they say, have moved into many areas of Ladakh in sufficient numbers to upset the economic, social, and religious structure. Ladakh, by virtue of its position on ancient trade routes, had a significant Muslim population for centuries, but these old families are not viewed with the hostility usually reserved for relative newcomers from Srinagar or Delhi who have parlayed their reasonably easy access into dominance in the tourist business, the largest money earner. Before the area was opened to foreigners, most Ladakhis lived on farming, growing grains, potatoes, and sometimes vegetables and fruit, wherever it was possible.

Others kept livestock herds, especially goats and sheep for wool. Apart from the bazaars of Leh and Kargil, there were few market centers with the extensive service industries that give birth to a comfortable middle class. Medicine and law were the leading professions, though the ranks of doctors and lawyers were small. A handful of land-rich families lived, and still live, well—though not in palaces or mansions. The most luxurious home I visited had perhaps six or seven modest rooms, plus a simple kitchen and bath. A few pieces of handcrafted wood furniture, including some fine antiques, were crammed into a parlor and dining room each not much more than ten or twelve feet square. In other homes, where there was no inherited wealth, wooden platforms covered with Tibetan-style rugs served as daytime couches and beds at night in the one or two rooms inhabited by a family.

Periodically, Ladakhis agitate to break free of domination by Muslim Kashmir. They know there is scant hope of regaining the wealth and independence they once enjoyed as subjects of a Buddhist kingdom, but many hope for some kind of special territorial status within India, separate from the rest of Jammu and Kashmir. When I first went to Ladakh in 1989, the Ladakh Buddhist Association was in the throes of an intense civil disobedience campaign. "Kashmiri dogs go back!" read one banner, an ironic echo of the slogan Kashmiris use in expressing their views of New Delhi's occupying troops: "Indian dogs go home!" For centuries in the Kashmir-Ladakh area, the image of a dog was associated with unwanted miscreants forced into banishment. Cunningham noted in the 1800s that Ladakhi criminals were sometimes branded with irons bearing a dog's head and the inscription "dog marked—expelled" before being run out of town with taunts and threats.

Although Ladakh had been under almost unending curfew for weeks, daily demonstrations intended to force arrests took place outside the Soma Gompa in the heart of Leh, which served as a command post for the Buddhist Association of Ladakh. The protests went like clockwork. The Jammu and Kashmir state police would line up buses at an intersection near the rallying point. In the monastery compound, demonstrators (sometimes all women) would form into a flying squad and march briskly through the gompa's gates into the street and, half a block later, into custody. With some struggle, they were herded aboard the waiting buses and driven away for a brief incarceration.

The short main street of Leh, its small, scruffy shops shut tight by the curfew, was a desolate place that day. As I waited for more action from the gompa, I could see above and beyond the police bus the facade of Leh Palace, a Tibetan-style skyscraper thought to be modeled on Lhasa's Potala. Hollow with disuse, it loomed over the bazaar like the ghost of a forgotten age, its windows like the eye sockets of so many skulls. The palace, on a rocky mountain outcropping that seems to hover above the town, is empty of courtly life. Leh's royal Namgyal family, long stripped of titles and power, is headquartered now at Stok, eight miles away, where a museum displays the defunct kingdom's remaining treasures. A scion of the Namgyal family recently found his way into the Ladakhi Buddhist Association and was urged by a new generation to become an active figurehead for their campaign of separate identity. He is, in a sense, the once and future king in a dynasty whose lineage flows from the rulers of a lost Tibetan empire.

The level Buddhist militancy can reach in Ladakh surprises outsiders accustomed to the image of a meek and pious people committed to a peaceful life of prayer and reflection. Even more startling than the demonstrations in 1989 were reports by Muslims that some of them had been captured and forcibly converted to Buddhism by having *chang,* the popular fermented barley drink, poured down their teetotaling throats. Muslim homes were surrounded, their inhabitants taunted. "There is terrible psychological pressure on Muslims," a businessman said over tea on his veranda. "No Muslim can sleep properly these nights." At his house, set in a wild garden on a winding back lane in Leh, no one in his Muslim family wanted to come out and sit with us in the sun on a warm autumn morning. The women had heard of Muslim homes in rural villages being surrounded and attacked by Buddhist gangs. An imam's house had been stoned near Leh, they said. Muslims had been forced on pain of death to fly multicolored Buddhist flags.

Though a few years later a lot of this hostility had cooled and there was more cooperation between Buddhists and Muslims, many Ladakhis still insist they are in a long-haul fight for cultural survival. Cut off from Tibet by a prolonged dispute between India and China over their trans-Himalayan border, Ladakhi Buddhists are stranded and isolated—"driven into a small corner between Islam on one side and Chinese Communism on the other," say the scholars David Snellgrove and Tadeusz Skorupski in their *Cultural Heritage of Ladakh.* Meanwhile, the Ladakhi homeland has become the base for a huge Indian army border force. The military makes most of the rules along the Indo-Tibetan frontier, where trade has been largely curtailed in the name of security. The army is everywhere in Leh—at the airport, in dusty jeeps on the few roads, along the passes, and in the mountains, where foreigners are not infrequently stopped and asked a little intrusively what brings them here.

The Chinese, intent on suppressing all forms of Tibetan nationalism after a 1959 rebellion (and continuing unrest ever since), are no friendlier. Ladakhis no longer move freely into and out of Tibetan monasteries, which are themselves being diminished and altered under Beijing's control. Trapped between the fears of India and China, the Ladakhis can no longer trek freely along the Himalayas through Nepal, Sikkim, and Bhutan to buy domestic and temple treasures from Buddhist artisans the likes of whom this barren land can no longer support. Families here once hung Tibetan thangkas, wore Chinese brocades, and treasured the creations of Bhutanese silversmiths. Without spontaneous travel, Ladakhis cannot easily refresh themselves at other spiritual wells of their faith or share in the life and worship of other Himalayan Buddhists.

All legal travel out of India into other nations in the Himalayan region must be by air through Delhi or by land through a limited number of border crossings into Nepal and Bhutan, though some routes into Tibet may open soon if peace prevails. Sikkim is more accessible to Ladakhis as Indian citizens, but then Sikkim is not only hundreds of miles distant but also caught in its own crisis of spirit and thus has scant solace to offer. In Nepal, where Tibetan Buddhism flourishes and draws devotees from all over the Himalayas, the Ladakhi presence is virtually nil, and few lamas immersed in the monastic life of Nepal have any idea of the status of the religion in Ladakh; some will say vaguely only that they heard it seemed to be in decline.

Denied an autonomous status in India, where they inhabit the only Buddhist-majority area, Ladakhis have no way to mitigate the dominance of Muslim and Hindu Kashmir at the state level or the economic and military control emanating from Delhi. They have limited hopes for Delhi's plan to establish a local governing council with some former state functions under its control; they would not, for example, have authority over the police.

"The Kashmir government has done us many injustices," said Tondup Sonam, an assistant to His Holiness Kushok Stakna, the Leh gompa's head lama and leader of the Buddhist Association. (A *kushok* in the Ladakhi language, a dialect of Tibetan, is the same as a *tulku* in Bhutan or Sikkim—an incarnate lama.) "We have been tolerating these things for too long," he said with passionate conviction. In a cluttered room above the gompa courtyard, Tondup Sonam had been watching the day's demonstration getting organized below, where banners were being unfurled and assigned. Many in the crowd were young people, motivated by a widely held fear that Kashmiri—specifically Sunni—Muslims were intent on capturing the economy completely and seizing all the jobs in tourism and commerce in Ladakh. "We are smelling that the Sunnis want to dominate people here," he said. "There have been intrigues for several years. The youth have to organize."

At Sankar monastery, a short drive through a valley running northeast of Leh, a lama talked about the roots of the Ladakhi Buddhist rebellion and why it had focused on only one Islamic community, the Sunnis. Around the Sankar gompa, families were living on the thin edge of subsistence. A number of children ran barefoot in the cool fall air, dressed in castoff foreign tourist clothes. A little girl of about seven or eight wore an oversize seersucker dress and the remains of a trekker's down-filled vest. Over her matted hair she had tied a brightly patterned bandanna. Her face was expressionless; malnutrition stunts the growth and robs the vitality of millions of children in poor parts of India. This is one such place, though far from the worst.

"When India opened Ladakh to tourism in 1974, shopkeepers from outside began to come here," the lama said. "Kashmiri Sunnis began to get a hand in everything. Travel agents in Srinagar or Delhi creamed off most tourist revenues, because the outsiders come through those places. The majority of local people in Leh, who are Buddhists, are not benefiting. But at the same time, costs are higher for our daily needs. We also think the Shia Muslims who have been living here peacefully for four or five hundred years are being incited by Sunni Kashmiris to turn against us."

Imam Mohammed Omar Nadvi—a Ladakhi Muslim whose family has lived around Leh for centuries, intermarrying with Buddhists—objected vigorously to that charge, which he classified as another provocative rumor intended to fan resentments against all Islamic families. Stories, all unfounded, were also circulating about gompas being desecrated or robbed by Muslims. A hotelier, a Ladakhi Buddhist, seconded the imam in discounting these incendiary reports. He said that more often than not, local Buddhist families and sometimes even monks had willingly sold religious treasures from their straitened monasteries to Kashmiri dealers or tourists. More important economically, he argued, was India's failure to ensure that Ladakh enjoyed at least relative prosperity within the growing national economy. Ladakhis see the difference in Sikkim, another former Buddhist kingdom, but one incorporated into India under much more recent and controversial circumstances. Millions of rupees pour into development in Sikkim, while in Ladakh, apricots fall from the trees and rot in the orchards because of inadequate transportation for marketing this highly perishable fruit. A middle-class couple talked about this one morning as they showed me their small farm, which they struggle to irrigate. Over the stone wall encircling the trees, a looming monochrome landscape of rocks and dry earth heightened the sense of hopelessness.

Two years after the 1989 outburst in Leh, tourism collapsed in the Kashmir Valley as a revolt against New Delhi by Kashmiri Muslims turned Srinagar into a battlefield. Fewer outsiders or Kashmiris came to Ladakh overland from Srinagar. Tensions dissipated a little in Leh, while the Indian government looked for ways to increase flights or improve alternative roads to the Ladakhi capital. With Kashmir effectively gone and hill stations like Simla and Darjeeling overcrowded and ecologically devastated, India needs new Himalayan tourist centers, and Leh is one prime candidate, along with previously closed areas east toward the Tibetan border and south in pristine Spiti, a Buddhist enclave on the upper edge of Himachal Pradesh. The prospect pleases many cash-strapped Ladakhis but worries others. Islam crept up the Indus, Kashmiris poured across the Zoji La. Both have altered the face of Buddhist Ladakh. But how much more damage to a fragile culture and ecology would large numbers of tourists—foreign or Indian—do?

Helena Norberg-Hodge, who in her most recent book, *Ancient Futures,* looks back over nearly two decades of life in Ladakh, says that tourism has already introduced begging and the growth of a get-rich-quick mentality. For Helena and her Ladakhi colleagues, there is a special sadness in this. She and her local partners have been working hard through a small foundation called the Ladakh Project to improve life without altering it beyond recognition by dependence on imports from the outside world. Dressed in her ankle-length Ladakhi robe, Helena and Tsewang Rigzin Lakruk, the project's president, showed me around their headquarters, which also served as a model building for demonstrating what developers like to call "appropriate technologies"—small, inexpensive, and fashioned of mostly local materials. Several hundred Ladakhi householders were learning from the project how to warm their homes with sunshine by constructing and placing windows to maximize light while insulating against drafts. Ladakhi carpenters had developed an efficient solar oven, which was on display in the project's garden, along with greenhouse frames that could extend growing seasons for fresh vegetables. Ladakhis, Helena said, were people born in extreme scarcity. This contributed to the high level of cooperation she found in villages. There was also a high level of tolerance for new ideas, an attribute foreigners find wherever Buddhism orders life.

Alas, that tolerance also makes Ladakhis too responsive to the lures of tourism, some say. "In one day, a tourist would spend the same amount that a Ladakhi might in a year," Norberg-Hodge, who speaks Ladakhi, writes in *Ancient Futures*. The impression left on local people was that the visitors enjoyed untold wealth that could easily be shared. She tells the story of Dawa, a fifteen-year-old village boy who in a matter of a few years had drifted to Leh and gone into business as a tour agent. She asked him how life in his mountain village looked to him now. "Boring," was the reply, in English. The people didn't have electricity, he complained, and some didn't even want it. He dismissed such thinking as out of step with the age: "We've worked in the fields long enough, Helena; we don't want to work so hard anymore." And off he went in search of his Dutch girlfriend.

Chapter 7

SIKKIM: "NO ONE HEARD US CRY"

THE GENTLEMAN was angry. The son of a former royal official, he had stored up nearly two decades of bitterness against the West. Now he had the unexpected opportunity to vent it. It was late on a winter afternoon in the Sikkimese capital, Gangtok, when we met; I had invited myself to his house, which was set in a quiet and secluded garden somewhere on the edge of town. A local merchant had guided me there, saying that this distinguished family had a store of firsthand accounts of the final years of Sikkim's last king, the Chogyal Palden Thondup Namgyal, and the shattering of Sikkimese independence. The chogyal, who died of cancer in near-obscurity in New York in 1982, is one of modern Asia's most tragic historical figures, the more so because his sorrowful story is barely remembered.

Even B. S. Das, the Indian official sent from New Delhi effectively to depose him in the 1970s, remembered the chogyal with respect and something approximating affection. "A lone and forgotten man who lost his kingdom, his wife and everything he stood for, stuck to his Palace, his People, his Sikkim till he breathed his last," Das wrote eloquently in *The Sikkim Saga,* an account of his ghoulish mission to this vulnerable Himalayan kingdom. "Unbending in his misfortunes, he dreamt of some one, some day appreciating the righteousness of his cause and placing him in history as a true nationalist who fought single-handed against all odds for what he believed in."

With Asian grace, the gentleman in Gangtok I met that afternoon showed his annoyance at my intrusion for only a moment before offering me a chair and ordering his servant to bring cakes and tea. But sixteen years after Sikkim was absorbed by India, he could barely disguise his contempt for the journalists he said had ascended to the mountain kingdom in 1963 with baggage full of adjectives to coo over the fairytale wedding of Hope Cooke, but hadn't stuck around long enough to notice that there would be no happy ending to the Sikkimese story. Journalists found plenty to say about the New Yorker who fell in love with a monkish Himalayan prince thrust into line for the throne by the death of an elder brother. They couldn't stop writing about the young American who was elevated to *gyalmo,* or queen, of Sikkim, not long after. But they were strangely absent a decade later when the kingdom collapsed and died. Where were you then? the gentleman wanted to know. By clinging to an exotic fantasy and averting its eyes and cameras in Sikkim's darkest days, he said, the democratic world had acquiesced in India's cynical destruction of his homeland, the second-to-last Himalayan Buddhist kingdom. "No one heard us cry," he said. "Or no one listened."

"The Shangri-la concept was dangerous for us," Cooke wrote in her autobiography, *Time Change.* "At every interview I'd given over the years, I'd tried again and again to drive the point home that however small and semiexotic we might be, we were real, we existed. If people didn't credit us with reality, we would perish very soon, the victim of very real power politics." And perish Sikkim did. No longer an independent kingdom with barely 200,000 people, Sikkim is now an Indian state with at least twice that number of inhabitants in a mountainous land of less than eight thousand square miles—somewhere between the land size of Puerto Rico and Canada's Prince Edward Island.

The Sikkimese gentleman and I reached an accommodation. I would not name him in any publication if he would talk awhile. And he did, sadly, now and then looking out the window toward the neat lawn and the trees that enclosed a small, slightly formal garden on a hillside terrace. In the days of the Raj, such gardens were often inspired if not created by compulsive British weekend horticulturalists determined to make the Himalayan hill stations take on the cultivated look of rural England. Gardens, along with amateur theatricals, tearooms, lending libraries, and stone churches with trellised gates, were weapons against homesickness. Gangtok, being the seat of an independent kingdom, escaped day-today administration by British civil servants and thus had no large expatriate colonial community. A resident political officer worked directly through the king. His functions were to oversee the affairs of the royal government while protecting British interests (a precedent India built on) as well as to set the general social tone and see that the appropriate flowers got planted.

John Claude White, the first political officer to take up residence in Gangtok in the late nineteenth century, when there were no roads or towns of any size, wrote in his journals about his efforts to build an appropriate house "in the midst of a primeval forest" not far from (but on a hill higher than) the royal palace. "By levelling the uneven ground and throwing it out in front, I managed to get sufficient space for the house, with lawn and flower beds around it," he recalled proudly in *Sikkim and Bhutan,* his record of his colonial service. "The garden was a great joy and an everlasting source of amusement and employment both to my wife and to myself," he wrote. "It was a lovely garden, the lawns always a beautiful green in winter, and perfectly smooth, with masses of flowers, the magnificent forest trees left standing about in clumps with feathery bamboo and groups of tree ferns adding a charm of their own. In early spring the lawns were fringed with daffodils, primroses, polyanthus, daisies, pansies—almost every spring flower you can name, flowering in a profusion seldom seen in England. By the end of April, the roses were in full bloom, a perfectly exquisite sight, excelling anything I have ever seen even in England. The house and all the outbuildings were covered with them."

A century later, these gardens that the British carved into hillsides remain a recognizable colonial legacy from the high valleys and mountainsides of Pakistan to the remotest resorts of Assam. There is always a lawn, usually rectangular and rimmed with flowering borders and bushes, sometimes planted in pots that give the whole affair portability as seasons change. On the lawn (regularly swept by servants) are chairs, tables, and sometimes large umbrellas set out for taking tea or enjoying meals in the open air. The most appealing characteristic of the climate in the Himalayan foothills is that while the nights may be harsh, the sun at midday and into the afternoon always seems to be warm and soothing, monsoon seasons excepted.

Cozy, understated gardens also survive around old British-era hotels, in Murree, Shimla, Darjeeling, and the balmier hill stations of South

India. These homey patches of grass and flowers are not the magnificent formal constructions of the Moguls, with their terraces and watercourses, or the more austere French garden landscapes of Dalat, the premier colonial sanitarium-resort in Vietnam. But no people so rhapsodized over their flowering plants as the British. Claude White went on for pages in his memoirs cataloguing all his flowers, season by season, and boasting of the size of their blooms. A stock flowering in front of his study window, he recorded methodically, was four feet six inches high and three feet six inches in diameter, and a *Lilium auratum* "grew to eight feet, with 29 blossoms on a single stalk."

Gangtok was so undeveloped in the 1880s that the Whites had to import dairy cattle for milk, sheep for meat, a baker, carpenters and furniture builders, a blacksmith, and a silversmith. But they built a house to match their status, even wallpapering the interior with an imported touch of home. Fine Sikkimese houses, like that of the gentleman talking over tea, caught the ambience of an English manse, with dark, heavy furniture and draperies in rooms designed to resist the sun along with the sounds, smells, and often even views of Asia. Roses in the dooryard bloomed. Beyond them hedgerows grew. It was a self-contained world.

When the life of independent Sikkim was snuffed out, the courtly gentleman was saying, it had been a small country on the way to controlled growth in tune with its size and heritage, much like Bhutan. But there were crucial differences. In Sikkim a Buddhist monarch and Tibetan or Bhutia people closely related to the Bhutanese ruled a population more than half Nepali by ancestry. Nepalis were largely Hindu, spoke a very different language, and were eager and mobile workers in a variety of occupations. They took quickly to new terrain, where they settled and expanded their families. In Sikkim, as later in Bhutan, they could be readily exploited as disaffected fifth-columnists.

Sikkim also sat astride the most accessible gateway to and from Tibet, an old trade route from Lhasa to Darjeeling through the pass called Natu La. This and other high but navigable trails might one day be used by India's enemies. Bhutan's mountain passes were more distant and difficult to traverse, and therefore of less concern to imperial Britain and later India. Bhutan was also larger geographically, and peopled by a martial race of strapping men and women who had proved their battle skills time and again over the centuries. They gave Bhutan a don't-tread-on-us quality that the Sikkimese did not enjoy, and especially not the Lepchas, the country's third major ethnic group, the gentlest of Himalayan people.

To the Indian establishment, allowing Sikkim to remain free and vulnerable when the British left India in 1947 was tantamount to exposing a Himalayan Achilles' heel. China was not yet the direct threat it would later become after its army had overrun the Tibetans and turned its attention to the Indian border, but Sikkim did have close ties with Tibet through culture and marriage. The Chogyal Palden Namgyal studied there as a monk and married a gorgeous Tibetan princess, Sangey Deki, who died in 1957, a few years before Hope Cooke entered his royal life. The Sikkimese long nurtured claims on Tibetan territory, and those might someday prove troublesome, Indians thought. Almost from the day independent India was born, many Sikkimese believe, Delhi plotted the kingdom's downfall, with little regard for a 1950 treaty of accommodation.

Indian ministers and administrators gave outsiders the impression that they were already in control well before delivering the fatal blow. They argued that they were simply picking up the reins (or, as one Indian official preferred, a leash) on Sikkim dropped by the departing British. In early 1960, John Kenneth Galbraith, then ambassador to India, recorded in his diary a brief visit to Gangtok and his meeting there with Bleshwar Prasad, "the Dewan Sahib, who is the effective head of the government and an Indian." He added the observation that all the top administrators in Sikkim seemed to be Indians. The *dewan,* by then an Indian-appointed adviser to the chogyal who introduced himself to Galbraith as prime minister of Sikkim, apparently had a reputation for tactlessness, the ambassador noted. It was a trait that flowered then and flowers still in Indians sent abroad to do their nation's work in the neighborhood.

Sikkimese could later make much of Galbraith's adopting Delhi's language in calling the aging ruler he met in Gangtok a "maharaja." Chogyal Tashi Namgyal, the king he met, was a frail man of sixty-eight and an artist more interested in his paints than his government files. His heir, who would marry Cooke, Galbraith called the "maharajkumar." As often in politically status-conscious India, the choice of title carries significant implications. "Maharaja," in Delhi-speak, was applied to heads of protectorate territories and incorporated princely states. It was a rank subordinate to that of a king, as "chogyal" was defined in Sikkimese. Indians, who argued accurately that the British also called Sikkim's king "maharaja," inevitably got out of sorts when the Sikkimese or foreigners addressed the chogyal as "Your Majesty," which was deemed more than he deserved. "Your Highness" would have been more than enough for India, which had abolished hereditary kingships.

Galbraith's Indian escorts must also have shared their considerable anxiety about Tibet with the ambassador, who at one point while visiting a Bengali plantation was apparently told that he was closer to Tibetan territory than he probably was. He noticed the numerous contingents of Indian forces in Sikkim, "located here, presumably, to discourage the Chinese." The level of paranoia in Delhi about the Sikkim corridor from Tibet soared after the 1962 Chinese attacks on India in the Ladakh area on the western flank and near the Burmese border in the east. These incursions, met disastrously by an ill-equipped Indian force, were mounted not long after Beijing had finally consolidated its occupation of Tibet in 1959. India's Himalayan line of security had never been so threatened.

And then, in 1963, along came the marriage of the heir to Sikkim's throne to an American, who, given the lively imaginations of Indian policymakers, might as well have been an agent of the Central Intelligence Agency. That same year, to the consternation of Delhi, Hope Cooke's new father-in-law, Sir Tashi Namgyal, the artist-chogyal whom Ambassador Galbraith had met, died and his son inherited the throne. It took more than a decade of treachery, dirty tricks, and the blatant cultivation of Nepali-Sikkimese to accomplish the task of decapitating Sikkim and dethroning its hereditary ruler, but Indira Gandhi finally succeeded in the 1970s. By then she had also drawn into her cause a few high-ranking Tibetan-Bhutia Sikkimese, most notably a schemer named Kazi Lhendup Dorji, to give the destabilization plot a less obviously ethnic coloration. *Kazi* is a Sikkimese title of inherent nobility, possibly with Central Asian or Kashmiri antecedents; in Kashmir a *qazi* was traditionally a learned expert on law, usually born into a substantial family. Until relatively recently, a Sikkimese kazi was more apt to serve the royal government than to enter opposition politics, but Kazi Lhendup Dorji was not cut from the old mold. Even less reticent about breaking fealty to the king was his ambitious European-born wife, the Kazini Elisa Maria. Thus three women played prominent parts in the dramatic undoing of Sikkim: the kazini; her innocent archenemy, Hope Cooke; and Indira Gandhi.

As prime minister of India, Indira Gandhi had none of the scruples or statesmanship of her father, Jawaharlal Nehru, who had given Sikkim assurances that its autonomy, if not independence, would not be disturbed. He died in 1964 and his immediate successor, Lal Bahadur Shastri, soon followed him to the funeral pyre, leaving the field to Nehru's ambitious but perennially insecure daughter. By 1975, a brief but violent invasion, the forced abdication of the chogyal, and an act of Parliament in New Delhi had made Sikkim an Indian state. By the time free Sikkim had plunged into its last two turbulent years of life, the American-born queen, Hope Cooke, and her influential friends from the United States were going or gone, my Sikkimese gentleman insisted, so nobody outside seemed to care.

That is not strictly true. Voices were raised in the United States and at the United Nations against this burst of Indian manifest destiny. Feelings in Delhi were bruised by American admonitions. Prominent among the critics of the annexation was Claiborne Pell, the Rhode Island Democrat who was already something of an *éminence grise* among foreign-policy experts in the United States Senate. Outrage was not sustained, however. In 1973, American troops were returning from a debacle in South Vietnam—Hanoi's regulars would overrun Saigon two years later—and there was no enthusiasm for rattling sabers over odd little Sikkim and its medieval crown.

Cooke, who left Sikkim and the chogyal in 1973, never to return, is remembered vividly in the region, though not for her spirited foray into Tibetan Buddhism and Sikkimese wifehood. Indian officials reached a sneering and unfair conclusion that the American interloper lusted after a crown, and decamped when she saw that she would lose it. In truth, her reasons for leaving Sikkim were far more personal, as her self-absorbed autobiography illustrates. In other Himalayan nations, especially in Bhutan, Cooke is recalled and occasionally still castigated among the elite for an article she wrote for the June 1966 *Bulletin of Tibetology,* of which she was also an editor. The Bulletin was published by the Institute of Tibetology in Gangtok, established in the late 1950s as Tibet was slipping under total Chinese repression. As gyalmo of Sikkim after 1963, Cooke had become an active partner with her royal husband in bolstering the identity of the little kingdom. Apart from supporting research into the religion and culture of the Tibetan peoples, the royal couple also promoted native Sikkimese crops and crafts, introduced more effective protection of an unusual natural environment, and fostered appearances of Sikkimeseness in architecture, decoration, entertainment, and public life.

This alone would have been observed with suspicion in some quarters in New Delhi, since Sikkimese nationalism could only enhance an affinity for things Tibetan. But Cooke did not stop there. She turned her considerable American energies and creativity from bolstering Sikkimese craftsmanship and restoring the bungalow-palace in Gangtok to reexamining history. Her now infamous article in the *Bulletin of Tibetology* reopened the acidic issue of Darjeeling, a former outpost of Sikkim that had been effectively annexed by India's British colonial administration in the nineteenth century. Following Britain's lead, India assumed control over Darjeeling and other hill areas at independence, despite Sikkimese protests. The issue of Darjeeling could only reopen wounds among the Sikkimese at a dangerously tricky moment. In her article, the gyalmo argued that the Sikkimese crown had probably intended to grant only "usage" rights in the Darjeeling area to the British, who wanted to build a sanitarium away from the pestilential plains of Bengal. Britain abused that grant, the gyalmo's argument concluded. The corollary was obvious: the Indians were perpetuating a violation. Cooke later acknowledged ruefully that she had "stirred up a hornet's nest."

The Indian press, too often willing to promote the government line whatever the facts, flew into a prompted rage. Himalayan statesmen were appalled and fearful, a Bhutanese told me two decades after the publication appeared. Cooke was also sobered by the reaction. "I was remorseful, scared," she wrote in her memoir of those years. Many Sikkimese, Bhutanese, and sympathetic Indians look back on that one well-intentioned if reckless act as the gyalmo's most dangerous mistake. To the bureaucrats and policy planners of India, this unpredictable American woman, whose very presence in the region had focused an unwelcome spotlight on Sikkim, now seemed to be fanning her husband's already defiantly nationalistic tendencies.

The tale of Sikkimese victimization and helplessness that the gentleman told me in his formal parlor in Gangtok, so at variance with India's official version of events, was familiar. Indeed, it was fresh in my mind, because a day or two earlier I had found, prominently displayed in a Gangtok bookshop, a copy of a book difficult to obtain in India, *Smash and Grab: The Annexation of Sikkim*. This riveting blend of chronology and personal observation was written a decade after the collapse of independent Sikkim by the distinguished Calcutta journalist Sunanda K. Datta-Ray, who had reported on the kingdom for more than a decade and was, in the end, a friend of the last chogyal. *Smash and Grab,* a lot of it read by candlelight in my room at the old Nor-khill Hotel during an electrical blackout, brought alive the miserable story of a king doomed by treachery and finally cancer, yet trailed to the end of his days by graceless Indian intelligence agents. Still, the book hadn't quite prepared me for the raw bitterness that welled up in the dark parlor of the aristocratic family whose son I was hearing out. Before I left, the gentleman walked around the room pointing out family portraits, some in ornate frames. The pictures also spoke poignantly of a lost world, but in those frames the past was safe and everyone smiled.

Other Sikkimese told me similar stories of a people deceived and a country stolen. They pointed to silent, lingering signs of protest: the continuing use of the old Sikkimese coat of arms on the buildings of what is now an Indian state, the pilgrimages to the memorial chorten of the last chogyal, where foreigners cannot go. Not all the disaffected are Buddhists, and not all the complainants want to see a return of the monarchy. Over the years since the debacle of 1973–75, the criticisms of Indian rule have polarized around concerns that too many people have been pouring in from the overpopulated Gangetic plain and Nepal, both densely populated and strained in resources. Marwaris, Kashmiris, and other high-intensity Indian merchants (present in smaller numbers even a century ago) had muscled out local businesses, people told me. Aid was spawning corruption of unprecedented proportions. In many quarters there was the half-assertion, half-question: Why, when everyone had been so much poorer before the annexation, did the quality of life seem better? Those days are remembered as a bucolic time when Gangtok's few streets weren't choked with jeeps and concrete monstrosities did not spring up at every turn to mar the soul-healing, spirit-lifting mountain views.

One morning on the way to Rumtek monastery—a roller-coaster trip from one side of the Ranipool River valley to the heights on the opposite bank—I stopped to pick up a well-dressed woman walking to work in some haste. She had missed a local jitney and was anxiously trying to flag down another ride as she struggled along in shoes not made for trekking. She wore a sari, and the red dot of a *bindi* on her forehead indicated she was a Hindu. "Nepali," said the taxi driver with the certainty of taxi drivers everywhere as we slowed to give her a lift. She was a minor civil servant, she said in the course of a conversation in which she lamented the overbuilding of Gangtok and the hills around it as Indian development money for building projects and a few small agriculture-based industries poured in to keep the restive Sikkimese reasonably happy. By 1990, India, which had used the Nepali majority in Sikkim to overthrow a Buddhist monarchy, had to worry that millions of Nepalis concentrated across the Indian north and east wanted their own nation. They call it Gorkhaland. In the hill towns of West Bengal—Kalimpong, Kurseong, and most of all Darjeeling—a strong Nepali separatist movement, armed and unarmed, had created havoc and economic disruption in the 1980s. Among other effects, this sent a warning to the Bhutanese, who decided to take a now controversial census to see how much Nepali migration they had absorbed.

The Gorkhaland movement for land and a national identity defined by the Nepali language took its name from the legend of the brave Gorkhas, soldiers from the lowlands of Nepal known for their ruthlessness, utter obedience to a cause or commander, and exceptional, legendary fighting skills. Gorkhas—they prefer that spelling to Gurkhas—were the people who produced the warrior-king Prithvi Narayan Shah, who united Nepal in the eighteenth century. They served the British well in several wars and now provide troops for the Indian army and paramilitary police. A dimestore novelist, Subhas Ghising, took up the Gorkhaland standard in Darjeeling. In Sikkim, a leading politician, Nar Bahadur Bhandari, leading another Nepali-nationalist party that eschewed the Gorkha label, responded with demands that Nepali-Sikkimese get special treatment—a quota of Indian parliament seats, for example—to keep them from being swept up in a Gorkha tide. The Gorkha movement naturally had an appeal in Sikkim among newer arrivals from Nepal and Indian hills and northern plains. Bhandari was beginning to drift toward quasi-separatism (while bogged down in lawsuits on charges of corruption). As chief minister of Sikkim before his personal and political troubles brought him down, he was regularly accused of autocratic behavior; tourists were told he chose which way the satellite dish was pointed (it made cable television possible in the isolated town) and everyone in Gangtok had to watch his programs.

How ironic, I thought, if some kind of autonomy should be restored to Sikkim at the insistence of a politician like Bhandari and his Nepali-Sikkimese followers, who were largely responsible for the overthrow of the stubbornly nationalist Buddhist king. From the early days of Sikkim's final crisis, Nepali-Sikkimese were having second thoughts about what a monster they had unleashed. The personal Sikkimese valet of B. S. Das, the Indian sent to Gangtok effectively to engineer the signing of Sikkim's death warrant, asked his master anxiously if this meant he would have to become an Indian. "I hope not," Das remembered him saying. To be Sikkimese then meant being a Buddhist Bhutia or a Lepcha who spoke a Tibetan dialect, and not the Nepali language, which is closer to the Hindi of North India. Das did not think total absorption of Sikkim by India was inevitable when he left in 1974, after gaining an agreement on an associate status for Sikkim. But things rapidly fell apart after his departure, and New Delhi moved swiftly and ruthlessly.

On the road to Rumtek, our hitchhiker gestured to this or that substantial concrete house that she swore had been constructed with the inevitable creaming off of development assistance. She sailed with some enthusiasm into a general condemnation of India and the destruction that had ensued since Sikkim was pried open to the people of the plains. The harshness surprised me, since she had no doubt been the beneficiary of a Nepali-led state government. About then, we passed a construction crew at the side of the narrow road. The faces were hard to identify and the saronglike garments some of the laborers wore were intriguing, so I interrupted to ask where those people had come from. "Maybe they are Nagas, or are coming from somewhere in Nepal," she said. "So many people are brought here to work on lowly jobs, too many people. A lot of Nepalis. None of these people belong here." But aren't you Nepali? I asked. "Nepali!" she replied with a hard look and a stage laugh. "No, no. I am Sikkimese. The Nepalis are foreigners." The late chogyal might have smiled sadly at the sound of history falling on itself.

"THIS OFFICE is belong to Sikkim," a cheerful young person at the Sikkim Tourism headquarters told me, explaining why she could not provide information on taxi fares direct from various Bengali gateways to Gangtok, the only routes in for foreigners since an ambitious helicopter service from Bagdogra, in West Bengal, was grounded for safety soon after a very scary opening. "Taxi are in West Bengal, so I can't tell." But she could tell me that because of the "trouble" in Kashmir—then approaching a fully developed war for independence—New Delhi was planning to open more of Sikkim to tourists, especially trekkers and those who wanted to visit mountain monasteries. For years, Indian security constraints had kept large areas of the country off-limits to foreigners. By the early 1990s, the numbers of tourists (many of them trekkers) began to rise significantly; Gangtok had as many as two hundred small hotels or guesthouses.

An outsider coming to Sikkim for the first time years after its incorporation into India has a tough time making independent judgments about the changes that have taken place. To me it all seemed a very un-Indian place, with a few exceptions, from the moment my taxi from Bagdogra reached the Sikkimese border at Rangpo. An archway welcomed visitors to Sikkim as if it were a foreign country. We were obliged to stop and register with local authorities; the Indians require special passes for foreigners traveling to Sikkim. While I waited for the inevitable paperwork to take so inexplicably but routinely long to complete, I had coffee and a snack in a cheerful lodge where flowering shrubs and trees added color to the green hillside beyond the windows. The spacious tourist center, which also had about eight guest rooms, was built in the largely concocted Sikkimese style, with elements of Tibet in the slope of its outer walls, tall windows wider at the bottom than the top, and an ornamented central tower. The rooftops of the lodge, the tower, and a freestanding shelter over the entrance were neither flat, as they might have been in Tibet or Ladakh, nor pitched, as in Bhutan, but somewhere in between, giving the green metal panels a pagodalike slope that blended nicely with the hills. The countryside all around was luxuriously overgrown and seemed devoid of people.

The paperwork over, we were back on the road and on the way to Gangtok, a route that at first follows the valley of the jade-green Teesta River before it veers away toward its origins in the hills. The Teesta, flowing down to the plains over and around white sandbanks and through rocky rapids, has always been an important symbol of Sikkim—though it hasn't been very useful as a waterway for transport; it is not deep enough for long enough stretches for boats. Its valley is serenely beautiful, neither wild nor overcultivated. As we passed through villages en route to Gangtok, I savored what made Sikkim so instantly different from the Indian state of Himachal or many stretches of the Himalayan foothills in Uttar Pradesh, where hillsides grow yearly more barren of vegetation and every roadside stop is a full-time bazaar broadcasting the ubiquitous warbling whine of Hindi cinema soundtracks. On the road to Gangtok we passed through hamlets that seemed all but deserted. In one, a woman stepped out on her roadside porch and stretched, face to the sun, to yawn and scratch about her person. Buddhist prayer beads dangled from one hand. There was so much silence. In the valleys we followed into the hills, there were occasional farming hamlets, clusters of whitewashed one-story buildings with tin or thatch or wood-shake roofs.

As we neared Gangtok, my initial enthusiasm at finding that Sikkim still had a singular character within the Indian union began to wane. The town was cacophony itself by late afternoon. Traffic crawled around the switchback roads and steep side lanes, much as it would in any Indian hill station. There was no serenity here, no unmistakable Sikkimese character or atmosphere left in the town or its dozens of shops and offices. When the first British political delegation came to Gangtok in the 1880s, they camped on open land in the area that is now the vehicle-choked bazaar, terminally polluted by fumes, sewage, and soiled old plastic bags. In the 1970s—according to photographs I found in an old book at the General Stores, near the crossroads that passes for downtown—the bazaar was still a somnolent, relatively open space with shade trees. People were using footpaths, not taxis.

The bazaar is no longer one stretch of road, but rather a winding affair that snakes up the face of a steep hillside in several stages, a pattern common in the Himalayan foothills, where towns rarely have flat surfaces to work with. Along both sides of the original main strip (some called it the Purana, or Old Bazaar), merchants pushed Indian textiles and processed foods and soaps—Amul and Nivea and all their kith and kin—as well as garish plastic housewares and Indian-made Bata shoes. At one end of the old bazaar, a bust of Mahatma Gandhi mounted on a tasteless concrete plinth was protected by a nasty metal fence about five feet high, its gate secured with a padlock, and a further cement-and-chain-link barrier. I asked why the Father of the Nation had to be so heavily fortified, and was told vaguely that there might be miscreants about.

There was very little that was identifiably Sikkimese about the bazaar; what lowland Indians weren't selling, Kashmiris or Tibetans were. Hope Cooke tells a good story about how an American television crew filming her little palace wanted to shoot a few Sikkimese treasures; she had to forage for something that wasn't Tibetan, Indian, or otherwise foreign. The experience helped fuel her interest in promoting the crafts of Sikkim. Behind the bazaar, however, in the alleys and on the steep hillsides, Buddhist prayer flags fluttered. Passing under a huge banner proclaiming an "International Year of Tibet," I escaped in a taxi to look for the official Sikkimese state handicraft center, away from the bazaar at the dead end of an alley near the Indian governor's residence. All was gloomy there, owing initially to the lack of electricity. The Sikkimese sales staff, gossiping merrily when I surprised them at the open door, fell utterly silent and unsalespersonlike.

There were no other customers, so I tried hard to find something to buy, watched as I was by at least four pairs of hopeful Sikkimese eyes. All manner of goods were brought out from glass cases for my perusal, but only at my request. Blankets and rugs were too unwieldy to cart away; so were the colorful little carved and painted *choektse* tables that are the coffee tables and often dinner tables in Himalayan homes from Ladakh to Bhutan. I settled on a rough, handwoven woolen jacket handsomely embroidered down the front in a kind of braid. The jacket was a nice browny tweed; unfortunately, someone had lined it in glaring sky blue. Lining notwithstanding, the garment proved later to have the qualities of a hair shirt, as shards of wool designed for alpine temperatures burrowed through a synthetic interior to inflict torture. Over a sweater, though, it's good for shoveling snow.

My first day in Sikkim—half of it spent tangling with Indian Airlines and another five hours of it on the road in a small taxi from West Bengal—was saved by the Nor-khill Hotel. The Nor-khill, which once belonged to the royal family, is a rattling old two-story lodge that was almost empty, even though Gangtok's annual orchid festival was in progress and it was still tourist season. The old building, bright white with a red metal roof and a red-painted cement veranda to match, was in good shape, but its spirit was certainly sagging. There was much more verve in the Hotel Tashi Delek nearby, and the lavishly decorated Hotel Tibet, near the bazaar. But the Nor-khill had a good location and a nice garden (straggly potted plants and wobbly metal chairs aside) for reading and writing. It also had provocative historical associations: it overlooked the Paljor Stadium, the site of antimonarchy demonstrations in 1948 and again in the 1970s.

Inside, the hotel was a mix of faded European style with bright splashes of Himalayan art. A corner of the long lobby-lounge had half a dozen or more small tables painted with the symbols of Himalayan Buddhism scattered among regal chairs covered in locally woven fabric. Warm rugs covered the floor, and on the wall a three-panel, almost-Chinese-style painting showed a scene of rural life in the hills. The effort to give the lobby a Himalayan personality didn't extend to the spartan dining room or the guest rooms upstairs, however. I was pretty much resigned to another spell of mild discomfort in the mountains, the hallmark of rugged hill station sojourns. Then, arranging things in my room, I opened the faded curtains hanging unevenly over a chest-high window above a rickety table and there, of course, were the Himalayas. There was Kanchenjunga itself, the holy Sikkimese mountain. I poured myself a drink from my Bag of Necessities for Traveling in India, and stood in its presence until darkness fell, as if before an altar.

The death of a nation is a terrible thing anywhere. And the demise of the kingdom of Sikkim was all the more tragic because it meant another important piece torn from the map of the historical Tibetan Buddhist world. It was the end of Sikkimese independence that left Bhutan the lone defender of that distinctive culture. In Sikkim, Himalayan Buddhism and a monarchy of Tibetan lineage had coexisted for many years with a Hindu population of Nepali origins and the communities of Lepchas, people thought to be related to today's Burmese or Assamese, who settled in the hills and practiced a localized animist faith long before the arrival of the Tibetans who would be kings. The Lepchas claim to have given Sikkim its first name, Denzong. Insignificant pockets of Lepchas, a name they say was given to them by outsiders, also live in Bhutan, Nepal, and the Himalayan foothills of India. But only in Sikkim, with a land area under 7,300 square miles, much of it difficult mountain terrain, were they a relatively substantial presence for centuries. The Nepalis came later, encouraged by British colonial administrators looking for people to make more intensive and productive use of the land. But the Nepalis multiplied quickly as new families arrived. The Lepchas and the Tibetan-Bhutias could not override the demographic tide.

Sikkim's ill-fated monarchy ruled longer and had deeper roots than the Wangchuck dynasty now on the throne of Bhutan. Although, as always in this part of the world where mythology and history slide effortlessly into each other's territory, there are some critical questions about the Sikkimese version of events, it is pretty much accepted that the royal Namgyal family could trace its ancestry to the Minyak dynasty established in eastern Tibet in the ninth century. Some say an even earlier ancestor of the Sikkimese Namgyals once reigned in what is now Himachal, an Indian state next door to Ladakh, later ruled by another branch of the Namgyal clan. The Minyak dynasty and its heirs were based in the Chumbi Valley of Tibet, at least part of which was Sikkimese territory until barely a century ago. Many generations after the founding of the Minyak kingdom, one member of the royal family, Mipon Rab, drifted down to the vicinity of Gangtok. Three or four more generations on, Phuntsog Namgyal, a prince of the Minyak line, became Sikkim's first acknowledged king, or chogyal, to use the Tibetan title. Palden Thondup Namgyal, the last ruler of independent Sikkim, was twelfth in that royal line. Bhutan's hereditary monarchy began only in 1907, and there have been only four kings, who do not call themselves chogyals, at least not to English-speakers.

Because of the long years of rule by a family of Tibetan origins and the influence of the Himalayan Buddhist sects that inevitably entrenched themselves in Sikkim, with the Nyingmapa school becoming the state religion, the town of Gangtok and outlying monastic settlements in the hills and mountains are full of historical associations with the Namgyals and their faith. The ghosts of a kingdom hover around the Tsuklakhang, the old royal gompa on a hill above Gangtok, which is mostly closed to outsiders. Royal ceremonies once took place at Tsuklakhang, where the chogyal's astrologer-advisers lived. Once a year, around September, monks still gather there to perform dances in honor of Kanchenjunga, the god-mountain guardian deity, which rises to a height of more than 28,000 feet along the border with Nepal. This dance to Kanchenjunga, called the *pang lhabsol,* also commemorates the pledge of a bond between Bhutias and Lepchas, who called themselves Rong-folk, or "valley people." (That name is a little confusing, because the Lepchas are Buddhists, and, especially in Nepal, the term "rong-folk" or *rong-pa* would be applied to lowlanders, who are more likely to be Hindus and Nepali-speakers.)

As in Bhutan now, Himalayan Tantric Buddhism was the state religion and the private faith of the Tibetan-Bhutia people and their kings. Most of the Lepchas who preceded them here were in the course of time converted from pure spirit worship and joined the Buddhist community, while also accepting a Buddhist king. Some Nepali-Sikkimese, members of tribes or clans outside the otherwise dominant Hindu world, are also Buddhist, among them the Rai, Gurung, Limbu, and Tamang people. But as in Nepal, Hindus and Buddhists in Sikkim often did and still do take part in each other's festivals and join in celebrations that are thought of more as Sikkimese than belonging to any individual community.

Because visits to Tsuklakhang, the palace (still in the Namgyal family's possession), and most other sites closely associated with Sikkimese royalty are barred to foreigners by skittish Indian officials, I went instead to Dodrul Chorten and the monastery at Enchey for a glimpse of Sikkimese Buddhism. Dodrul, on the airy crown of a wooded hill near the Institute of Tibetology at Deorali, can be identified miles away by its soaring white central chorten capped in gold with the omnipresent symbols of Buddhism—thirteen parasols representing the Thirteen Stages Toward Enlightenment, fire, a sun cradled in a crescent moon for air and sky, and a small flame or orb signifying ether, an element believed to be found in the upper reaches of space. The ground around the base of the chorten is all but enclosed by walls of prayer wheels. A temple nearby is the base of Sikkim's highest lama, the Dodrup Chen Rinpoche. When I reached the chorten, at the top of a steep path lined with prayer flags, the scene was alive with dozens of novices clowning around on a cool spring day. Two were launching paper airplanes with gleeful shrieks. A dozen or more raced each other up and down a driveway. Others climbed balustrades and threw stones into the trees, I imagined at birds.

At Dodrul, the Guru Rinpoche reappeared in all his glory. There are two famous statues of him here. The Sikkimese, to claim a piece of the action surrounding this legendarily hyperactive guru who brought Tantric Buddhism to the Himalayas, believe that the saint buried some of his famous holy treasure for posterity in Sikkim centuries before this was a Buddhist kingdom. The sacred books were then duly discovered hundreds of years later by monks from Tibet who settled in Sikkim and founded its monasteries.

Because of Sikkim's small size, geographically and in population, and because there seemed to be no urge to build fortifications, despite invasions from Tibet, Nepal, and Bhutan over the centuries, the Sikkimese centers of religion and government are more modest and accessible compared with their counterparts housed in the great dzongs of Bhutan. Rumtek, fourteen miles from Gangtok, is the exception, because it has been the international center of the Kagyupa Karmapa school of Buddhism since 1959, when the Chinese took military control of Tibet. Many thousands of Himalayan Buddhists and well-wishers overseas support Rumtek's temples. Supporters are also helping to rebuild the former seat of the Karmapas at Tsurphu, near the Tibetan capital, Lhasa, which was sacked in the 1960s by the zealots of China's Cultural Revolution. The Indian government takes justified pride in helping to upgrade and maintain Sikkimese temples and monasteries. There are several hundred of them, some of which officials in New Delhi say were in advanced disrepair in 1975.

Enchey monastery, which seems to have been restored recently, is on yet another isolated hilltop a few miles from town. The monks were at prayer, so I sat apart at the temple doorway, among heaps of worn little shoes belonging to the novices who were perched cross-legged and attentive in two rows leading away from the chief monk at his prayer table. Enchey is one of about half a dozen leading monasteries of Sikkim. Its site was chosen by a lama with the power of flight who descended from the sky to build himself a hermitage. The spot is now marked by a three-story, yellow-roofed temple that is something of a cross between a classic winged pagoda and a solid Himalayan gompa. Though its roofs soar, its base is planted solidly and heavily in the earth with that inward slant of its thick walls that Bhutanese architects tell me makes structures resistant to most earthquakes. The temple was built early in the twentieth century, of stone blocks now plastered white. Wide bands of bright red define the tops of the outer walls, a hallmark also of holy buildings in other Himalayan Buddhist lands. The elaborate windows on the ground floor are, to the unrefined eye, stunning works of art. Each window frame, easily six or eight feet tall and perhaps five or six feet wide and extravagantly ornamented in floral and other natural symbols drawn from the Buddhists' artistic canon, is surrounded by a section of dark stone left unplastered and unpainted in roughly the form of a huge garment with short sleeves above an A-line robe, rather like a kimono hung splayed on a wall. The effect created is that of a traditional, irregularly shaped window, wider at the bottom, even though the three modern glass panels within are perfect rectangles. On the upper floors, windows are trimmed in bright yellow, giving the temple top a glittering golden look.

Prayers ended, and novices poured over me and my doorstep to race into the corners of the courtyard. The boys whooped as if to welcome recess, shuffling impatiently into their shoes and tussling with each other as they ran. A monk appeared from the dim interior of the temple and offered to show me around. We walked past the monks' living quarters, more a hostel than cells, to a pavilion filled with offerings and warmly glowing votive lamps. An annual festival is held in the monastic compound at Enchey at the end of the Sikkimese year, usually in December-January. Other monasteries concentrate their festivals around either the Sikkimese New Year, called Loosong, that soon follows, or the Himalayan Buddhist New Year, Losar, a movable holiday that normally falls around February.

Like most Buddhist communities across the Himalayas and the Tibetan plateau, the Sikkimese name their years for animals according to traditional cycles, then prefixed with one of the elements. There are twelve prescribed animals—rat (or mouse), bull (or ox), tiger, hare, dragon, snake, horse, sheep, monkey, bird, dog, and hog—and five elements—earth, water, fire, wood, and iron. Each element is good for two years, so that, for example, a Year of the Earth Rat would be followed by the Earth Bull before moving on to the Water Tiger and Water Hare. The combinations are obviously not the same in succeeding cycles, because repeating the names of elements still leaves us two units short of the number of animal names. This makes the calendar business tricky and, as I learned in Bhutan, best left to experts.

The Rong-folk or Lepchas of Sikkim had calendars of their own. Though like many Himalayan people they combined Buddhism with their nature-based beliefs and the veneration and appeasement of local spirits, these indigenous calendars were based on the observation and interpretation of purely local natural signs. As in rural Bhutan and other places in the mountains of inner Asia, the Lepcha calendars illustrate why the foreigner's measures of time and season may hold no particular attraction. The invention and use of calendars based on the blossoming of trees, the flight of birds, or the activities of animals also demonstrates how deeply the patterns of life and livelihood are interwoven into the environment and, sadly, how much culture can be lost with the extinction of plants and animals. A. R. Foning, in *Lepcha My Vanishing Tribe,* recalls how his particular clan worked out what season it was and what tasks that season demanded.

"Natural objects like the sun, the moon, and the stars, trees and plants, animals, birds and insects, act as our infallible calendars, time-keepers, direction-indicators and guides," he wrote. "They tell us when to sow our seeds, when to harvest the crops, and what things to look for, and at what times, in forests and rivers. When we see the *tuk-po pot boor,* the peach blossoming, we know that our Nambum, our New Year's Day celebration, is approaching and we look forward to it expectantly and start making preparations for it. Similarly, when we find the *konkee boor,* or cherry blossom, we know it proclaims to us that now, after the *so sa,* dry season lull, we have to get busy with the work of cultivation. Likewise, the flight of the pathetically wailing *kurngok* bird overhead, immediately after winter during starry nights, tells us that it is just the time for putting down cucumber, pumpkin and other such seeds. Likewise the advent of the *ka-ku,* the cuckoo, heralds the sowing time of the dry-land paddy, the *dumbra* and the *ongray zo.* We start preparing the field and depositing the seed in holes made with sticks. Some months later, the *chyak-dun* bird appears, giving a call telling us to 'now hurry up' for the harvesting of the paddy. In other words, our very existence is inextricably bound up and interwoven with these things, things that God has given us."

These seasons were then broken down into months they called *lavo,* based on the cycles of the moon (also the method of Tibetan Buddhists), and years, *nam,* composed of roughly twelve twenty-nine- or thirty-day lavos—with an extra one thrown in about every three years to even things up and not get ahead of the seasons. The Lepchas called the extra lavo a *lavo shyoke,* a "moon added on." This does make Nambum, the New Year, mutable, but the celebration is, in any case, not begun until everyone agrees that many other tasks have been successfully performed, including the giving of varied offerings to deities and demons to keep them occupied. While the deities are busy scrambling for goodies, the humans can enter a new year unencumbered by busybody, troublemaking spirits.

The natural world the Lepchas found here may be the lushest and botanically the most prolific in the Himalayas, similar to the environment of Bhutan. Crossing from West Bengal into Sikkim at Rangpo, the traveler feels that the subcontinent has been left behind and that some kind of rain forest has strayed here from its moorings in the Caribbean or the South China Sea. Flowering bushes and tree ferns droop over the embankments along narrow mountain roads, and groves of bamboo spring from the hollows. Farther north—or at higher altitudes—oak, walnut, and maple trees grow, with large rhododendrons plentiful above nine thousand feet. Birds are still in profusion, although Sikkimese say that their numbers are rapidly dwindling under the pressures of population. Sikkim once had 550 species of birds, some extremely exotic, and nearly 650 kinds of butterflies. More than four thousand species of plants have been identified in the former kingdom, including hundreds of varied types of orchids. I went to see the annual orchid show, held in a small park on a ridge above Gangtok. There seemed to be nobody there, except for the ladies selling tickets at the door and a young woman whose job it was to walk around the exhibits misting the waxy plants, so I wandered alone through skillfully re-created natural gardens with pools and trees festooned with only a sample of Sikkim's orchid varieties and a wild bird or two. The birds may have come uninvited; it was hard to tell.

The curse of reading too much history followed me around Gangtok, even to the flower show, which was held on a small exhibition ground called Whitehall, about midway between the palace and the old British Residency, seat of the Indian governor—two camps that fought for the soul of Sikkim. In between, geographically as well as psychologically, lived the dewan, the Indian who played the role of prime minister during the limbo period between the withdrawal of the British and the Indian annexation of Sikkim. This was the period of the scholar–civil servant—like John Lall, who took office in 1949—when dewans lived in a royal bungalow a stone's throw from the orchid festival. Appointed by India but serving the chogyal, dewans had a disturbing tendency to side with the palace, doing so on enough occasions to make New Delhi rue the system. Worst of all, Indian officials noted in their reports, their dewans had taken to dressing in Sikkimese costume, which for men was an ankle-length Tibetan-style robe.

There were more than just trace elements of cultural and racial prejudice in India's relations with the Sikkimese and other Tibeto-Burman people. B. S. Das, who while dismantling Sikkimese independence in 1973–74 bore the title of chief executive of Sikkim, cited his earlier experiences in Bhutan as giving him the psychological wherewithal to deal with the Sikkimese as they tried to cling to their nationality. "Luckily, Bhutan had taught me enough patience to put up with the Mongoloid monologues without much damage," he wrote. Sikkimese and Bhutanese students have told me how when they go to Indian universities—particularly Delhi University—they have to get used to being called Chinkies, a pejorative for those with East Asian or Southeast Asian features. Himalayan Buddhists and many of the ethnically similar people of India's own northeast—Hindus, Christians, and Buddhists alike—find their tolerance and openness is often mistaken for licentiousness in India's pathologically puritan society of arranged marriages and the near-absence of dating or casual sex—though not of sexual assault, which is the scourge of northern Indian campuses. Indian friends of Sikkim who try to understand these cultural differences often come away sympathetic to the mountain people and their ways.

At Rumtek monastery, I asked an Indian monk in residence what he thought of Sikkim and its tortured relations with India. The monk had come to Rumtek from Bihar, where, he said, despite his religion he would always be viewed as a Hindu outcaste because his ancestors were lowborn. He was what Indians call an Ambedkar Buddhist, a follower of the lowborn but highly educated legal scholar Bhimrao Ambedkar, who presided over the writing of the Indian constitution but who despaired of erasing the inequalities of caste in Hindu India and converted to Buddhism before his death. As the monk and I sat on a stone wall and talked, a procession of elderly Sikkimese women circumambulated the temple compound and its spacious, gleaming buildings in bright red and gold. The monk said he appreciated Sikkimese simplicity and lack of deviousness. He feared the intrusion of Indian-style politics, which he called "the playground of rogues and crooks and thieves." He thought the Sikkimese may have been a little too relaxed, too transparent, too naïve to see intrigue until it was too late. They were, he said, never a match for either the quick-witted Indians or the clever Chinese. He suspected Sikkimese were a little on the ethereal side, unwilling to get involved adequately in the world around them and too willing to accept feudalism, whether in monastic life or in government.

He saw the state's present Nepali-led administration playing on this, and dismissed Indian claims of having liberated and reformed Sikkim, making it democratic after centuries of monarchy and domination by a Tibetan Buddhist minority. "This so-called reform was done at the point of a stick, and by paramilitaries," the monk said, eyeing me with a sidelong glance, as if I seemed to be arguing New Delhi's case by suggesting positive motives for the annexation. Then he looked away and ruminated. "The Sikkimese may be wacky in many ways," he said, "but they have one overwhelming saving grace, and that is Buddhism."

Chapter 8

BUDDHIST NEPAL

LAKPA NURU SHERPA was happy to be back in his two-room house in Chaurikarka, a hamlet deep in a sheltered valley a couple of thousand feet below the village of Lukla, a starting point for treks into the Mount Everest region of Nepal. The Himalayan kingdom of Nepal, nearly the size of Florida, must support a population of almost twenty million people scattered over difficult topography; life is hard for most. Lakpa Nuru, a mountain guide like many of his fellow Sherpas, was lucky. Fit and healthy in middle age, when many other Nepali men are dead or spent beyond their years, he was able to retire from the trail and come home to tend a small plot of land. He sent his children to school. And then, with what money was left from his years of trekking and climbing, he went off to India, several hundred miles away, to buy books.

The Sherpas are Buddhists, descendants of migrants from eastern Tibet who settled centuries ago in the Solu-Khumbu region of northeastern Nepal, the region best known to foreign trekkers. Before he died, Lakpa Nuru said, he wanted to own the most precious thing he could think of: a set of Lord Buddha's teachings, produced in all their authenticity by Tibetan monks in the northern Indian hill town of Dharamsala, the headquarters of the Dalai Lama's government in exile. Like all traditional Tibetan Buddhist books, these volumes are assemblages of narrow loose-leaf pages inserted between boards, wrapped in colorful cloth and secured by a bright ribbon. The script, read horizontally, is in a classical Tibetan language unknown to Lakpa Nuru. He spent his life savings knowingly on a set of books he will never read. That didn't matter. "Maybe my children and grandchildren will read them one day, because they are more educated," he said, as he asked to be photographed with his treasured library. When I told the story later to His Holiness Ngawang Tenzing Zangbo, abbot of Tengboche monastery, in the shadow of Mount Everest, he was not surprised. "Every Sherpa home is a cultural center," he said. "How much so depends on each family's means."

"The government may call us a Hindu kingdom and His Majesty may be an avatar of Vishnu," a businessman once told me in Kathmandu, "but if you scratch the surface of Nepal almost anywhere, you'll see how Buddhist we really are." Buddhism came to Nepal early, as might be expected, given the religion's origins in nearby northern India, and was soon adopted by the people called Newars, who are as close to an indigenous population in the Kathmandu Valley as anyone will probably ever find in the darkness of barely explored Nepali history and legend. The Newars were not alone in their faith. All over Nepal there were other Buddhist minorities, particularly along the Tibetan border. All or most of Nepal apparently fell under Tibetan dominance in the seventh and eighth centuries, but with or without conquest, Tibetans and Newaris cross-fertilized each other's highly developed Buddhist cultures for hundreds of years.

Much of this history can be politically inconvenient not only in Nepal, where most of the kings and all the hereditary Rana prime ministers of the nineteenth and twentieth centuries were Hindus, but also in India, where upper-caste Hindus have dominated politics since independence and Buddhism is more coopted as part of history than honored as a living religion. Not a few Indians argue that Buddhism is no more than an offshoot of Hinduism; Hindu priests have control over some of Buddhism's holiest places, including the temple at Bodhgaya, where Buddha reached enlightenment.

Back in Chaurikarka, Lakpa Nuru had invited me to visit his *lheng,* or prayer room—in effect, half his house—where he had constructed a traditional bookcase of deep cubbyholes beside the family altar to house his new library. He was wearing a trekker's abandoned T-shirt that read "Enjoy Victoria B.C." and a woolen stocking cap that said "Aspire" as he sat down behind a rough reading desk to unwrap a sacred volume. His altar was a wondrous thing, covered in part with aluminum foil and festooned with paper chains, gauzy white *khata* scarves, a peacock feather, more than a dozen Buddha images, statues of the much-traveled Guru Rinpoche and the goddess Tara, incense burners, butter lamps, and offering bowls. A photograph of the Dalai Lama shared a large picture frame (its glass cracked) with various postcards of people and places important to his faith. Though his small house, built of stone and wood, was roughly finished elsewhere, the prayer room had religious paintings on two walls; these were inherited from his father and grandfather, who had lived in the house before him and employed an itinerant artist to do the work. The room next door, where his family lived, ate, and slept, was a much more spartan place, except for a collection of Chinese ceramic rice bowls and copper plates displayed (along with two Chinese thermos flasks and two glass tumblers) on shelves along one wall. The family cooked on a stove made of stone and fueled by a wood fire. There was no running water.

Chaurikarka is a small hamlet with a few dozen houses, almost all built of stone, their roofs of loose wooden shingles held down by more rocks. In simple villages like this, Himalayan Buddhism is lived in its most down-to-earth form around countless family altars by people who speak Tibetan dialects, far away from the great lamas of their faith, who disdain their rustic ignorance and superstition. There are compensations, though, in a setting that is both physically magnificent and spiritually alive. In the center of Chaurikarka, a solid chorten sat astride the path leading away in the general direction of Khumbila, the Khumbu Sherpas' sacred mountain, whose distant presence bestowed blessings on those within its view.

This path toward the distant holy landmark is also Chaurikarka's main street, a porters' highway from the last market town—several days' walk back down the trail—into vast alpine regions without roads or airstrips. In a patch of open space near the chorten and a cubbyhole general store with very little for sale, about a dozen porters, Tamang people from farther west, plodded into town and paused to rest along a stone wall just high enough to serve as a shelf for the huge woven backpack baskets of consumer goods they were hauling to the storeless interior. The porters backed wearily toward the stone ledge and eased the weight of their burdens onto it without having to unstrap from their shoulders the cargo of blankets, small jute rugs, at least one bolt of cloth, tins of oil, boxes of crackers, sacks of rice, instant noodles, and a few plastic utensils and toys.

The loads, most of them extremely heavy, were borne by young men, some still in their teens, and by one or two white-haired porters in faded, shredded clothes, too old to be doing this job but too poor to stop. Tamangs from north-central Nepal, who are also Buddhists, are a cut below Sherpas in the world of mountain people. Sherpas are the guides and mountaineers, talents they have developed to an art in recent decades of climbing Mount Everest—called Chomolungma by the Sherpas and Sagarmatha by other Nepalis—and the Tamangs are the heavy lifters.

Later, on another trail leading to Namche Bazaar from Lukla, a Tamang porter passed by carrying a thick plate-glass window four or five feet square roped to his back in a wooden frame; he had to turn sideways to let others on the route go by. His face was a portrait of strain as he shouldered this piece of air freight, yet he was barely out of Lukla, with its crazy little grass-and-gravel ski-slope airstrip, and had at least another day to march, most of it uphill. Porters have delivered all kinds of cargo to Namche, including a whole dental clinic, disassembled. They also serve in emergencies as human ambulances, rushing trekkers stricken with altitude sickness to lower levels or ferrying their own lame or elderly up steep and rocky tracks.

The porters pausing in Chaurikarka had thin, sinewy legs from years of walking. Some didn't own shoes, but maneuvered along the stony trail in rubber sandals or the remains of flimsy Chinese sneakers. They spoke little as they paused to stretch and relieve the weight they bore, except to exchange a few pleasantries with Sherpa women bent over their short hoes planting potatoes in a small walled field beside the trail. Each porter carried a walking stick with a T-shaped top, which could be used (when there wasn't a handy wall) to rest the large basket long enough for a breather. They were dressed in tatters, the shoulder seams of their thin cotton shirts lacerated by the straps of their baskets despite the thicker sleeveless vests most of them wore to protect their skin. These men are the human trucks and freight cars of Nepal. They are not the porters who work for trekkers and have the down vests, baseball caps, satin team jackets, and English, Italian, German, French, or Japanese phrases to show for it. These are the long-distance haulers, passing through a landscape hardly changed since ancient times—instant noodles notwithstanding. Chaurikarka is like that: no bicycles or other wheeled vehicles make movement easier (the mountainsides are too steep for bikes or carts), no electricity lights the houses, no cooking gas or kerosene eases the burden of gathering firewood.

On the climb out of the hamlet toward Lukla on the ridge above, the hiker is struck by the deathly silence of the forest. It is forbidden to cut most trees in Nepal—a desperate measure, patchily enforced, intended to hold back rampant deforestation—so people unwilling or afraid to break the law scavenge for anything else that will burn. The wooded slope I climbed exuded a strange unreality: there were no leaves or twigs on the ground, no small animals or birds to be seen or heard. The trees stood alone, as if constructed for a natural history museum diorama; a stuffed squirrel would not have been out of place. The contrast to the teeming woodlands of Bhutan or Sikkim could not have been more stark. Nepal is one of the world's most densely populated countries, and even here, in the shadow of holy mountains, life illustrates the statistics. A lack of environmental consciousness has no religious connection when people need fuel to cook their meals or warm their houses. It would have been lunatic to run around Chaurikarka pressing people to explain how Buddhists, protectors of nature, could allow this vacuuming of the woodlands to take place.

Not too long ago, Lakpa Nuru's devotion to Buddhism, and moreover his hope that his offspring would follow his example, might have seemed pitiable, given the headlong rush of young Nepalis, including Sherpas, into urbanization and a taste for the material goods foreigners tote casually into Himalayan villages for all to admire. Before the Chinese suppression of a Tibetan uprising closed the Nepali-Tibetan border in 1959, Sherpas had been the Solu-Khumbu region's commodity traders, bringing salt and wool from Tibet to barter for manufactured goods from Kathmandu and India. Nowadays they run teahouses, trail lodges, trekking and mountaineering services, and shops where trekkers' castoffs may be sold along with a variety of unexpected imported goods shopkeepers have been quick to realize there is profit in stocking: toilet paper, track suits, canned beer, scented soap, and trail mix. Rustic cafés in Lukla serve French toast and muesli.

Some Sherpas who don't succeed turn to job-hunting in Kathmandu (where richer Sherpas are investing in hotels) and run into competition with other Nepali Buddhists from the hills also searching for an income. Over the course of not very many years, Kathmandu has turned from a dozy, slightly ethereal town left over from a distant century into a warren of exhaust-choked, garbage-strewn streets and byways where thousands of shops tumble over one another, pouring out into the patchily paved lanes the cheap clothes, sweaters, and jewelry (almost none of it Nepali) bought by bargain-hunting backpackers, the descendants of the hippies who once made this town the narcotics nirvana of the Eastern world. More than a million residents scramble for space in hives and warrens above stinking gutter-sewers which foster the spread of epidemic diseases; the warnings were out for cholera and encephalitis on my last visit. Low-budget tourists, charmed by small lodges where a few dollars will still buy room and board, succumb with increasing frequency to gut-wrenching maladies. Japanese tourists and some international aid workers ride or pedal around wearing masks to filter the particle-heavy air. Oddly, a lot of us still love the place, though affection is tested a little more each year.

The mountain people are a particularly sad sight as they hang around the capital looking for work or for a foreign woman with a hankering to try some exotic Eastern sex. On a winter evening over dinner in a guesthouse in the capital, the French Tibetologist Françoise Pommaret pointed out several of her compatriots who had stayed behind to marry porters or trail guides, only to discover they didn't quite belong in Nepal. They drift into budget restaurants to drink a good deal and find European company. On their laps they hold the tiny children who have given them a stake in trying to make life work here despite disappointments. At night, during one of the frequent power cuts, they stumble out into the potholed streets or the few treacherous patchwork sidewalks to bump into knots of young men lurking around some of the better-known nightspots—usually small restaurants of indifferent upkeep but reasonably safe and tasty food. All of this teeming world, it should be noted, exists outside the cocoons of the major hotels that shelter the higher-priced crowd. It is possible to spend days in Kathmandu and never have to walk its noisome streets; the sellers of wares and services will come to your gate, and air-conditioned vans do the rest.

The prosperous Sherpas—more than other Buddhists from the mountainous north who still struggle for a livelihood—are one of the engines pushing a Buddhist revival in Nepal, though Buddhism itself took root here long before the Sherpas were a significant presence. The Kathmandu Valley's creation myth (or at least the most popular one) tells of a turquoise sea where the capital now stands. Out of the water grew a magnificent phosphorescent lotus recognized as a manifestation of Swayambhu, yet another form of Buddha. The Boddhisattva Manjushri, wishing to reach the flower, which radiated an entrancing light, grabbed his sword and sliced through the valley wall to drain the lake. When the water had receded, he built a stupa on the hill where Swayambhunath's cluster of shrines now stands, capped by a golden spire with an eye on all four sides of its base to watch over the valley. No one knows exactly how old the first buildings at Swayambhunath are, but an ethnic Gurung Buddhist happily and ecumenically named Krishna Lama assured me as we walked around the main stupa that it had been there at least three thousand years.

Though the borders of Nepal encompass the birthplace of the historical Buddha, this is a nation where Buddhism and Hinduism—much of the worship of Shiva and his omnipresent phallus, the *shivalinga*—coexist to an often confusing degree. Bodhnath seems to nurture a rigorously Buddhist milieu, yet Hindus come to worship and leave offerings there as well as at Swayambhunath, where it is not uncommon to find a nearly naked sadhu daubed in vermilion sitting cross-legged in front of a side altar. In the Durbar squares of Kathmandu, Patan, and Bhaktapur, Buddhist and Hindu shrines and iconography mingle in endlessly fascinating ways and places.

In a Kathmandu neighborhood where I once stayed for a month, every morning began with Buddhists igniting fires in bowls of incense on their rooftops and the Hindus pausing at a small crossroads shrine to pray, light a candle, or leave an offering. Then Buddhists and Hindus (and their Muslim neighbors) merged and mingled on the dusty lanes on the way to work, school, or the daily shopping. The scholar David Snellgrove, whose *Indo-Tibetan Buddhism* provides the most exhaustive and lucid early history of this region, thinks that Nepal's Buddhist-Hindu symbiosis provides the last living example of what religious life in northern India must have been like before aggressive Hindu Brahminism and the Muslim conquests changed the landscape forever. "One realizes," he wrote, "how much has been lost in India, and how fortunate we are to have a small surviving replica in Nepal."

With the arrival of many Tibetan exiles in the 1950s, especially after 1959, Buddhism got a critical if unexpected boost in the valley, where new religious centers sprang up, existing communities expanded, and monasteries proliferated. Tibetans, successful in a variety of businesses, most of all carpet-weaving, give generously to monks and shrines. An articulate and cosmopolitan Tibetan middle class, larger than that of any other Himalayan Buddhist community, has been successful at explaining and promoting Tibetan Buddhism internationally. So apparent was the resurgence by the 1980s that some influential Nepali Hindus sought to curb the growth of Buddhism. In the royal government of King Birendra Bir Bikram Shah Dev, the call resonated among those who saw the high profile of Tibetan Buddhists in Nepal as a potential irritant to China. Many Tibetans vow openly to see their homeland liberated from Chinese rule, a thorn if not the hoped-for dagger in Beijing's side. Consequently, in deference to China, the Dalai Lama has never been able to make an official visit to Nepal, except for Lumbini, and public celebrations of his birthday are banned or severely restricted. For Nepal, good relations with the Chinese are a necessary balance against pressures from India, which is forever seeking a dominant role in Nepali affairs.

Not long ago, Tibetan refugees in Nepal worried that their welcome was wearing thin. Searching for information on events in Lhasa, where an anti-Chinese movement is always rumbling beneath the surface, exploding now and then in demonstrations, I met new émigrés from Tibet nearly surreptitiously in the late 1980s, so great was the concern of host Tibetans who had established themselves in Nepal and did not want their livelihoods jeopardized. But in 1990, a Nepali democracy movement forced a change in the country's constitution to reduce the power of the monarchy. New elections brought secular parties into office, and threats to Buddhism seemed to dissipate, just as they did when Nepal first tried democracy in the 1950s.

The Buddhist renaissance has probably had the least effect on the Newars, despite long years of good relations with the Tibetans, says Purna Harsha Bajracharya, a Newar from a family of Buddhist scholars. Bajracharya was instrumental in beginning the Nepali Archaeology Department's first excavations of Lord Buddha's birthplace in Lumbini in the 1960s. His name, *vajra-acarya* in its Sanskrit form, literally means a Tantric master. I went to see him at his small home above a busy bazaar near the center of Kathmandu. The high-pitched product advertising of the street vendors and loud arguments of barter combined with bicycle bells and the horns of motorized rickshaws were so pervasive that Purna Harsha's soft voice was hard to hear when I played back my tapes of our first talk that evening.

But this cacophony was probably appropriate, for the Newars have always been Nepal's most committed urbanites, thriving at the heart of commerce. For more than a thousand years, they dominated trade routes between India and China from their family bases in the Kathmandu Valley and their trading houses and mercantile associations in Lhasa. Wool, silk, tea, rice, precious corals, works of art, silver, and finally manufactured goods moved along Himalayan trails on pack animals. Along the same routes, Tibetan Buddhists came south to visit the great shrines of Nepal. Newar lamas, including Purna Harsha's forebears, went to Lhasa to exchange learned opinions. The Newar trade monopoly was not broken until early in the twentieth century when the British encouraged the opening of new routes to Tibet from the northeastern Indian hill town of Kalimpong through Sikkim.

Purna Harsha's house backed onto a much quieter zone built around a Newari Buddhist *vihara,* a small temple-monastery marking the home of an important family. This vihara was in a state of decline, its owner having died some years ago "without issue," in Purna Harsha's words. He has informally taken over responsibility for the small enclosed square with delicately carved wooden doors and lintels that enclosed the shrine to a god now gone. A tailor has moved in on one side; other families fill the rest of the space, using the pump that Purna Harsha's family installed over a centuries-old well that still produces good water. In front of the shrine stands a *chaitya,* the Newar equivalent of a chorten or stupa. Purna Harsha, a man of great dignity and generosity, says that his duties amount to little more than "putting a few flowers there from time to time." In truth, he seems to take pains to salvage this corner of history, abused as it is by newcomers without an appreciation of its value.

Many other Newar compounds have suffered amid the general decay of old Kathmandu, where buildings collapse and mounds of fly-covered garbage fill once-sacred pools and pile up at many an intersection, repelling tourists. Newars, with their considerable intellectual and design skills, were responsible for the architecturally remarkable cores of the valley's three magnificent medieval cities—Bhaktapur, Patan, and Kathmandu—and were sought after across the Himalayas and in Tibet as craftsmen for both Buddhist and Hindu buildings.

Newars believe that one of their own, the young Princess Bhrikuti, carried a civilized form of Buddhism with her to Tibet when she became one of two wives of the Tibetan king-emperor Songsten Gampo in the seventh century. Indeed, Newars say that she took with her to Lhasa a statue of the Lord Buddha so valuable and exceptional in its execution that the famous Jokhang temple was built (by Newar craftsmen) to house it. Purna Harsha says that Newari women have always taken important parts in religious ceremonies and family affairs. They were traditionally free to move around the town and sometimes took lessons from monks—at least until the Rana period, when they became the targets of licentious officials whose militant Hindu upbringing conveyed little understanding of the Buddhist social order. A kind of self-imposed purdah set in, and is only now being broken down.

That the Newars' Tibeto-Burman language became Sanskritized, and that the Newars were apparently forced beginning in the fourteenth century under the Malla dynasty to adopt a Hindu caste system completely alien to Buddhist teaching, did not diminish their firm commitment to Buddhism, even after the Gorkhas, Hindus of Indian origin from the Terai, took over the Nepali monarchy in the eighteenth century. Purna Harsha Bajracharya argues that the caste system was forced on Newars out of necessity by the Malla kings, some of them Buddhists or sympathetic to Buddhism, who feared Newari solidarity. "When the rulers found everyone united among us, they were angry. The caste system became useful to divide us." It was enforced more rigorously after the end of Malla rule by Gorkha rulers, who also imposed caste on the Tibetan-speaking people of the north and assigned most of them a low status.

Purna Harsha says again and again that the Newars never had a quarrel with Hinduism, which some of them adopted. The problems were political. He adds that in any case the term "Hindu" is too broad to apply to most Nepalis, who concentrate their devotion on one god in the Hindu pantheon, Shiva, and should rightly be called Shivaites. "In the histories of Nepal you won't even find the word 'Hinduism,'" he said. "Buddhism and Shivaism grew side by side here. Both hold each other in great respect. We speak of the *Shiva-dharma* and the *Buddha-dharma*."

Purna Harsha Bajracharya, now retired, talked about how the persecution of Newar Buddhists during the century dominated by the Rana dynasty of hereditary prime ministers had inevitably led to a lack of self-assertion and a paucity of research into their own history and culture. He tells of scholars unable to publish or forced into exile because they did. Newar Buddhist culture can never really be obscured, however, because of the extraordinary public architecture and religious institutions it contributed to Nepali life. The child goddess Kumari, whose temple in Kathmandu's Durbar Square draws sightseers hoping to catch a glimpse of the living deity, is a Newari ingredient in the Nepali cultural mix. The prepubescent Kumari, to whom by legend the valley belongs and to whom, therefore, everyone, including the king, must pay tribute once a year, is one of several such goddesses; Newar temples once had many more.

News of the vigor of Buddhism in Nepal is fast spreading beyond the Himalayas. Because Nepal, once closed to outsiders, has in recent decades become one of South Asia's most open societies, easily accessible by air from both Western nations and East Asia, Kathmandu is attracting more international scholars and new believers from several continents. Go to prayers at almost any gompa around Kathmandu and there is likely to be, in addition to a few American or European voices, a handful of respectful Japanese, Thai, Malaysian, or Singaporean worshippers. The Westerners are no longer the stock characters who once drifted in from the fringes of the drug-taking, hippie Freak Street culture that was prepared to get high on just about anything the Nepalis could offer in the 1960s and '70s, including the erotic Tantric Buddhist art whose proliferation a nineteenth-century Englishman had labeled a "filthy custom." That carefree scene bottomed out sometime in the 1980s after the overland route from Europe was closed by war in Afghanistan and by a Nepali decision to raise the costs of travel in Nepal and to reorient tourism toward more affluent visitors and serious trekkers. The casual age has not entirely passed, of course. In a Kathmandu garden café I heard two backpacking Americans discuss what to do with their day. "Let's go to Swayambhunath," one said. "A lot of really cool things go on there."

At the well-heeled Orgyen Tolku Gompa at Bodhnath, Chokyi Nyima Rinpoche said he had noticed a continuing evolution of tourism in recent years. "Before, tourists came to look at the mountains. Then some started coming to see the monasteries. They see Kathmandu is a special place. Very holy. Tourists changed. Some began wanting to hear some teaching, to study with us," he said. With new interest obviously came money. The rinpoche's private quarters include a private chapel of evident affluence, decorated in the brilliant colors traditionally favored by Tibetans. The high ceiling was painted a bright aquamarine, with rafters lacquered red. Stylized paintings of religious motifs covered the walls, along which six brass and crystal sconces had been installed for light. From the rafters hung two large crystal chandeliers. At the altar, dominated by a larger-than-life image of Buddha, there was a collection of gold statues and fine ceramic temple guardian lions. The floor was carpeted in Tibetan rugs. The one unharmonious note was the hideous three-tiered plastic waterfall with a trick faucet and plastic flowers installed on a corner table. The faucet seemed to be suspended miraculously in midair, producing a stream of water from no visible source. (The water was being pumped up to the shiny golden tap from the bottom collection dish, through an unseen clear tube obscured by the stream flowing back down around it.) Incongruous kitsch though it was, it certainly caught the attention of disciples. Two boys sat riveted in front of it.

One of the most powerful and beloved of contemporary Tibetan Buddhist lamas, the late Dilgo Khyentse Rinpoche, established his base in Kathmandu, where he and his followers built the impressive Shechen temple and monastery. His Holiness, who had at one time instructed and inspired the Dalai Lama and served as a personal guru to members of Bhutan's royal family, was the internationally recognized ranking lama of the Nyingmapa school and one of the last—if not *the* last—of the great Tibetan-born teacher-saints and *tertons,* discoverers or revealers of holy treasures. Twenty-two years of his life were spent in meditation, some of them in isolated caves in the manner of the great lamas of the past. He established and consecrated temples in Bhutan, India, and the West as well as in Nepal and set up a school of classical studies at Bhutan's Simtokha Dzong. (His daughter Chhimi Wangmo is assistant director of Bhutan's National Museum.) Though rooted in the Nyingmapa school, the rinpoche devoted much of his later life—he fled Tibet for Bhutan in 1959—to preaching a nonsectarian Buddhism, drawing on the holy writings and philosophies of all schools.

I had often heard in Bhutan about the blurring of sectarian divisions. I remember in particular what the abbot of Tashigang Dzong told me as we stood by a huge, complicated, multifaceted sculpture in one of his temples that looked at first sight like a confusing jumble of images piled on a giant plant. "This is the holy tree," he said. "Here is the lotus grown from the lake. On the leaves the different Buddha scholars are. We have different sects. Here is the leader of Nyingma and how he achieved enlightenment. And next is another sect called Karmapa, and this is its lineage. And this is Guru, and this is the sect that was followed by Shabdrung. Up there at the top is Buddha himself. So you see no matter what denomination or what sect, the root is same, the body same, and ultimate truth is one. Root is same, ultimate goal is same. Only approach is different."

In poems, essays, and talks in Asia and the West, Dilgo Khyentse Rinpoche went beyond mere nonsectarianism. He gave the religion that recognized him as a leader in 1910, while he was still in his mother's womb, a true sense of universality. After he died in September 1991, Bhutan spent more than a year praying and preparing for his final funeral rites. Present at the *purjang* or cremation ceremony in November 1992—during which, Bhutan's weekly newspaper said, "the last mortal remains of His Holiness dissolved into the state of luminosity"—were the Bhutanese royal family, more than fifty thousand monks and tulkus, and thousands of other followers and admirers from around the world. Many more would have come if Bhutan could have handled them. The cremation took place on a meadow in Paro, in view of the Taktsang monastery, where the Guru Rinpoche was believed to have descended on a flying tiger in the eighth century bearing the Nyingma Tantric teachings. The cremation pyre of Dilgo Khyentse Rinpoche was a work of Bhutanese artisanship at its best: a carved, roofed pavilion bedecked in silk, with altars around the clay coffin overflowing with the finest offerings of food and religious objects. Tibetan Buddhism may never again see this exalted ceremony performed with such purity of ritual and in such an unspoiled cultural and natural environment. While Himalayan Buddhists await the rinpoche's reincarnation, his legacy lives on in Kathmandu in the shadow of Bodhnath.

"Kathmandu is developing into an important center for Buddhist study," another Tibetan lama, Khenpo Rigzin, said during one of our conversations at the Nyingma Institute of Nepal, a new monastic school just outside Kathmandu memorable for its quiet, superserious atmosphere. The institute has a Tibetan-American patron, Tarthang Tulku, a publisher of Buddhist texts in Berkeley, California, Khenpo Rigzin said. Novice monks—still all boys, no girls—from across the Himalayan region and India come here to take a nine-year course that is heavy on Buddhist philosophy. So far, no Westerners had enrolled as students, Khenpo Rigzin said, though they are admitted for research. He added politely, even sweetly, that Western students might pose a problem, given the very different intellectual and spiritual environment that produced them. In his experience, he said, he found it took them a little longer to grasp things. A concept he could teach a Bhutanese, Sikkimese, or Sherpa in a week would take two or three weeks to penetrate the mind of an American, he thought.

Khenpo Rigzin has turned down many offers to teach in the West, because he believes the Himalayan milieu is important to him. "I know that the standard of life is very good in America. But we need something different. According to our philosophy, we must realize the dharma. The way of living must be there. It is good for monks to stay in a group, to practice prayer together. Here I feel sure, secure. It's easier to live as lama in Nepal."

If anything, Nepal is already becoming spoiled by success, Khenpo Rigzin said, reflecting the burgeoning sense among some leading Buddhist lamas that too much luxury is creeping into monastic life. In some cases, that is already an understatement. A Kathmandu businessman told me how when he tried to sell a Mercedes-Benz, he got no takers in the royal family or among wealthy houses, but found a Tibetan rinpoche ready and willing to pay cash for the car. One day, leaving a Kathmandu restaurant after lunch, I saw two monks head toward a new Hyundai parked out front. The older one got into the back; the younger one (wearing a cowboy hat) folded his robes, slid into the driver's seat, and sped away. The ideal life of a monk, Khenpo Rigzin said, is to follow the Lord Buddha's own advice to avoid cities, corrupting influences, distraction. He said that only the greatest of lamas would be able to concentrate in the busy atmosphere of some gompas these days.

His Holiness Ngawang Tenzing Zangbo, the Sherpas' Tengboche abbot and overseer of all Buddhist gompas in Nepal when I met him, said pithily that these days too many monks "prefer electricity to butter lamps." He expanded on this to say that there was nothing inherently bad about new inventions and modern life in general. The problem came when these things became preoccupations. "Good clothing, for instance," he said. "In other times, lamas never wanted the best garments. They could go barefoot and possess nothing. Now they are asking for better robes. At Tengboche, I am trying my level best to keep things as traditional as possible. I want to improve life a little bit, make it more comfortable, but stay always within tradition. I believe that when you learn the harder way, when you experience hardship, this means more and is closer to our teaching."

He said that he is not surprised to see Westerners flocking to Tibetan monasteries in Nepal. "In the West, there are too many distractions," he said. "People long to come to these mountains. Here you can learn things through your heart." He noted that Kathmandu also drew many Himalayan people because of its proximity to sacred places, but was confident that many lamas among them would return to remote areas and practice a wholesome religion, free of urban temptations. He hopes that the spiritual boom will result in higher levels of religious life all around the region and not the further degradation of monastic life through materialism. He sounded as if it might be touch-and-go in some places.

Almost all Buddhists in the Himalayas, not just lamas, are coming into frequent contact with wealthier Buddhists, both Mahayana and Theravada, from Southeast Asia, Hong Kong, and farther east. A glimpse of their obvious affluence has a powerful effect. Bhikku Nirmala Nanda, one of a small number of impoverished Theravada monks in Nepal and the abbot of a temple in Lumbini, is grateful for the gifts brought by Thai pilgrims, but alarmed at their materialism. "They come with so many baggages full of things," he told me as we shared tea, he in his chair of honor near the altar and I on the steps nearby that led to his mango grove in the sunny courtyard. "I have to tell them, 'If you carry so much heavy baggage, it will be very difficult to get to Nirvana. Reaching enlighten-ment will take a longer time than if you are free of this weight.' " I told him the biblical story in which Jesus declared that it would be easier for a camel to pass through the eye of a needle than for the rich man to enter heaven. He said he hadn't heard that one, and chuckled at the symmetry.

IN DISCUSSING theology, Khenpo Rigzin and Ngawang Tenzing Zangpo both dared to venture the opinion that because of the political nature of the Tibetan exile movement, the Dalai Lama's base in the northern Indian mountain town of Dharamsala, harder to get to than Kathmandu, is no longer a universally accepted center of the Tibetan Buddhist universe in scholarly and spiritual terms. The Dalai Lama is a Gelugpa reincarnate, and much of the activity in Kathmandu is associated with other Buddhist orders, but that is not the issue. "His Holiness has one foot in the dharma and one in politics," Khenpo Rigzin said. "He can't move on either side. We Tibetans have to be militant, but I don't believe my religion should bring me into politics. The political activity has weakened the Dalai Lama as a religious teacher."

Himalayan Buddhist lamas and abbots are now free to return to Tibet, where most of them were born or studied, and many are making the spiritual journey. They help restore monastic links and sometimes support the rebuilding of shattered gompas. His Holiness Dilgo Khyentse Rinpoche was among those who returned to Tibet in peace in the 1980s. He led an international campaign to restore the original Shechen monastery in Kham, in eastern Tibet, one of the six leading Nyingmapa centers. The monastery, where the rinpoche had gone as an incarnate tulku at the age of eleven, was ruined like many others in China's Cultural Revolution. Such a trip for the Dalai Lama would be all but impossible short of a significant change of heart in Beijing. And so Dharamsala grows ever more remote from the Tibetan Buddhist mainstream.

Robert Thurman, a Columbia University Buddhist scholar who was ordained as a monk in his youth, agrees that Tibetan Buddhists are making a big impact on Nepal in both economic and religious spheres, though he deplores the damage the chemical dyes of the Tibetan carpet industry, now Nepal's largest foreign-currency earner, have done to the environment of the Kathmandu Valley. Buddhists should be protectors of nature, he says. But Thurman, who has known the Dalai Lama for many years, gave a sympathetic accounting of the exile leader's predicament when we met in Bumthang, in Bhutan.

"His Holiness the Dalai Lama is the only one who has had to combine intellectual and religious leadership with responsibility for a community," he said. "He had to oversee the setting up of a curriculum for schoolchildren in exile that would give them both some preparation for the modern world and would restore their culture; give them some sense of pride in a situation where they had nothing. They literally came out of Tibet in rags, and barely survived. Many family members died in the exodus. And so that experience has made His Holiness very practical and very firm about certain things. He has constructed large monasteries. He also supported technical education and innovation. He's had to really think through a lot of these things. I don't think he's done a perfect job, and I don't think he thinks he's done a perfect job. I don't think he has been able to implement everything he's wanted to implement.

"Around him and the various ministries, one of his problems now is that a lot of the more capable Tibetans—amongst the Tibetan refugees it's considered a kind of patriotic duty to serve the government in exile—put in their years of service, then take off into business or go abroad. They can't really earn any money—or hardly a living wage if they have children they want to put into school—by working there. It's become such a meager government in exile. So there is a little bit of mediocrity there. However, there is a very good spirit, and His Holiness himself sort of keeps after them, and he manages to do a good job."

Furthermore, the Dalai Lama, winner of the 1990 Nobel Peace Prize, has periodically had to deal with pressure from younger Tibetans who want Buddhists to be more militant in efforts to regain their lost homeland from the Chinese, a course of action His Holiness described in an interview with me in Delhi as "suicidal," given the might of Beijing's army and the hostility of the Han Chinese. The battle to keep the Free Tibet campaign on a nonviolent course has consumed a lot more of the Dalai Lama's already stretched time and energy. "The Dalai Lama feels militancy is immoral from a Buddhist point of view, and he's not a militarist," Thurman said. "He worries about militancy among his followers. I think the Nobel Prize postponed more militancy, violent militancy, among the young, both outside and inside Tibet. It gave the young Tibetans the view that maybe there was a way out through a kind of Gandhian militancy, a nonviolent militancy."

While Tibetans have raised awareness of Himalayan Buddhism internationally, Sherpas have been contributing significantly to what an American anthropologist calls the mainstreaming of Buddhist culture within Nepali society. James F. Fisher, a former Peace Corps volunteer in Nepal who occasionally returns to live for spells in the region, said in his 1990 book *Sherpas: Reflections on Change in Himalayan Nepal* that religion is intensifying, not fading, among the newly rich Sherpas. Fisher recounts how in 1981 the Tengboche monastery was able to raise twenty thousand dollars in two days to open a gompa in Kathmandu, where many Sherpas were living.

Although the Tengboche abbot, Ngawang Tenzing Zangpo, doesn't always share Fisher's optimism that Sherpa culture can survive affluence,

Fisher is convinced that Sherpa men and women are proud of their community, a pride reinforced by foreign climbers and trekkers who come in contact with them in the hardworking hamlets of Solu-Khumbu. "Sherpas are so massively reinforced at every point for being Sherpas," he wrote, "that they have every reason not only to 'stay' Sherpa but even to flaunt their Sherpahood." Poorer Tamangs, impressed by Sherpa success, often try to pose as Sherpas, Fisher says. "This process of 'Sherpaization' counters the momentum of the much-vaunted Sanskritization (emulation of high Hindu caste behavior) that has absorbed the upwardly mobilizing energies of the subcontinent for centuries," he wrote.

This is an intriguing observation. If the trend persists, it would have implications throughout the Himalayas as small nations feel a need to define themselves against the wave of Hindu revivalism rising in India or the outbursts of Hindu Gorkha nationalism within their own borders. Hope Cooke seems to have sensed the need for Himalayan Buddhists (and Tibeto-Burman people) to form a closer inner Asian community. This kind of thinking added to her troubles with India. Visions of a pan-Himalayan Buddhism with political overtones are consequently held at arm's length in other places, notably Bhutan, for fear of Indian reactions. But if the sense of community were to surge upward from a more prosperous, better-educated grassroots Buddhist society, who's to tell what the results might be?

Charles Ramble, a British anthropologist who speaks and reads Tibetan and who had been studying the Tibetan people of northern and western Nepal for more than a decade when I met him in Kathmandu, interjects a cautionary note when the subject turns to the glorification of Sherpahood and other forms of Tibetanization. He thinks that in the rush to retrieve, enhance, and promote a Tibetan-Buddhist culture there is always the danger of invention. From Ladakh to Sikkim and Bhutan, he sees arcane and sometimes completely artificial rites or "traditions" being introduced in the name of cultural restoration. But he says there is little doubt that Tibetanization has a wide appeal.

SHERPAS and other northern Nepali people inhabit a region that is more Tibetan in culture than South Asian. Himalayan Buddhist legends have resonance here. This is where the fabled saint Milarepa, who was born about 1050, was supposed to have meditated on numerous occasions. Though large areas of the Tibetan border regions of Nepal are still very isolated and difficult to reach, there is a good Chinese-built road from Kathmandu to the border hamlet of Kodari, the first leg of the overland route to Lhasa. It passes through glorious green valleys with terraced fields and warm red-brick Nepali homesteads. Though the going gets tougher on the other side of the border, the easy trip to Kodari leaves a lasting impression of how close Nepal, more than any other Himalayan nation, feels to Tibet. Geographically, the exception to that observation would have to be Ladakh because of its location on the Tibetan plateau. But the state of military readiness around the edges of Ladakh creates a certain psychological barrier. In Bhutan, where there are numerous passes and some vestiges of trade, one nevertheless gets the feeling that these gates through the high Himalayas have been walled shut since 1959, and that Tibet could be somewhere else on earth.

It was while meditating in a cave near Nyanam on the Nepali-Tibetan border that Milarepa was supposed to have told the story of his life to disciples, who passed it on to posterity. The tale reveals that Milarepa, a great traveler, had more than a few Nepali acquaintances. (Not to be outdone, the Bhutanese believe he may also have meditated in their country, and Tibetans naturally have a long list of places associated with his long and pious life, long stretches of it spent in hermitages.) Milarepa's story, incidentally, is peppered with references to strong and clever women who could apparently read and write, a hint that in some circumstances the status of women may have been reasonably high in Himalayan Buddhist societies, even in ancient times, even though women were generally barred from monasteries.

Until he gave up the black arts, Milarepa claimed to be able to inflict hailstorms on his enemies—causing, for example, much disarray, destruction, and terror among those who had wronged his mother and sister in the village of his youth. In later life, he calmed down and turned to poetry that is both pithy and instructive. In one hymn, dedicated to considering the usefulness of thoughts and actions, Milarepa wrote these stanzas, in a translation refined in the 1920s by W. Y. Evans-Wentz:

> *Unless all selfishness be given up from the very heart's depths,*
> *What gain is it to offer alms?*

and:

Unless pure love and veneration be innate within one's heart,
What gain is it to build a stupa?

Until the unification of Nepal by Gorkha kings in the eighteenth century, most Tibetan borderlands were not really a part of the country. Psychologically, many pockets still are not. The kingdom of Mustang, nearly 150 rugged miles from Kathmandu in a protuberance thrusting into Tibet, was one of them until Nepal opened the territory to development and trekking. In upper Mustang, the Buddhist kingdom of Lo, with its walled capital, Lo Manthang, broke free of Tibet in the fourteenth century, reached its height about a hundred years later on the strength and income of trade with Tibet, and enjoyed an independent existence for nearly four hundred years. During that time temples and a few palaces were built in what was called Mustang Bhot—Tibetan Mustang. "Bhot," "Bhotia," "Bhutia," and other variations of the word often mean Tibetan to South Asians in the same way "Hellenistic" meant not quite Greek but within the influence of the Greek world. The word, probably a variation of "Bot," originally meant Tibet in the Tibetan language.

Although the kings of Mustang had lost all their residual powers and the formal use of titles in the 1950s, Mustang was a wild card as late as the 1960s, when Nepal was unable to do much to stop a Tibetan exile guerrilla force based there with what is widely assumed to be substantial help from the United States Central Intelligence Agency. The guerrillas, known in Nepal as Khampas because most were from the Kham region of eastern Tibet, obviously never stood much of a chance against the Chinese army in Lhasa, but they could serve as an annoyance to Beijing. Tibetan exiles in the Indian hill town of Darjeeling told me, with lingering bitterness, that American enthusiasm for their cause ended as suddenly as it had begun when President Richard M. Nixon recognized the Chinese Communist regime. Some Tibetans went on fighting until the mid-1970s, when Nepal sent soldiers to wipe out the bases of the rebellion. About the same time, the royal government of King Mahendra introduced some development to Mustang, which had lost its Tibetan trade.

A fine account of the confusion Mustang experienced as tourism arrived is found in the journal of a long trek through the roadless region by an American-educated Nepali writer, Manjushree Thapa. She was discovering Mustang herself; she later became involved full-time with conservation and sustainable development in the old kingdom, working with the Annapurna Conservation Area Project. In her small book *Mustang Bhot in Fragments,* she tells of long days on the trail with a friend, an engineer who was checking on the progress of small electricity generators, and evenings in teashops, village halls, homes, and lodges with people who were her compatriots but thought she must be a foreigner. "You're from Am'rica?" a little girl asked her, seeing her camera. She wrote of a fragile desert ecology in one place and a lush valley in another, of people eager for tourism despite the damage it could do; life seemed to offer no other economic opportunities.

She described the king's palace in Lo Manthang, with linoleum on the floors and men who drank themselves into nightly stupors while rolling dice. But she also wrote of the piety and devotion of people who had maintained their Buddhist temples and monasteries undisturbed by politics over centuries. She sat down for tea with monks eating Chinese candy brought back from Tibet, where temples are once again open to them. One of their lamas made regular trips to Tibetan gompas, they said, where he was much in demand to say prayers. In return he brought back butter for the butter lamps of impoverished Lo Manthang. It was an interesting trade-off: the wisdom and piety of an unbroken Tibetan Buddhist tradition for the biscuits, sweets, and butter of soldier-rich, monk-poor Tibet. Tibetan gompas aren't alone in looking toward Lo for a rare cultural purity, Thapa wrote. With the barriers to outsiders coming down, Mustang, like Bhutan, will draw a special breed of tourist. "Because it promises a Tibetan culture more pristine than in Chinese-occupied Tibet, Lo is the darling of discoverers, adventurers and Tibetophiles," she said. But the outside world is alien, no matter what its motive for coming to Mustang. And outside influences were already making a mark before tourism began, as more people from this hidden kingdom traveled beyond its mountain walls.

"People had gone the way of money, and whether that entailed Hinduizing or westernizing or Nepalizing mattered little," she wrote. "Their travels and exposure brought back into the restricted area fragments of the world beyond: transistor radios, smokeless stoves, electricity, walking shoes, windbreakers and new languages. And through these imports, even those who remained in Mustang all year long took leave of their impossible, traditional way of life." Is this good or bad for Mustang? Thapa wasn't sure, but she had seen in village after village how hopes for rapid development had been dashed so often when projects went awry, and she agonized: "Must development come riddled with pain and contradictions and aborted opportunities? Is that the way change comes?"

These are the questions that Bhutan, the last living kingdom, is now wrestling with.

Chapter 9

BUDDHA AND THE BHUTANESE STATE

MAKING ANY SENSE of the fears Bhutanese hold for the future of their country requires a little knowledge of where Bhutan came from. Not so easy. Right away, we spin down the rabbit-hole of fantasy. The history of Bhutan begins in mythology and will probably end someday with more questions than answers, more legends than facts. Here is a land where children's schoolbooks open not with accounts of explorers or emperors, but with tales of spirits, demons, and saints. This is a country where a founder of the faith traveled on the back of a marvelous flying tiger, temples were erected to pin down the extremities of a malevolent she-demon, and the unifier of the nation was believed to possess the power to scare away hostile armies with a show of terrifying magic. Through this history flow most of the shared legends and legendary characters of Himalayan Buddhism, but here no modern political superstructure has yet tinkered with this cosmos.

When Lord Ronaldshay, the British colonial governor of Bengal, visited Paro in 1921 and inquired in passing who had built a chorten he saw along his route, he was told, matter-of-factly, a fantastic story. He recorded it in his book *Himalayan Bhutan, Sikhim and Tibet:* "The builder, a famous lama, on coming to Paro, found the hand of death heavy upon the valley. By virtue of his miraculous powers he divined the cause. A monster of the mountains, a ghoulish frog which battened on human blood, had made its abode in the valley. The monster's mouth was detected by a hole in the ground, and was effectually stopped by the erection over it of a chorten. In later days, a rich man came along and protected the monument, whose preservation was of such vital importance to the people of Paro, by encasing it in an outer covering. And so, as the Elder naively remarked, the people of Paro were saved."

To travel in Bhutan is to suspend not only disbelief but also rationality, consistency, the comfort of an agreed chronology, and any tendency toward impatience. Historical dates become mere suggestions, along with certain definitive measurements like the distance to Ura (or anywhere else from where you are) and the height of Gankar Punsum (or most other mountains)—not to mention dates on the notorious calendar. Accounts of both ancient and contemporary events can vary wildly. Statistics gathered by worthy international agencies often seem weirdly out of sync with what one hears and sees. In one of the great understatements of recent scholarship, Leo Rose of the University of California at Berkeley wrote in *The Politics of Bhutan* that the country posed "a novel methodological problem." Working in Bhutan in the 1970s, Professor Rose found the country "data-free," lacking even rudimentary research facilities and all but devoid of the intense South Asian–style political gossip that often helps fill in the blanks of recent history. By the 1990s, he probably would notice a marked increase in gossip, a good deal of it political because it feeds sumptuously on the activities of the half-dozen or so extended families who have come to dominate public life and the economy.

It is easy enough to trace the bare outlines of Bhutanese history as understood by the Bhutanese. Until perhaps the sixth or seventh century there is darkness—or, as the British political officer John Claude White wrote at the turn of the twentieth century, "the early history of this remarkable country is enveloped in great obscurity." Then Buddhism arrives, and for nearly a thousand years, the legends of saints and philosophers, of miracles and manifestations, of theologians and marvelous discoveries of holy texts, dominate the story of Bhutan. Buddhism is written into the national anthem:

> *As the doctrine of the Lord Buddha flourishes,*
> *May the sun of peace and happiness shine on the people.*

Three names dominate Bhutan's formative early years: the ubiquitous Guru Rinpoche; Pema Lingpa, a native saint; and Ngawang Namgyal, the seventeenth-century unifier of Bhutan known to most Bhutanese as the Shabdrung. Their images in statuary, portraits, and murals dominate many a temple and shrine at the expense of more familiar images of Buddha—with whom in the Bhutanese mind they are one.

Bhutan has a holistic history in which religious legend and political reality are tightly interwoven, and what historical records survive were written in the dzongs and safeguarded mostly by monks. Furthermore, because at least some of the oft-told stories serve to buttress the reputations of cherished heroes, the monarchy, or the contemporary monastic hierarchy, there has been little to gain from revisionism or intensive historical research. The best foreign historians know when to back away from pointless controversy. Michael Aris, the Oxford University scholar who probably knows more than any other Westerner about the early years of Bhutan's recorded history, having discovered some of its documentation himself in unexplored archives, considered the available evidence about the Guru Rinpoche, with whom history begins in a serious way in Bhutan, and came up short on most of the Guru's numerous manifestations. "For this reason it has been thought best to leave him mostly in the heaven from whence he came," Aris wrote in *Bhutan: The Early History of a Himalayan Kingdom*.

The Guru Rinpoche, whose image in paintings and statues can be either benign or terrifying depending on what he was up to at the moment being portrayed, is credited with bringing the Nyingmapa school of Tibetan Buddhism to Bhutan in the eighth century, although other Buddhists from Tibet had taken up residence at least a hundred years earlier. The country's name, Druk Yul, and its state religion, the Drukpa order of Tantric Buddhism, a branch of the Kagyupa school, took root in the seventeenth century when the Shabdrung Ngawang Namgyal, packing his fear-inspiring magic powers, fled to Bhutan from the Ralung monastery in eastern Tibet under pressure from competing Gelugpa monks.

Druk means thunder in Tibetan, and thunder was widely imagined to be the voice of a dragon. The Drukpa order apparently got its name because at the moment of the consecration of one of its earliest monasteries in Tibet, the monks heard auspicious rumbling in the heavens. (Or by another account, the founder of the new monastery, at Namgyi Phu, saw nine dragons flying in the sky.) Thus by extension Druk Yul, the Land of the Drukpas, is also the Land of the Dragon or, more poetically, the Land, or Kingdom, of the Thunder Dragon. Bhutan's religious minorities—read "Hindus"—refer loosely to all Bhutanese Buddhists as Drukpas, though they are not. Several schools of Buddhism flourish in Bhutan, with the Nyingmapa perhaps the most popular, spread over a number of ethnic and linguistic groups. There is much overlapping of ritual and devotion among followers of various schools, even within the extended royal family.

Bhutan—earlier rendered Bootan, Boutan or sometimes Bhotana—is another extension of that Tibetan word *bot,* which became Indianized to refer variously to highlanders or anything Tibetan or on the fringes of the Tibetan world, a usage that was picked up by the British and other Europeans. The Bhutanese would prefer not to call the country Bhutan, but the name has stuck internationally, so there it is. Arguably, Bhutan is a less troublesome name for the country's non-Drukpa people in the south and eastern regions, who are collectively actually the majority (though there is no immediate chance of them finding common cause). Bhutan's major official language, Dzongkha, is drawn from the modified Tibetan spoken in the dzongs, within whose walls religious orders and civil administrators still work side by side. The country's other official languages are now Nepali and English.

There are almost no universally accepted facts about the earliest human life in Bhutan, only stories and conjecture. The cultural historian Françoise Pommeret says that the country was probably inhabited by about 2000 B.C., a date deduced from the examination of stone implements found on the surface of the ground in several places. There has been no extensive archaeological research in Bhutan. The British colonial agent John Claude White was told a hazy, uncorroborated story of a seventh-century-B.C. Bhutanese king who was the terror of the neighborhood until he fell afoul of a Tartar warrior. Government publications say that many of the historical manuscripts called *namthar,* which tell of early events, were lost in fires at a printing works in Sonagatsel in 1828, in the old capital of Punakha in 1832, and in Paro Dzong at the turn of the twentieth century. In addition, an earthquake shattered many buildings in 1897, destroying more records.

But even without cataclysmic events, archaeologists and historians would have considerable problems with mountainous Bhutan, because people have always lived scattered across isolated valleys on one-family farms or in small hamlets, often with fewer than a dozen houses. Concentrations of artifacts or other records would at best be small and hard to find. Biodegradable homes made of mud, wood, and woven bamboo are simply abandoned to recycle themselves when no longer needed. Because there were far more trees in Bhutan than in, for example, Ladakh and most of Tibet, Bhutanese houses, while often more substantial and sophisticated than many in other Himalayan regions, were also more fragile or vulnerable. Near Wangdiphrodang, I saw the earthen remains of a hamlet deserted not very long ago after a flood or fire. It looked at first glance like a colony of giant anthills; the outer shells of the disintegrating buildings matched the reddish color of the ground under them. Inside, walls still bore the soot of cooking fires.

And then there are the problems of tying up the loose ends of the neighborhood histories of those people not rooted in the heartland of western Bhutan but living on the sidelines over the last three hundred years as Bhutan's Drukpa rulers, ecclesiastical and temporal, gradually forged a nation across the sharply corrugated landscape from the Chumbi Valley of Tibet eastward to the border of what is now the Indian state of Arunachal, and from the glaciers and peaks of the high Himalayas down to the tropical zones abutting sultry West Bengal and Assam. A lot of people inevitably got left out of the political story line. To be fair to Bhutan's leaders, some of them, including King Jigme Singye Wangchuck, are aware of this, and pledge to rectify the lapse with the promotion of regional scholarship. Bhutan's first college was consecrated in the 1970s in eastern Bhutan, outside the traditional Drukpa world.

For centuries between the arrival of Buddhism and the introduction of secular education in the 1960s, Bhutan's intellectual elite was found entirely within monastic walls, where writing was in *choekey,* an old ecclesiastical form of Tibetan. Teaching was the domain of monks and lamas. Again, the two are not synonymous: a monk, or *gelong* in Bhutan, is in holy orders and celibate; a lama may or may not be ordained. Lamas are teachers; monks, not necessarily so. A monk may be a lama, but a lama—who may lead a secular life and have a wife and family—is not by definition a monk. The Shabdrung Ngawang Namgyal, a towering religious as well as political leader, did not take monastic vows until he had produced a son. The Bhutanese also have *gomchens,* or unordained village priests, who are in fact laymen authorized to perform certain ceremonies, and a few clusters of nuns outside the traditional monasteries.

The establishment of Sherubtse College, Bhutan's first institution of higher education, means that a secular environment for local scholarship has now been created on a spacious, sunburned campus at Kanglung in eastern Bhutan. Under Zangley Dukpa, Sherubtse's first Bhutanese principal, students and faculty are being encouraged to write about their environment and culture for publication in newsletters, an academic journal, and locally produced books. Zangley Dukpa says he exhorts the college community rigorously to separate the sacred and secular in their studies and writings, though the lines will in a Bhutanese mind always be a little blurred. He has introduced courses in Bhutanese history and promotes the writing of short stories with Bhutanese themes. The principal, who was educated in Singapore and is fascinated by the evolution of education systems worldwide—he can talk with expertise about the Oxbridge model in England or American land grant colleges—says he looks for links between how nations educate their elite and how those societies develop. In talks with teachers at all levels of education in Bhutan, he tries to impress on them the need to differentiate between pure knowledge and culturally weighted instruction. This is a subject of critical debate as Bhutan moves out of a scholarly world enclosed in monastic walls and into a secular intellectual environment.

"What I tell my friends is that sometimes we tend to confuse the curriculum with indoctrination," said the principal, a short, exuberant, generous man. "The distinction between scholarship and indoctrination has to be clear-cut. Take a boy fourteen years old—he may not have the ability to grasp the distinction. Our culture can be taught, but what you have to keep in mind is how to make a lasting impact. This can be done through the story form. For example, I went to see the teachers of Dzongkha, who had been teaching about lighting butter lamps and offering water to the monks. I said: No, that is indoctrination. At eleven, twelve years old, the students are being told, Do this, do that. The teachers asked, Then how? And I said: Once upon a time, there was an old man and an old woman, and early in the morning they would wake up, brush their teeth—teaching hygiene also—then they would go to the temple altar with butter lamps and water. Then they would go to the fields. The religion, the culture, is part of the story.

"You may ask, Then why do you need these cultural aspects at all?" the principal went on. "The answer, as sociologists proclaim, is that you and I may have very different perceptions, but in a society we have to live comfortably, and there are cultural strengths that bind us together. The structure of a society includes cultural aspects, and that is how we live, and what we believe. To be peaceful, to make our society stable, that culture is a stabilizer—and that is important." Half conviction, half plea, this observation is heard all over Bhutan in these troubled times. The troublesome question to Hindu Bhutanese is, whose culture?

The principal and I were talking over tea in the waning light of a golden afternoon in the eastern town of Tashigang. It was the eve of Sherubste College's fourth convocation, and the principal was excited about what his college was struggling to achieve in shaping a modern culture for Bhutan as it prepared to graduate a new batch of educated young men and women from all over the country. (As prizes were awarded, I noticed that some of the highest achievers came from the restless south.) He invited me to sit with the faculty during the convocation as an official guest. I told him that this was embarrassing. He pressed. We compromised: I would go (in academic regalia) as a representative of Columbia University's Southern Asian Institute, of which I was a research associate. Miraculously, they found me a Master of Arts hood, cap, and gown in less than a day.

As we talked over tea in a small screened pavilion on the guesthouse lawn, about half a dozen young men suddenly appeared on the grass and broke into an extraordinary dance to the accompaniment of a strange song, a plaintive chant in a musical language of its own. The principal said that the dancing and singing were in celebration of a great victory in a *kuru* competition. Kuru is a game of darts—but what darts! In this game, players throw larger-than-average feathered missiles at small targets placed scores of meters away. The strength of the players' arms, the speed of the darts, and the precision with which they reach their targets is astonishing. The whole operation is so improbable that a spectator seeing kuru played for the first time thinks it must be an illusion or trickery. No dart should go so far so fast, with just the power of an arm, even helped by a few quick steps into the throw. The young men on the lawn were also dancing in the hope of cajoling donations from the principal's aides, who had come up to Tashigang from Kanglung to check on the accommodation of convocation guests, including Prince Namgyal Wangchuck, an uncle of the king and one of the royal family's most popular members. They were spending the night in Tashigang's two official guesthouses before proceeding to the campus the next day. A gaggle of small boys, standing at a respectable distance, had followed the kuru heroes to our lodge as a kind of cheering section. Theatricality had overtaken a lazy afternoon.

In Thimphu a week later, I watched a kuru match that produced much more graceful yet muscular dancing. When one of two competing teams performed after scoring a bull's-eye, the victory dance was an entertainment in its own right. Spectators pointed out that the effortless choreography was understandable, since this was the National Dance Company's kuru squad, and the player-dancers were apparently trouncing a less nimble-footed team from the Ministry of Agriculture. The dancers in Thimphu were obviously more polished than their country counterparts. But the rustic enthusiasm of the barefoot Tashigang squad, performing in the hope of a windfall to sustain their team through another season, was more touching in its earnestness. I saw a couple of the Tashigang kuru heroes later that day telling tall tales to an admiring group of little children on a path near my guesthouse window.

The dancers gone from the lawn, the principal returned to his discourse. "We bifurcate the subjects we teach, international subjects and noninternational subjects," he said as his aides drifted into snoozes on lawn chairs. "Take a subject like history. We don't mean to say that we don't want to learn the history of other countries. But the problem is, first let us know about ourselves before we learn about others."

The next morning, under a brilliant winter sun, I went to see the past and future come together in Bhutan at the Sherubtse convocation. The day began with a traditional procession called a *chhipdrel*. Monks and students in classical dance costumes and masks, barefoot young men dressed as ancient warriors, and an orchestra of temple instruments greeted Prince Namgyal Wangchuck at the gateway to the college, perhaps a quarter of a mile from the auditorium where the ceremonies were to be held. They led him toward the campus assembly hall in a glorious procession of sound and color. The abbot of Tashigang Dzong, a gentle monk with a cherubic smile, waited at the door to chant an invocation. The faculty was drawn up in ranks on the edge of the path along which walked the prince and the prochancellor of Delhi University, Sherubtse's parent institution. After the taking of many photographs, we were ready to form up to enter the dark assembly hall. More blasts from temple horns, the beating of drums, and the clanging of cymbals reverberated through the crowded auditorium to announce the start of the ceremonies. A low rumble of monks responded from the back of the platform, behind the rows of guests and officials, but not until there had been a sharp exchange among them over whether it was time to start the chants or not. A quick glance from the abbot fixed that. They chanted.

I was assigned Seat 13 in the section reserved for faculty and government officials. I remarked that I seemed to have drawn an unlucky number. Oh, no, my neighbor in the gallery assured me. To the Bhutanese, thirteen is a very auspicious number, as are several other odd numbers, and I should feel honored. Mostly I felt like a bird in the wrong nest, sitting there behind Prince Namgyal, facing students who had never seen me before and must have wondered where I came from and what I was doing there among the dzongdas and professors. The event progressed, or rather swung back and forth between the Middle Ages and contemporary life, for a couple of hours. The awarding of degrees in the arts, sciences, and business was interspersed with more prayers, chants, gongs, and trumpets. There were students who wanted to be engineers or scientists as well as scholars of the humanities. The graduates came robed in silk to collect their degrees; one young man was wearing a dazzling gho in black-and-gold Chinese brocade.

When it ended, we decamped to the gardens for sweetened rice, hot butter tea, and a tour of the school, then moved to a magnificent enclosure of decorated tents for a lunchtime feast. Someone pulled me forward to present me to Prince Namgyal Wangchuck, a tall, handsome man of breathtaking presence and exuberant personality. I thought how corny but true it was that the Bhutanese aristocracy really did look like the fairy-tale royalty of childhood story books. The introduction gave me the opportunity to apologize for crashing Sherubtse's party, since I certainly stuck out as an unknown foreigner. He laughed away the apology. Later, full of vitality and enthusiasm for the day's festivities, he would lead a mass folk dance around a playing field, drawing in well-dressed invited guests and village people in threadbare ghos and kiras who had inched down a grassy bank from the road that traversed the campus to watch the fun.

As we formed up into a buffet line, I attached myself to Father William Mackey, the Canadian-born Jesuit who is not only the founder of the high school that became Sherubtse College but also a Bhutanese citizen and therefore the country's only Christian priest. He had been asked to set up Sherubtse as a high school in 1968 by the late King Jigme

Dorji Wangchuck, who gave the institution its name: *sherub tse* means "peak of knowledge." It became a college of higher education a decade later. As we entered the traditional banquet enclosure walled with fresh-cut evergreens, where bowls of hot food waited on a long table, Father Mackey stopped to greet the chief monk from Tashigang, who had led the convocation prayers. The abbot had come to lunch holding the hand of a little tulku, a shy boy of about five or six who had been identified as the incarnation of a departed monastic scholar. The boy never left the abbot's side, occasionally burying his little face in the monk's robes. Prince Namgyal, seeing Father Mackey and the abbot together, strode over and announced enthusiastically: "My two gurus!"

Father Mackey enjoys this. He has made his peace with Bhutanese Buddhism, and he says he tells his fellow Jesuits in Canada that he is a better Christian for it. He came to Bhutan in the early 1960s after running into trouble in India, where he taught in the hill stations of Darjeeling and Kurseong before foreign missionaries came under nationalist and Hindu chauvinist pressures. Christian missionaries were not encouraged by the Bhutanese either, but Father Mackey had come to know Bhutan's late first prime minister, Jigme Dorji, who frequently visited young Bhutanese students in the Indian hill station schools. Bright children, mostly boys, were sent to these schools in an area of the Himalayan foothills that had once been Bhutanese or Sikkimese before falling under British rule. There were no high schools in Bhutan when Father Mackey arrived in Himalayan Asia, though many monasteries provided education to novice monks and occasionally other children. Jigme Dorji, who urged Father Mackey to move to Bhutan and help establish public schools there, was assassinated in 1964, a victim of what most think was internecine plotting among members of the ruling elite (possibly related to the perception that he was too close to India). Since his death, there has never been another prime minister. But Father Mackey stayed on, learning to speak Dzongkha and promising never to proselytize among the Buddhists or convert Bhutanese to his faith, a pledge he had not found it hard to make. Recalling that promise, he says with a chuckle that we would all be in spiritual trouble if we thought that "salvation comes from a little bit of water being poured over your head."

With a college and many new schools to attend, Bhutanese are eager to learn more about their own country, but new teaching materials have to be created to fill big gaps. The earliest written accounts of Bhutan have been found in texts from Tibet, in which scholars refer to the country by various names, all related to its geographical or botanical distinctions—as, for example, Lho Jong, meaning "Valleys of the South," and Lho Mon Kha Shi, "Southern Mon Country of Four Approaches." Scholars say "Mon" was the Tibetans' general designation for all non-Buddhist Mongoloid people on the southern side of the Himalayas. As in Tibet, the early people of Bhutan were practitioners of spirit worship with propitiatory ceremonies and superstitions. The term "Mon" also appears in other names for what we now call Bhutan: Lho Mon Tsenden Jong, "the Southern Mon Valleys Where Sandalwood Grows," or Lho Jong Mon Jong, "Southern Valleys of Medicinal Herbs." The last description is still particularly apt.

In the Bhutanese monastic tradition, the earliest authenticated manifestation of Buddhist civilization in the country came with the construction of two temples, Kyichu in Paro and Jampa in Bumthang, in the seventh century. The temples are believed to be the work of Songsten Gampo, one of the greatest of Tibetan kings. It was a century later, in A.D. 747, that the Guru Rinpoche arrived from Nepal to aid a king in trouble with the gods, school textbooks say. The Guru was then on his way either to or from Tibet; like many other stories from Bhutanese mythological history, this one has variations. Some historians, for example, say he came to the Himalayas through what is now the Indian state of Assam; others trace his trip through Kashmir, at the other end of the Himalayan world. There are many legends about the Guru Rinpoche; and some accounts of his travels, if taken literally and collectively, would make him an exceptionally long-lived and extraordinarily peripatetic man.

A modest booklet published by the royal government under the title *The Guru Rinpoche, the Great Culture Hero,* takes the view that the Guru, a saint whose appearance had been foreordained by the Buddha himself, arrived via India at the invitation of a King Sendhaka of Bumthang. He later went on to Tibet, where he spent a mere 111 years. (By which time, according to another story, he was well over a thousand years old, having been born a reincarnate of the historical Buddha sometime not long after the founder's death early in the sixth century B.C.) In both Bhutan and Tibet, this Himalayan Methuselah battled and vanquished demons and shamans and spread the Nyingmapa interpretations of Mahayana Buddhism, which consolidated in Tibet. "As a direct result of

Padmasambhava's efforts," says the booklet, "the people of Tibet were elevated from a state of barbarism to a state of unsurpassed spiritual culture. He is therefore truly one of the greatest of the world's culture heroes."

Lopen Pemala describes in the same booklet how twelve miraculous or magical episodes in the life of Guru Rinpoche became the twelve themes of the Bhutanese festivals known as *tshechus*. Because the Guru is the unseen guest at these religious celebrations, held on the tenth day of each month, when the Guru takes the form of the waxing moon, certain prayers must be said to him. Guru Rinpoche was supposed to have assured his followers of his continuing presence in this world by these lines: "Every morning, every evening, I will come for the salvation of all sentient beings. I will come as a rider mounted on the crown of rays of the rising sun."

To me and perhaps many other outsiders, the spirit of Guru Rinpoche dwells most powerfully around the temples at Kurjey Lhakhang, near Bumthang. In a dark grotto in one of the shrines, the faithful say, the outline of his body is imprinted on a rock, now all but obscured from view by a large likeness of the saint. Near the temple grows a giant evergreen, sprung from his walking stick. The miracles that Guru Rinpoche performed at Kurjey are important because the events, enshrined in legends, are keys to understanding how Buddhism meshes with spirit worship in the Bhutanese psychology, and how a Buddhist more often than not prefers to coopt an enemy rather than destroy him.

As one widely heard version of the story goes, the Guru Rinpoche arrived in Bumthang at the desperate call of Sendhaka after a troublesome neighborhood deity, Shelging Karpo, had stolen the ruler's "vital principle" and rendered him seriously ill. Sendhaka, who was reputed to live in Jakar castle, now the hilltop administrative headquarters of Bumthang, gave his daughter to Guru Rinpoche either before or after the saint rendered assistance; accounts vary. John Claude White was told in 1905 that the woman was named Menmo Jashi Kyeden, that she "possessed the twenty-one marks of fairy beauty," and that she and the Guru together were able to save the king's soul with their effortless goodness.

In a longer version of the tale, the Guru thought up a few tricks to draw the attention of the demon Shelging Karpo, hoping to surprise and overpower him. First, the Guru sent the king's daughter into a meadow to draw water in a golden vessel. While she was on this errand, he turned himself into his Eight Manifestations (a few of them certainly scary) and drew an audience of rapt deities from their natural hiding places all around the nearby valleys—save one, Shelging Karpo himself, who refused to be tempted or tricked. Upping the ante, the Guru turned the king's daughter into five women, each with a golden pitcher that reflected the sun toward the absent deity's sanctuary. This was too dazzling to ignore. Shelging Karpo crept out in the form of a lion to have a surreptitious look at the source of the golden glow. The Guru struck. He turned himself into a mythological bird, the *garuda* (or griffin), and grabbed the demon-as-lion and made him say uncle. To regain his freedom, Shelging Karpo was forced to renounce all threats to Buddhists and Buddhism and to take up residence as a guardian deity of the place. According to the monks at Kurjey, Shelging Karpo, who was never obliged to become a Buddhist, is still the monastery's protector. The demon-turned-deity is immortalized in paintings in several places within the temple complex, as are other local gods who tangled with and were outwitted by the Guru.

As for Guru Rinpoche, he went on to meditate at Taktsang, now a monastery on a cliff above Paro, where a temple safeguards an image of him riding a flaming tiger. In time he vanished from the earth, but he lives on in unending reincarnations. Before his departure, he asked his disciples (five women, according to Rigzin Dorji) to collect his teachings and hide them in various places, to be found after the passing of time by tertons, the discoverers of treasure. The terton phenomenon, says Michael Aris, remained very much a hallmark of the Nyingmapa or "old order" Buddhists. The discoverers of written treasures were busiest making finds all over the Himalayas from the eleventh to the sixteenth century. In studying the "text discoverers," Aris made an interesting discovery of his own: that some of the works found were Bon texts. He agrees with those other scholars that as the Bon religion was integrated with Buddhism in Tibet and elsewhere, a largely animist faith took on the trappings of a Buddhist sect or school, a trend clearly discernible by the tenth century. In everyday storytelling in Bhutan, Sikkim, and elsewhere, tales of tertons are invariably stories of those who found texts hidden at the bidding of Guru Rinpoche, not of a Bonpo.

Foremost among the tertons who discovered treasured teachings of the Guru was Pema Lingpa, a rather more down-to-earth saint who was born in Bumthang in the middle of the fifteenth century and who began his career as a blacksmith or metalworker. Aris calls him the "discoverer par excellence" of the Bhutanese, who moreover wrote in language that was "simple, direct, and untutored" as befit a village lad of limited formal learning. If Guru Rinpoche, whose name literally means "the precious teacher," exists as much in mythology as fact, Pema Lingpa was without doubt a real being. His story in children's schoolbooks comes complete with a family tree that links him to the royal family of Bhutan through one of three consorts. He was also an ancestor of the sixth Dalai Lama, who lived in Tibet at the end of the seventeenth century.

A very short fellow reared on two well-known Bumthang products, flour and honey, when his mother's milk ran dry, Pema Lingpa built the doorways of his temples low, using his own stature as a guide, or at least that's what the monks say as we dip to enter the sanctuaries associated with him. Always at heart the metalsmith, Pema Lingpa crafted a cape of chains to be worn by worshippers with strong backs as they circumambulate the altars (preferably three times) at Tamshing Lhakhang, a monastery in Bumthang built by the great terton somewhere around the turn of the sixteenth century. Pema Lingpa's craftsmanship must have been born as much out of his own creative genius as from the lessons he received as the childhood ward of a blacksmith, because he also composed marvelous classical dance sequences to tell religious and mythological stories. The dances are still performed according to his stage directions.

The presence of Pema Lingpa is very real at Tamshing, because the monastery has escaped the Bhutanese urge to refurbish periodically by painting over old works of art, and therefore has been changed very little in five hundred years. Again, the atmosphere is medieval, or what we imagine medieval to be. No motorized vehicle can reach the portals of the monastic walls. The last few miles of stony track leading in the general direction of the monastery are about as much as a Land Cruiser can manage. We—a young civil servant deputed to introduce me to the chief monk, and I—dismount and walk atop a shifting bed of roundish river rocks that have been used to form a path as we approach the monastery, set in a vast meadow not far from the Bumthang Chhu, with Kurjey Lhakhang on the opposite bank. The rocky walkway looks suspiciously like the work of Pem Dorji, the Bumthang dzongda, who is dedicated to abolishing mud paths. Near the outer gateway to the monastery grounds, a weaver is working. In the next courtyard, monks and lamas rest on the porches of their cloister, chatting and drinking tea an old woman serves from a teapot so big she struggles to carry it. There are stray cats, and knots of children. Tamshing is a religious school, and so there seem to be more than the usual complement of novices for such a small monastery. In the next, innermost courtyard, boys are horsing around as they sew and fill chalkbags for writing. These are little pouches of sturdy cloth stuffed with white powder that is squeezed out through a small hole in one corner. The boys write with the little hand-held bag, forcing the chalk dust onto slates.

Inside the temple, a series of priceless paintings are blackened by age and the fingerprints of the faithful, but are still thrilling links to a barely understood age. One was described to me as the image of the founder and great terton. I wanted to take his picture, but that was out of the question. My photography permit from the royal government, always politely examined, was again rejected by an independent monk, probably (but not necessarily) because the official I had with me was not of the sword-bearing rank. As I stood before a monk in a dimly lit corner of the sixteenth century, it seemed both crass and foolish to whine, "But the king said . . ."

Late on the same afternoon of my visit to Tamshing Lhakhang, we found a monk from Pema Lingpa's monastery resting at the small shop next to the Swiss Dairy's cheese-and-wine factory across the river from Jakar, where a few benches and tables serve to turn the general store into a rustic coffee shop. Over a plate of fresh cheese and biscuits, ordered by the dzongda, an official before whom everyone quailed, or at least thought twice about making a contrarian decision, the monk was easily persuaded to tell me the legends of his monastery and its founder. He spoke in a kind of stream-of-consciousness style, almost a recitation, as Pem Dorji translated *sotto voce*. When he had run out of stories, the monk suddenly stopped, gathered his things into a cloth bundle, and took his leave, heading back in the fading light to his distant home.

"At the age of twenty-five, when Pema Lingpa came to Bumthang, he thought about how the foundation stones of the monastery should be laid," said the monk. (Never mind that I had been told Pema Lingpa was as much as six or eight years younger at the time. By this point I had stopped fretting over details.) "When Pema Lingpa was in this process of thinking, a pig appeared. On the four sides of the site, the pig came and with his nose he made four holes, and that's where Pema Lingpa decided to lay the foundation stones of the present monastery. The land was given to him by Chokoteba, the deity of that place. All that land used to be the field where he trained his horse to gallop, this guardian deity of Tamshing. Inside the shrine, the main statue is Guru. It was built by one hundred thousand *kendums,* angels. The painters from Tamshing asked Pema Lingpa for work in the monastery. Pema Lingpa said, 'You paint-ers cannot enter this temple, because the Guru inside was built by the angels.' And they were wondering why is it so. These local painters and sculptors were curious, and they went in the temple and all the angels disappeared. So when the angels flew away, the Guru from inside the statue—you know the face of the statue is facing up in the sky—so he was watching the angels disappearing and flying away. The hat on Guru's head was made by Pema Lingpa himself.

"If you look, when you enter inside our temple, you see the height of the ceiling is very low. That is the exact height of Pema Lingpa. When you enter the main gate, in the courtyard on the left-hand side, there is a prayer wheel. This prayer wheel was made later on, over the seat where Pema Lingpa sat. When he used to give preachings, he used to sit where the present prayer wheel is. The foundation stone is his seat. This also was made by the angels. Outside the temple in the compound, you can see on the paving the footmark of the pig, and some of the hand and forehead of Pema Lingpa, where he used to do his prostrations. Did you see the deer mask inside the temple? Pema Lingpa made the face of the deer, and at night in his dream, an angel told him that there were a pair of antlers waiting on a hill, waiting to be put on this mask. So Pema Lingpa sent his attendant up there and the deer horns were there. So that's how the mask was made. That is another one of the treasures made by Pema Lingpa himself.

"After he constructed the temple, then he went to Mebartsho to bring the treasure back." In other words, his base secure, Pema Lingpa took up the duties of terton.

Mebartsho, the Burning Lake, is no more than a shaded grotto over a bottomless pool deep in a forest glen not far from Jakar on the way out of Bumthang to Ura. It is a powerfully holy spot to the Bhutanese and a place of almost supernatural enchantment to the curious outsider who goes there and listens to its story. You walk to Mebartsho, a good thing. People should approach places of religious or mythological drama softly, cut down to human size. The path follows the rim of a gorge, since

Mebartsho is a pool formed by the Tang River. Near the end of the walk, the path begins to descend, passing shallow caves in the rocky wall of the glen where faithful Bhutanese have placed dozens of tiny clay *tsha-tshas* or chaityas, miniature stupas, as sort of material prayers for forgiveness, better health, or other crucial needs. Then comes the stairway down to the deep, dark well of water where the miracle took place. Here is how a Bhutanese schoolbook explains what happened:

"When Pema Lingpa was around twenty-three years old," it says (there we go again with a relative number), "he had a vision of the Guru Rinpoche giving him a scroll of prophecies for discovering hidden treasures. Following the directions given in the scroll, he went to the gorge of Tang Chhu below his village with some of his friends. He appeared to be somewhat strange to his friends. Immediately on their arrival at the gorge, he jumped into the pool in the river. He clambered out of the river clutching a box containing several religious texts. People were surprised and amazed when they heard about the incident and began to doubt the truth. On the next auspicious day, when he was about to jump into the lake, a crowd gathered on the rock to witness the sight. He held a butter lamp in his hand and prayed: 'If I am a demon, I will die. If I am the spiritual heir to Guru Rinpoche, I will fetch the treasures and come back with the lamp still lit.' At this, he jumped into the lake. He reappeared after some time holding a ritual skull, a statue of Buddha, and the lamp, which was still burning. The lake came to be known as Mebartsho (Burning Lake). People's faith in him began to grow and his fame as a terton began to spread."

Like Guru Rinpoche and Pema Lingpa, the Shabdrung Ngawang Namgyal, the last of Bhutan's three great historical figures, was a man of religion. But with the Shabdrung—literally, "the one at whose feet all submit"—we enter the kind of recorded time verifiable by reasonably good Bhutanese records and the relatively objective accounts of the first European visitors to Bhutan, two Portuguese Jesuits, João Cabral and Estevão Casella. The Jesuits were passing through on their way to Tibet in 1627 when they inadvertently got put under something close to house arrest for a number of months and had a lot of time on their hands to observe the daily life of the Shabdrung's court. Casella's written record of their "visit"—the Bhutanese regarded them as honored guests whose hosts just didn't want them to move on—gave historians a benchmark by which to judge the later years of the Shabdrung's rule and to measure the extent to which this exile from Tibet was able to consolidate his power while unifying the state. Still, the mysteries of Bhutan persisted. When the Shabdrung died in 1651, his death was kept a secret for exactly fifty-eight and a half years. Anyone who asked about him was told he was in retreat.

Shabdrung Ngawang Namgyal had been a Drukpa abbot when he arrived in Bhutan in 1616, but his fame as a civil administrator in his adopted land soon outshone his religious reputation, save perhaps for his ability to call up magic and perform superhuman feats in tight spots. The Shabdrung had no sooner arrived in Bhutan than a series of six Tibetan invasions took place, all aimed at preventing him from establishing a power base so near the Tibetan border. In every case, the Tibetans went down to defeat, sooner or later. That left the Shabdrung free to begin organizing a kind of central government for Bhutan based on a division of labor between a *desi,* or secular head of state, and the *je khenpo,* or chief abbot, the national religious leader. Below the desi were three *penlops* or governors of large regions: the Paro penlop in the west and southwest, the Dagana penlop in the south-central area, and the Tongsa penlop in the east and southeast. A few semiautonomous subregions were left to the administration of *dzongpons,* local officials who like the penlops were based in the massive fortresses the Shabdrung constructed at strategic points around the country. Although there were fortified monasteries in Bhutan before the Shabdrung's time, they were never on the scale of those he built, nor were they designed for so many secular and religious functions. In planning his mini-capitals, the Shabdrung sent word across the Himalayas, to Tibet, Nepal, and Ladakh, to find the finest craftspeople to construct and ornament the fortresses and the temples sheltered within their walls. These fortresses alone would demonstrate the genius of Ngawang Namgyal in pacifying, securing, and uplifting the country and its people. To be sure, there continued to be regional feuds and battles after his death, but the system held. The dzongs remain a unique Bhutanese institution architecturally, socially, and administratively.

The Shabdrung didn't stop at desis and dzongs. He also codified laws and established an ethical system for officials, the spirit of which Bhutan may have to draw on heavily if it is to stay above the sea of corruption swamping the rest of South Asia. Under the Shabdrung's rules, seventh-graders are taught by their history books, "no officials or priests are allowed to send out alms-begging parties." Neither can any administrator "accept or demand any present for marriages or separations for which he is the civilian representative." In short, anyone with power "should not give the subjects unnecessary trouble."

The Shabdrung, while reputedly living a simple life, able to exist on a diet of fruit and milk, was not short of self-confidence. During his rule, he wrote a treatise extolling his strengths and virtues known as "The Sixteen I's," which was reproduced on his personal seal, a wheel with sixteen spokes. It goes like this in Bhutanese schoolbooks:

> *I am he who turns the wheel of the dual system.*
> *I am everyone's good refuge.*
> *I am he who upholds the teachings of the glorious Drukpas.*
> *I am the subduer of all who disguise themselves as Drukpas.*
> *I achieve the realization of the Goddess of Compassion.*
> *I am the pure source of moral sayings.*
> *I am the possessor of an unlimited view.*
> *I am he who refutes those with false views.*
> *I am the possessor of great power in debate.*
> *Who is the rival that does not tremble before me?*
> *I am the hero who destroys the host of demons.*
> *Who is the strong man that repulses my power?*
> *I am mighty in speech that expounds religion.*
> *I am wise in all the sciences.*
> *I am the incarnation prophesied by the patriarchs.*
> *I am the executioner of false incarnations.*

When the Shabdrung died, or his death was finally acknowledged at the turn of the eighteenth century, three reincarnations of him began to appear more or less simultaneously, representing his body, speech, and mind. Over the two hundred years that followed, these reincarnations have been gradually downplayed and phased out. But the power of the Shabdrung lives on. When a rumor swept Thimphu in 1992 that a Bhutanese exile from India claiming to be a contemporary incarnate was about to pay a brief visit, crowds gathered outside a hotel where he was expected to stay, but the rumor was never more than that.

Ngawang Namgyal's administrative system survived the founder's death, however, staffed by an ever-expanding class of civil servants who, then as now, shared the dzongs with monks. In the fields around, farmers labored under a feudal system that traded labor for sustenance and protection. In a cashless economy, landless peasants were essentially serfs or even slaves to landowners. Taxes were paid in crops of rice, barley, or buckwheat, supplemented by supplies of wood and butter. The tradition lingers in symbolic ways.

Dasho Rinzin Gyetsen, the dzongda of Tashigang, told me that when he took office in that remote eastern dzong, people walked for as long as five days from distant villages to bring him gifts of butter, hard-boiled eggs, vegetables, and other products of their farms. He in turn was expected to visit their communities. "A dasho takes a vow before the king to serve the people," he said. "And a dzongda has very close links with them. On my trips to their villages, the people provide food, drink, and horses all along the way. When I arrive, the best house in a village is emptied for me; the family moves away all its possessions and leaves it clean. If there is no suitable house, people construct a shelter of firs or leafy branches and stand guard all night while I sleep. They will roast a pig and ask that the food be served by the dzongda's own hand."

Because regional feuds continued to disrupt the otherwise bucolic life of Bhutan well into the twentieth century, the arts of war were not neglected. Every Bhutanese man learned archery and swordsmanship and could be called up at any time to garrison a dzong or march against a troublesome neighboring lord. There were few guns of any kind, so Bhutanese soldiers were able to protect themselves reasonably well with iron helmets and shields made of hide or thickly woven vines or grasses. Battles began with ritual dances and prayers to the guardian deities of a place—much fiercer gods than any in the Buddhist pantheon of incarnations. Soldiers were often barefoot.

It was such an army that took on the British in the hope of saving a valuable belt of rich land that served as a buffer between the Himalayan foothills and the higher elevations of Bhutan. The area, several hundred miles in length, was known as the Duars, literally the "doors" or gates from the plains into the hills running along river valleys. The strip of land, divided into the Bengal Duars and the Assam Duars, corresponding to those Indian states, included not only fertile plains but also a number of hill towns. The British, administrators of an armed commercial empire in India in its early years, quarreled intermittently with the Bhutanese in the eighteenth and early nineteenth centuries over trade, access to Tibet, and occasional Bhutanese incursions into territory deemed to be under the protection of Calcutta, the headquarters of the East India Company.

Peter Collister, in his excellent book *Bhutan and the British,* looks to the temper of the age to explain why Britain saw fit to pick fights with this small country, especially in the nineteenth century, when relations dropped to an all-time low. The Victorians, he found, combined a heightened fear of Russia and China (both just over the Himalayan horizon) with "the evangelistic and moralising spirit of the times." Ashley Eden, one of the least sympathetic of the emissaries sent to deal with the Bhutanese, prepared a report whose language Collister described as superficial and scathing. Eden went so far as to make the suggestion that the country might be successfully colonized.

Meanwhile, the British nibbled away at territory. In 1772 the Bhutanese fought and lost a battle with Britain over the small kingdom of Cooch Behar, now in India's state of West Bengal. In 1841, the Assam Duars were annexed by the British, setting off two decades of skirmishes with the Bhutanese. Near the end of 1864, the British issued a proclamation of complaints that amounted to a declaration of war on Bhutan. Six hundred elephants and countless bullocks were assembled for the task of breaching the mountain kingdom's defenses in the Bengal Duars, according to Collister. Artillery was moved into place, and the Anglo-Bhutanese War began with an attack on a Bhutanese fort at Dalingcote, near the forested meeting point of Sikkim, Bhutan, and India. The Bhutanese defended themselves with bows and arrows and rocks.

In a few months, all the Duars were in British hands, and peace was restored with the 1865 Treaty of Sinchu-la. The British turned to other projects. The Bhutanese, bruised and humiliated, retreated to their mountain domain. But Bhutan had escaped colonization; the British were never able to station even a resident political officer in the country. Bhutan could turn to new projects, the most important of which was the stabilizing and reunifying of a country torn by civil strife and foreign wars for nearly two centuries. Jigme Namgyal, penlop of Tongsa, almost completed the task between 1865 and his death in 1885. The final victory was left to his son and heir, Ugyen Wangchuck, who became Bhutan's first king, the Druk Gyalpo, Precious Ruler of the Dragon People.

Chapter 10

THE DRAGON
PEOPLE

WHO ARE the Bhutanese, the people who have the maybe impossible task of saving the last Himalayan Buddhist kingdom? Other Himalayan Buddhists think of them as aloof, proud, and generally conservative. Even sympathetic people who share their religion are critical of Bhutan's initial intolerance in dealing with its southern, mostly Hindu, rebellion, and there is a surprising lack of passion in the region for protecting the sovereignty of Bhutanese Buddhists, who have managed to look after themselves pretty effectively through the centuries. Long years of isolation have apparently left permanent imprints on Bhutanese thinking, especially in the monasteries, where change is resisted. Throughout the region, there is a sense that the inflexibility of Bhutan's monastic leadership—not the monks themselves—could endanger the country whose unique religion and royal rule they most want to save.

Although Bhutan's supreme religious leader, the je khenpo, and the government-subsidized (and -pensioned) monks he leads are followers of the Drukpa Kagyupa school which established a theocratic state in Bhutan in the seventeenth century, many Bhutanese, including royal family members, are Nyingmapa Buddhists or followers of lamas who are Nyingma teachers. Furthermore, the Drukpas are considered a western Bhutanese phenomenon, and are thus resented by many eastern Bhutanese, who see them as a privileged group. Bhutan does not need an east-west division at a time when the north and south are involved in something approaching civil war.

But there is yet a more tragic consequence of Drukpa domination. It prevents Bhutan from using its protected religious environment to lure Buddhist philosophers and scholars to the kingdom, or so monks outside the country say. Logically, this last Himalayan Buddhist realm might well become an intellectual center for the faith. But no, a Bhutanese monk told me in Kathmandu. "I have to come out for new ideas," he said. "The great lamas from outside are not welcome in Bhutan." The monk had come to study with Khenpo Rigzin at the Nyingma Institute of Nepal. He saw the Drukpa monastic order not as a force for the vigorous propagation of Buddhism and exciting debates on its philosophy and direction but as a stumbling block to learning among the last people to live in a Buddhist kingdom. Foreign lamas and students are denied visas to Bhutan, the khenpo said. Bhutanese in power deny this, but, whatever the truth may be, there is certainly a perception in the Himalayas that clannishness and exclusivity are perpetuated by the Drukpa monastic hierarchy. Foreign monks insist that as the country and its king modernize, the Bhutanese people's most important heritage, the Buddhist religion, is officially in Drukpa blinkers.

Attitudes could not be more different among the Bhutanese in secular life—in law, medicine, agriculture, civil administration, and other civilian professions—who have been charged by the king with bringing Bhutan into the contemporary world. They are acutely aware that they are a generation standing somewhere on the frontier between medievalism and modern nationhood. People in their forties and fifties can still remember a country without roads or schools or money; they are the last of the old order, and the creators of the new. This could be exhilarating, if that were a sensation in more general currency in this country where reserve and moderation are more the norm in public life. More often, a Bhutanese just accepts, matter-of-factly, the extraordinary task of trying to construct an institutional future true to the best of Bhutan's heritage. Moreover, they do it with a sense of humor.

Sonam Tobgay, chief justice of Bhutan, is one of those citizens whose work could significantly change national life. But he isn't puffed up or pompous about the prospect of an immortal reputation. Although he can discourse at length about the origins and accretions of Bhutanese common law or about the code of the Shabdrung Ngawang Namgyal, he is at his most animated when telling rural jokes.

For instance, there was this backwater town where panic had set in over the imminent visit of a high-ranking government official. The rustic folk, certain they would commit crass infractions of etiquette, sought advice from an elder in the vicinity who was a shade more worldly-wise. Don't get worked up, they were told. Just turn out for the visit properly dressed in your best clothes and then watch what I do and imitate my every act. The day arrived, and so did the great dasho. The townsfolk came out to line the road in respectful welcome, all eyes on the elder, who was making an extravagant show of knowing the correct ritual. But in his zeal, the elder overdid it. In a grand gesture, he accidentally managed to shake loose the shallow wood-and-silver drinking cup that every well-accounted Bhutanese carries in the folds of his robe. Since the village was on a steep slope, the hapless elder was unable to stop his little bowl from rolling to the edge of the road and plunging merrily down the hill, gathering speed as it went. The rustics waited only a second before pulling their treasured cups from their ghos and bowling them down the same incline, proud of not having missed a cue.

Before the short, stocky justice reaches the end of the story, he is convulsed in laughter. Not necessarily because the joke is such a rib-tickling thigh-slapper, but because it is a beautiful example of a tale designed to illustrate the extreme stupidity of a region of Bhutan notorious for breeding dimwits. He launches directly into another joke about the same region. Two men went hunting. When they first spotted their prey (I think it was a handsome deer) some distance away, they chose arrows and drew their bows to shoot. One hunter, anticipating a feast, asked his companion, Did you bring the salt, pepper, and chilis? The second, focused on the deer, said, What? Did you bring the salt, pepper, and chilis? the first asked again, a little louder, worried about a lack of seasoning for their barbecue. What did you say? asked the second once more. *Did you bring the salt, pepper, and chilis?* the salivating first hunter shouted. The animal heard the outburst, of course, and, warned of its danger, ran away.

"There are in every country, every place, always some jokes," Justice Tobgay said during a chat in his chambers at Bhutan's High Court, as he digressed into an exposition on the importance of humor in understanding a country's psychology. The High Court is no ordinary courthouse, but a magnificent traditional structure built not long ago in pure Bhutanese Buddhist style, right up to the loose-shingled roof held down by rocks. The main courtoom is a riot of color, with familiar paintings on

Buddhist themes covering the low desks behind which the nine justices sit at the bench, the pillars holding up the ceiling, and whatever other spaces were available to the artists' brushes. The bench itself is a raised platform covered by Bhutanese rugs in bright primary hues. Trials are conducted in one of the three official languages, English, Dzongkha, or Nepali; the choice is made by the principals in each case. The justices take pains to make this clear, since ethnic Nepali exiles have charged disingenuously that the use of their language is banned or curtailed in Bhutan. The chief justice studied the principles of human rights in Australia and international law in London, and he is aware of the need to keep the High Court, an appellate court of last resort (with the king the only higher authority), as objective as possible in a climate of ethnic tensions. Justice Sonam Tobgay describes himself as "the most independent man in the kingdom."

I had heard around town that he had begun an oral history collection of the life and folklore of Bhutan in his spare time. That was an exaggerated rumor, he told me with a rueful smile. He certainly wanted to promote the collection of folklore, both jokes and moral tales, but he was too busy computerizing court records, reviewing the country's legal codes, and putting centuries of customary and religious law into new contexts to do much collecting himself. Where jokes are concerned, there is only a brief moment left in history to record this gentle humor, before videos blanket the land with the slapstick of Indian cinema and sophisticated (and not so sophisticated) sitcom silliness of Hollywood. The Bhutanese have a wry, understated sense of humor, a knack for seeing the amusing or absurd in many ordinary situations, and good timing when telling funny stories. People seem to smile and laugh easily, habits toddlers learn as parents and grandparents play cheerfully with them.

"Jokes are entertaining, and should be laughed at," the justice said. "But they also can have tremendous meaning. Those that do, I think, should be preserved. No one here has written on that. Our jokes are very short, basically five, ten lines, which we can laugh about." The chief justice then slipped inadvertently into one of those Bhutanese tangles with numbers. "There are two kinds of jokes or funny stories," he said. "One popular one written in Tibetan. Number two, advice and moral values taken from the various religious textbooks. Third, and basically it is in this area I have interest, which can be bifurcated into two:

A—which is seemingly truly Bhutanese. B—it must tell certain things about that place. Now, for instance, some stories of a stone, of a place, gives names which neither exist in our Tibetan classical working grammar or in the dictionary. This speaks a lot about the language and the culture that once existed. The Himalayan range was the abode of aboriginals who had distinct culture, language, unwritten language. If I can find and save these old stories it will be a service to the country, to a future generation.

"We all talk about culture and tradition, and the richness of culture and traditions," Sonam Tobgay continued. "But it would be an empty tribute unaccompanied by any action. Our oral folk tales or stories all have moral values. And tremendous rationality. At a certain stage in life you tend to mock these tales. But you learn. For instance, the trees near the source of the river or the stream: we were constantly drummed at a younger age that there are gods in them. Not really gods, but guardian deities. If you cut that tree, the *nagas* will be very angry. This was basically a deterrent measure propounded or expressed in folk tales. It was just a tale, but in retrospect—and, also if you analyze it—it has the scientific values for the environment. And anything that has value I think must be treasured."

The justice is fascinated to see what still-living folktales reveal about the subtle social or political messages conveyed, especially to children. "Now, for instance, last year the Dzongkha Development Commission conducted a survey. They have asked the children to submit folk tales, to write folk tales. Some of them—it was three hundred and something they got—had certain messages to pass. The kings were always venerated. But they were writing about a time when we did not have the kings. The concept of king was not there. A lot of light that throws."

The chief justice's more pressing task now is the rationalization of the legal system and the computerization and analysis of court records—no small challenge, since, like everything else in Bhutan, some of the historical lawgivers' lives and deeds are obscured by a mythological overlay. His casual account of his source material is astonishing. "The first codified law of Bhutan was in 1651 or 1652—the dates are disputed," he said. "That was in Shabdrung's time, in his last days. But if you look into those documents, they have drawn sources from the laws of Lord Buddha, which were pronounced in 1913 B.C. Those are the treatises of Lord Buddha. Of course, you may ask, in 1913 Lord Buddha was not born. According to Buddhist philosophy, Lord Buddha was born five hundred times good life and five hundred times difficult life. And in one of his five hundred times, in the kingdom of Madgadanya Bodhgaya, presently called Bihar, there was a king called Mirputchinand, and Lord Buddha was a reincarnation of that. So it appears that the first material source of law was based on that law.

"Secondly, the fifteenth king of Tibet, who was born in around 627 A.D. or 629, he had done one of the best and most elaborate code of laws," he went on. "In fact, those laws are better than those of the ten tables of Cicero and Augustine and others. They are very elaborate. Then Guru Padmasambhava also had made some laws—somebody asked Guru Padmasambhava: 'You have taught everything to us. Would you say something about law?' And Guru Padmasambhava then relates certain laws.

"In 1951, when the third king ascended the throne, the National Assembly was instituted. From 1952 onward there were discussions on the various provisions of the laws of Bhutan, which we call the General Law Book. We have yet to do a search to try to draw similarities on sources of each article of the law, comparing and contrasting with some of the articles or principles initiated by the persons or sources that I have mentioned. We have yet to do that. However, the General Law Book is a very good law book. There were extensive discussions from 1952 until 1959; it was not enacted in one session. It came in 1959. Therefore we called it the General Law Book of 1959."

The 1959 code combines local customary law for civil procedures with internationally accepted criminal codes, the chief justice said. "There seems to be a lot of similarities with the British penal code." He added that Bhutan does have the death penalty on its books, contrary to Buddhist precepts, but that it has not been applied, though there have been calls for capital punishment for terrorists. There are some other dark spots. When leaders of Amnesty International, on a visit to Bhutan, raised objections to the shackling of prisoners, the Bhutanese were chagrined, a minister told me, because they weren't aware that shackling was not common everywhere. A new prison was built to meet many of Amnesty's standards.

In civil cases, codifiers of the 1959 law book tried to follow local practice. "At village level, mediation and conciliation were primarily given a lot of importance," the chief justice said. "At the district level there seems to have been a basic principle of fairness and justice employed." Since many cases brought to courts arise from disputes between neighbors or even members of the same family, there is no need for adversarial litigation demanding that one party win and the other lose. With legal representation at a minimum, a judge or magistrate is free to suggest compromises, which in many Asian societies are preferred to destructive victories by one side, causing humiliation to the other party.

Violence has been rare in Bhutan, murder almost nonexistent, which is why the new rash of crimes around Thimphu has thrown legal experts into a quandary over whether the old systems can go on working effectively in a new environment. "From our religious values, we believe our body is the embodiment or edifice of many other unseen gods and other beings, so we were constantly reminded, you are not hitting just a person, but you are hitting other things," the chief justice said. "Resorting to violence has never been our Bhutanese culture and it is not appreciated. So therefore, we do not normally do that." Most of the cases that come to court, he said, are land or property disputes.

In his large private chambers, the chief justice asked me to look at the High Court's coat of arms, which dominated one wall. "Right in the center you see the circle, which is His Majesty," he said. "Basically that concept came from Lord Buddha's time; the circle was the embodiment of Lord Buddha. Then you see a rod covered with a silken knot. The rod is a yoke: it's called a golden yoke. The yoke represents the penal offense, and the silken knot the religious law. In other words, the more crimes you commit, the more you carry the yoke. The longer you carry it, the heavier it becomes. But law must always be tempered with compassion, because a silk knot can always be untied, however tight it is. So therefore compassion and forgiveness are of primary importance to our legal system."

Not far from the High Court, another major ingredient of Bhutanese life and culture is under cautious scrutiny at the National Institute of Traditional Medicine. When I first went there, before they had mechanical desiccators for drying medicinal plants, the buildings and courtyards of the institute were fragrant with the pleasing and healing scent of herbs drying in the morning sun. Great carpets of medicinal leaves were spread over concrete floors in the pure air at an altitude of over 7,500 feet. A woman sitting on a low wall watched over the herbs, her back to a large prayer wheel with a gilded mantra painted on its revolving drum. The wheel is turned by anxious patients and their relatives as they wait outside the pharmacy and the doctors' consulting rooms nearby.

Paolo Morisco had been in Bhutan a decade when I met him at the institute, where his office is perched at the top of several flights of steep monastic stairs. An Italian doctor working for the nongovernmental Italian aid organization DISI, Morisco was deep in an ambitious effort to elevate traditional Bhutanese medicine to the level of a science without altering age-old remedies or supplanting them with modern drugs. Like the legal system rooted in Buddhist concepts, the ancient medical remedies of the Bhutanese—known to the world as Tibetan medicine—are very important to them, and the government is pledged to save and enhance the system.

"The Bhutanese are trying to strike a balance here, taking the things they need from modern, technological society while keeping a pace that is humane, that is livable, that is based more on spiritual than materialistic values," Morisco said. "Now whether they will succeed or not in the long run, that's a different problem. The fact that they are trying is, I think, very good."

Once on the way back from Punakha to Thimphu, I was drawn to a local clinic on a hill above the road that seemed to have attracted a long line of patients. It was winter, when respiratory infections were at their worst. The clinic had two sections, one for modern medicine and the other for traditional cures. On that day, everybody wanted to see the traditional doctor, Tshering Tashi, a dispenser of herbal medicines and an expert in a particularly Bhutanese kind of acupuncture using a gold needle heated over a flame or a burning herb. I watched him treat an elderly woman, said to be eighty-one years old, who complained of giddiness. If she really was eighty-one, this was an amazing age for Bhutan, where average life expectancy probably still hovers around fifty. Finding the right spot on her skull through a measurement based on the length of one of her fingers, he touched her small white-haired head several times with the hot needle. He also talked with her quietly, reassuringly, about her health in general. After the treatment, she left content, and the line of waiting patients inched eagerly forward.

"There's no fear in Bhutan of losing the culture," said Morisco, who was wearing wool gloves with the fingers cut off as he fiddled in his cold garret office with an Apple computer that had blown its fuse. His work quarters at the Institute of Traditional Medicine, a teaching, treatment, and research center on a hillside above Thimphu, were primitive, dark, and chilly. But his years of work among the Bhutanese had made him optimistic, and his enthusiasm warmed the room. "The work we are doing is not at all to try and save the culture. The culture is pretty much saved. It's pretty much alive here. What we are trying to do, especially in medicine, is to help the Bhutanese to approach traditional science and traditional knowledge with a more modern mentality, so that they can make the best out of it. That's really the idea."

Bhutan, known through its history as a land of medicinal herbs, still has these plants in abundance—so much so that there are hopes of an export market in the future, when herbs can be gathered in large enough quantities without endangering their existence, or be cultivated rather than just plucked from the wild. But first, the plants have to be catalogued. "The plants used in the traditional Tibetan and Bhutanese systems are written down in books, and the books have been preserved. So you have a list of six hundred to nine hundred ingredients that are used in Bhutanese and Tibetan medicine," Morisco said. "But when you go to find the description in the original book, you see that the botanical description is not systematic. So you have diversity of interpretation in different parts of the Himalayas. Sometimes the practitioners know that it's not the original plant and they use a substitute because they don't find the original, which is okay. But sometimes they no longer know what the real plant is and they even have contests among themselves because one says this is the real plant and another one says no. So here we come in and say: Let's do a botanical identification, a systematic botanical identification. We form a committee of traditional doctors who will sit together and talk and standardize. Now, we don't mind whether under the same medicinal name they use two botanical species—as long as we know that under that name there may be two plants used.

"I'm sure we have here some resources that have already disappeared elsewhere, especially in Nepal and Sikkim," he said. "That is why we are going into a project of cultivating medicinal plants, so that we avoid using the natural resources from the forests. One of the big aims of this project is conservation and protection. Then we will also be able to identify and preserve varieties of plants which are rare and which may be unique to Bhutan at this point."

Morisco—a tropical medicine specialist who worked for five years in Thimphu's General Hospital before moving to the institute, which gets help from the European Community—said that the traditional systems of medicine common in Bhutan are also used in Ladakh and Nepal, "and these people don't like the trend in Europe to call this all Tibetan medicine." Bhutanese prefer to call it "the art of healing," and they believe they have made unique contributions to it. One of their specialties is moxabustion, the treatment I saw used on the elderly woman at the rural clinic near Punakha. Moxa is the herb burned to heat the gold needle.

"The two big differences in Bhutanese acupuncture is that they won't stick the needle beyond the derma; the puncture, it will be quite superficial," Morisco said. "It's not like the Chinese system, where they go quite deep. The second thing is that most of the time—actually all of the time—they heat up the needle with a type of fire, so there will be a little cauterization on the skin, which is actually very good because this is a good hygienic practice. The idea is that the meridians, the acupuncture points, can be stimulated not only by going deep into the flesh but also with just touching the point with the golden needle and heating it up. Even in some schools of Chinese medicine you will see now that they do pressure with their fingers, or scrape with horns on the acupuncture points. There are different things developing. It seems it doesn't really matter what you do with the needle, so long as you catch the acupuncture point."

Morisco, who like virtually every foreigner working in Bhutan spontaneously lauds King Jigme Singye Wangchuck for his enlightened but restrained attitudes toward progress and development, says that his experience in infectious diseases in Bhutan taught him that the greatest health threats to the country remain poor sanitation and smoky rooms. "Traditional medicine does not have concepts of public health," he said. "One of the subjects we have just introduced in our five-year curriculum in traditional medicine is modern hygiene and health sciences. We are also introducing courses in botany and biology to give their work a scientific base."

With certain inevitable variations, the general system of traditional medicine practiced across the Himalayas focuses on identifying symptoms springing from a broad range of causes. Yeshi Donden, a Tibetan-born master who became the Dalai Lama's physician in Dharamsala, recalled in his book *Health Through Balance* that Buddha had listed 84,000 afflictive emotions alone that can lead to disorders in the body, even before we get to physical malfunctions. Yeshi Donden looked closely at

404 disorders, dividing them into 101 caused by the accumulated karma of earlier lives, 101 linked to something in this life that has taken a while to manifest itself, 101 involving the interference of spirits, and 101 superficial problems linked to bad diet or behavior. In other words, each person's whole being and history (material, psychic, and karmic) must be considered in diagnosing symptoms and prescribing treatment. This holistic approach has begun to attract attention in the West, where a growing number of physicians and scientists are looking for ways to adapt the philosophy to vastly different settings.

"Holistic medicine is quite a new approach for modern medicine, but of course it's an ancient approach, and it's an approach with which we'll have to deal very soon, because there are many diseases that modern medicine cannot cure, could not cure ten years ago, twenty years ago," Morisco said. "We've had very little in breakthroughs in the last ten, twenty years, I think. Of course, antibiotics was the big thing, surgery's a big thing. But beyond that, in any diseases that are related more to human behavior—not only psychotic and psychosomatic diseases but even diseases that are kind of less easy to pinpoint to one specific agent, like a bacteria—modern medicine hasn't really gone anywhere. Modern medicine may not be doing very much with holistic medicine yet. But doctors say, yes, immunity and immuno-stimulation have something to do with the will of life, spiritual values, and internal qualities. All these things have been de facto recognized. Holistic medicine says that everything that you do in your life has a consequence, and can be the cause of suffering or disease—I'm talking about spiritual behavior or social behavior; killing somebody or behaving badly or being too jealous or too backbiting or those kind of things—all those have a direct influence on your health, which might come immediately or after years. According to Buddhist belief there are effects even in the next life, which is a little bit less easy to prove. But definitely there is relevance in this life; it is true."

For Morisco, who says he changed a lot of his own thinking on the role of traditional medicine during his decade in Bhutan, a few adjustments still need to be made in the Bhutanese system. Traditional practitioners must recognize when a patient may need modern surgery or another type of Western diagnostic test or treatment, a campaign Bhutanese doctors themselves have taken on by linking traditional and modern wings of clinics and hospitals. The well-educated and affluent already pick and choose from the best. When Rigzin Dorji, head of the National

Cultural Commission, became ill with abdominal cancer, he was first treated in Bhutan, then in a state-of-the-art hospital in New York City, and later by Buddhist priests in Japan. He extended his life for several years, though no one would venture an opinion on what form of medicine helped him.

Morisco says—as do many Bhutanese—that the rural lamas to whom many Bhutanese first go for medical help must open their minds to a few new ideas, especially in promoting sanitation and healthier community living. But there is not much else in the Bhutanese system Morisco would change at this point, he says. "Here you are a traditional doctor and you know everything from taking the pulse to doing a diagnosis to going into the forest and taking your ingredients to making medicine and giving it to the patient. Now you find one doctor in the West who can do that and you would have Nirvana."

If the Buddhist Bhutanese still live in harmony with a holistic past—not just in matters of medicine but more generally in a culture that has no special compartments for religion, law, music, art, or environmental protection, all of which grew up and still revolve around the monastery—they are also, almost paradoxically, more adaptable to new ideas than many people encountered elsewhere by international development experts. Learning English in childhood because it has become the language of instruction in all Bhutanese public (but not monastic) schools, young men and women are prepared to navigate smoothly through the world beyond the Paro airport—and to meet foreign tourists and aid experts with great poise and confidence on their own turf.

When Bhutanese young people return from education abroad, especially those who want to enter government service, they are sent for a course in *driglam namzha,* or national culture. This includes how to dress, talk, eat, and behave toward others in a traditional society. The training includes visits to historical sites and classes in how to conduct ancient ceremonies. "We want college graduates to know the Bhutanese way," Rigzin Dorji told me. "We want to make sure our cultural backbone is there, that manners and etiquette should not be neglected. How to love your parents. How to treat your masters or servants. Not to kill. Not to harm. All these are Buddhist concepts. Children should actually grow up on this system of ethics from the age of six or seven."

Thus, when all goes well, the Bhutanese enter professions with a deep grounding in their own culture as well as the linguistic and educational tools to learn what is new. But there is more to the shaping of the Bhutanese character; a lot more. Buddhism has certainly contributed to making the Bhutanese more tolerant and curious than their Hindu or Islamic neighbors in South Asia. Thais and Sri Lankans, also Buddhists, have been open to new ideas and quick to change course if they feel the change makes sense. The clever, literate Burmese were once thought to have a bright future, until a series of stifling military dictatorships snuffed out their hopes. A century ago, when Bhutan was almost entirely sealed off from the world, the British political officer Claude White was fascinated by their social sophistication. "I have always found the Bhutanese, as well as the Sikkim people, very appreciative of English food, and as they are Buddhists with no question of caste, they consider it an honor to be asked to meals, and are most anxious to return any hospitality they receive, in marked contrast to the natives of India, who are defiled and outcasted by such intercourse with strangers," he wrote on his first expedition to Bhutan in 1905.

Though the Bhutanese may be wary of their more powerful neighbors, the Indians and Chinese (and for obvious reasons the Nepalis), they do not exhibit a corrosive inferiority complex or a tendency to run themselves and their country down—an annoying characteristic of the gabby Pakistani elite, among other members of the South Asian talking classes. The Bhutanese can be sure of themselves without resorting to combative arrogance. Once after I spoke on Bhutan to an Asia Society audience in Washington, D.C., a Bhutanese student introduced himself after the slide show. I asked him if I had got Bhutan right in my remarks. "Most of it," he said kindly, and then changed the subject. He would not be drawn out on my mistakes, though I really wanted to know what he thought. Had this been an Indian audience, I would have been pressed vociferously and with considerable bombast to recant publicly at least one statement or another.

"The Bhutanese are a very special people," said Dr. Kees Goudsuaard, the Dutch coordinator of a wildly successful UNICEF vaccination drive whom I met some years ago at the Hotel Druk in Thimphu. "They are receptive to new ideas without ever throwing away what they think is valuable. The achievements made in health here are the achievements of the Bhutanese people; our part is the easy part." Michael O'Hara of the United Nations Development Program told me later that the Bhutanese "don't buy everything you say the first time." They are more deliberative and analytical. "They listen to you and ponder, and then decide. Development here is by Bhutanese government plan, not by the decisions of donors."

Eva Nisseus, who headed the UNICEF office in Bhutan for more than five years, said that in only a few decades of work—starting from a medieval base in 1960—the Bhutanese had pulled ahead of all their neighbors in creating modern health services. While she noted that there was much to be done—women needed to be taught more about their bodies and about hygiene in the home to cut death rates among babies and young children, especially in isolated rural areas—the Bhutanese had set up more than seventy clinics, twenty hospitals, and a system of "walking doctors" and medical technicians who visit the remotest settlements. Basic childhood inoculations were universally available by the early 1990s, an extraordinary achievement given the terrain and the scattering of fewer than half a million people over a country the size of Switzerland. In receiving medical attention or nutritious meals, girls enjoy equal treatment with boys in the family, she said, adding that this national pattern had been adopted even by the Hindu-Nepali Bhutanese of the south. This presents a striking contrast to the debilitating, even life-threatening deprivation girls often face in India or in Hindu communities of Nepal. A new education system for the primary years was, meanwhile, reinforcing Bhutanese tradition and the values of life lived close to the land.

Everyone with experience in Bhutan seems to have a wonderful story or two to illustrate the Bhutanese nonchalance about taking on the world single-handed. Apart from Ugyen Dorji—the baker in Thimphu who walked out of an impoverished life in the hills and a few years later was training with an Austrian pastry chef in Bregenz—my favorite character is Phuntso, a Bhutanese monk of about thirty whom I met in Kathmandu. In 1990, he told me, he left Bhutan to visit America. In Kathmandu, with the help of some Bhutanese with the funds to assist him as an act of faith, he got an American visa and a ticket to Bangkok. There he managed somehow to get a Thai International flight to Seattle. Monks always receive a great deal of deference and help from Thai airlines, though Phuntso wasn't too clear about how the flight was paid for. Anyway, he arrived in Seattle with no money and in debt for his tickets. He did have one phone number belonging to an American Buddhist in Los Angeles. Immigration officials must have been aghast at this slender, single-minded man in dark crimson robes with almost no possessions. They questioned him for three hours in Seattle and then gambled and sent him on to southern California, where someone from a Buddhist center was summoned to meet him and give him a place to stay for a week while he looked for his Los Angeles contact, whom he identified as Arthur Schanche or "Dr. Aht." According to Phuntso, this generous benefactor enrolled him in an English-language school and gave him a place to stay for two years, strictly as an act of devotion.

Free of material cares, Phuntso had a good deal of time to size up American Buddhists. "Some were good and some not so good," he said. "Some seem to be looking for something for themselves, not for mankind." He was most impressed with Chinese-American Buddhists, he said, because they seemed the most genuine. Thai-American Buddhists were too clannish to penetrate, however. Thais had their own temples, he said, which were Theravada Buddhist, not Mahayana, in any case. And New York, he decided, was too cold to visit when a trip became possible. For these and other reasons, he was unable to see nearly as much as he would have liked of America and its Buddhist communities. Back in Kathmandu at the small Nyingma Institute, Phuntso was pondering his next move. He was due to undertake the traditional three years and three months of meditation in retreat. He couldn't decide where to go.

Once on a visit to the Bumthang district in central Bhutan, I went looking for something like a model village, to see what improvements rural Bhutanese families would make if they wanted to live better lives by earning money in farming or business, but on a smaller scale than the new capitalists of Thimphu. I was sent to Jalikhar, close to Jakar town, where a gentleman named Ap Singye owns one of the grandest houses. At its back, the house overlooks one of Bhutan's most bucolic scenes, a broad expanse of meadow along the aquamarine waters of the Tang Chhu, where horses grazed among the willows. In front are more pastures on gently sloping hills. The ground is so good here that a little farther down the road environment and agriculture specialists were able to restore a deforested hill in a few decades through natural regeneration. That taught them to fence off other land to stop the free grazing of cattle.

Ap Singye's house is a two-story affair that we entered from the back, through a farmyard. Singye has done well in farming and from dabbling in other businesses locally. In fact, he wasn't home when we arrived, so someone sent to town for him. Singye was conversant with the world. A relative—I seem to recall it was his son—had gone to study in Hong Kong. He was eager to show me his house. The ground floor, as always in rural Bhutan, was left unfinished for storage space. The main rooms were on the floor above. We tarried longest in two of them, the kitchen and the family prayer room. The kitchen's centerpiece was a large smokeless stove made of clay, which dominated a corner of the room. This luxury gave the family clean air to breathe indoors, a marked improvement over traditional smoke-filled kitchens. Next to the kitchen was an empty room, with only a few long wooden poles suspended on ropes from the ceiling "to dry things," Singye explained. Later in another home, someone explained that the empty room would be given to a visiting monk or other distinguished guest. Monks are regularly invited into Bhutanese homes to perform special ceremonies for a family, not all of the rites strictly Buddhist. Monks can be called to cleanse a home of troublesome spirits or illness. They may be specialists in building talismans to ward off evil. They are there in birth, illness, and death.

A door from Singye's empty guest room toward the back of the house led to the family prayer room, which also served as the formal parlor. He ushered us to a rug-covered couch while his wife prepared hot buttered tea for us, with bowls of roasted grains to thicken the salty drink. While we waited, Singye talked about his family, and I had time to absorb the family altar opposite where we were seated. It was an exceptionally elaborate construction of wood, perhaps six feet wide, with gilded panels reaching to the ceiling. On the altar itself, there was an image of a sainted lama swathed in yellow silk, a silver pitcher of holy water topped by peacock feathers on its lid, a vase of cut grain, and a bowl of roasted cereals. There was also a stylized torma confection in gold or brass and the seven offering bowls filled symbolically with water. At the center of the assembly of religious objects was a sizable painting, about twelve by eighteen inches, of the Dalai Lama standing as if in a preaching pose, radiating light in rays above and around his head. It was framed in silver. Over the Dalai Lama's shoulder, several gilded images of Buddha looked down from niches in the altar's panels.

Singye and his family had most certainly invested a substantial part of their wealth in this altar. It stood alone in the sturdy but simple house as a kind of glittering chimera or a vision beheld in a dream of heaven. For

Bhutanese of middle age, the advent of a cash economy and the chance to accumulate a disposable income has meant the opportunity to glorify their homes and lives with altars worthy of their gods and deities. It has provided the wherewithal to give more generously to monks and monasteries and to undertake pilgrimages. For this first generation of beneficiaries of development, religion and the more rapid salvation of the soul have been the highest priorities.

But now what?

The signs of the future are already evident in Thimphu and Phuntsholing, where members of the next generation, now in their teens and twenties, are spending more time in shops, cinemas, and cafés than in temples. At the Institute of Traditional Medicine, Dr. Morisco didn't think anyone should be too complacent about Bhutan. "The Bhutanese face the same threats and dangers we have in the West," he said. "I mean, many of them, if they had the chance, they would go straight to New York and live in New York as a probably one hundred percent New Yorker. I don't think being Bhutanese there would make a difference. This is a society that has grown and formed itself over the centuries on the basis of Buddhist teachings, and that has given it special qualities. But the Bhutanese of today have inherited this without any merit of their own. Now they have to make their own choices. There is one good thing about the Bhutanese government, that is that it is an enlightened government, because it has an enlightened king. Definitely, the government is much more ahead than the people in controlling development. With more freedom, what choices would the people make? Like now there is a trend to go toward private businesses. That poses a lot of intrinsic problems because the government has been able to keep back all the negative development. Once the initiative goes to private business, I have serious doubts that many Bhutanese businessmen care a thing, for example, about nature."

Sonam Gyatso is a young monk who also worries about the future of Bhutan. At the age of twenty-eight, he gave up his career as an accountant, still a new profession, and turned back to religion. "I changed my dress and became monk," is how he described it. He had gone to Kathmandu to immerse himself in the study of classical Tibetan and the Buddhist philosophy, rejecting a chance to study in the South Indian city of Mysore, also a center of Buddhist scholarship, because it seemed too far away for him. He wanted to stay closer to Bhutan. In Kathmandu, he lived among other mountain people, mostly Ladakhis and Sherpas, while he studied and thought about how to help prop up his country's spirit.

"I pray to see our country in peace," he said. "There are so many struggles in Bhutan now. We are becoming unhappy people."

Chapter 11

ALL SENTIENT BEINGS

THE MONKS at one of Bhutan's most venerated temples were having a spat with the security officer assigned by the district's civil administrator to guard the shrines and enforce new rules against littering and the harboring of stray dogs. On a winter morning when sunshine bathed the temple courtyard and glinted off the golden-brass butter lamps set out to dry after a scrubbing, the administrator had lined up the abbot and half a dozen monks like so many schoolboys for a dressing-down. The ineffectual security officer, standing a few feet away, head down almost to his chest, had reported that he was the victim of a monkish conspiracy. Nobody in holy robes obeyed him, he said, though at this temple they were wards of the state. Monks refused to tidy up their quarters. They gave leftovers to the pariah dogs. Worst of all, the caretaker-guard alleged, they threatened him.

The administrator was livid. Striding back and forth in front of the silent, expressionless monks in their maroon robes and assorted running shoes, he admonished them sternly, told them that their campaign of noncompliance was over and they would henceforth pick up their trash and stop feeding stray animals. He then turned sharply on his heel and strode out of the monastery yard. As he approached the gate of this sacred place, a tiny, velvety-brown puppy loped happily toward him out of curiosity, hunger, or a search for affection, as baby animals do. As their paths crossed, the administrator, without missing a step, kicked the little dog out of his way, sending it rolling and squealing in pain and fright across the stones.

"In this place, there will be no dogs and no pigs," the administrator later explained calmly. "They are filthy and spread disease."

Bhutan has a stray-dog crisis, and it goes to the heart of the conflict between piety and progress in a Buddhist universe, where sparing the life and sensibilities of an animal is supposed to be an act of faith. Not infrequently and in many realms of activity in Bhutan and elsewhere in the Himalayas, monks and lamas are running into conflict with an increasingly intrusive and scientific state. The argument may be over opposition to modern medicine or the growth of secular education outside the monasteries, the spread of tourism to holy sites, or the treatment of animals, domestic or wild. As Rigzin Dorji made clear time and again, some topics may be open to debate, but there is really no latitude on the issue of protecting nonhuman life. All of us, down to the smallest mouse or insignificant insect, are sentient beings and therefore sacred in Buddha's eyes.

"Today my mother may be human," Rigzin Dorji said. "But when I die, I may be reborn as a dog, and then my mother may be a bitch. So therefore, you have to think that all living beings are my parents. My parents are infinite. Let my parents not suffer."

Carried to extremes, the rule defies reason and overrides instincts of human kindness, leading to cruelties no less painful than outright abuse. On a path to Sherubtse College, a dog had collapsed and was obviously dying slowly and agonizingly, its hairless body riddled with open abscesses. Why not put it to death? I asked. Buddhism tells us not to take life, was the reply. I heard that again when I encountered along the road a horse turned out of a village because it had broken a leg and could not work. The bone-thin animal was hobbling clumsily along the bed of a stream beyond the farmers' fields, dragging a useless back leg as it hunted for anything green and succulent on which to graze. No one apparently wanted it, or could afford to feed it just for pity's sake. Yet no villager dared risk the karmic consequences of an act of euthanasia.

Horses and ponies are having a tough time with modernization too. Twice on the stretch of road from Tongsa to Tashigang, we pulled over to help local people calm village horses that had been brought down to the paved road to shorten the route to market towns and were driven wild with fear as they encountered advancing buses and trucks for the first time. Bhutan had begun to join those developing nations where ruthless drivers, forgetting the rules about sentient beings, bully defenseless animals off the roads with misplaced bravado and even cruelty. We stopped because my Bhutanese companion on that trip was a village boy at heart and hated to see either farmers or animals suffer. First he ran to the assistance of a bewildered woman trying to recapture a crazed horse that had decided to escape the highway and run back to its village home after encountering a rattling, horn-blowing truck. That encounter passed off well: the horse recovered after the offending vehicle had disappeared around a bend. "Toot, toot!" the horse's owner shouted venomously, shaking her fists at the back of the receding truck.

The second case nearly ended in tragedy. An overloaded bus with a thoughtless driver honking his horn and screeching his brakes as he came toward us had no sooner passed by than we drove into the chaos he had left in his wake. A horse was rearing and whinnying in the middle of the road, its baskets of produce overturned and emptying in the dust and exhaust. A woman near tears was nearby, watching her son try to rein in the frantic animal. The boy soon lost control, and the horse began to gallop away senselessly, with the wild eyes of a beast possessed by demons. We crept along behind them in our car and asked the young man if he wanted to ride with us, thinking we could catch up with the horse and persuade it to stop. "No!" he said decisively. "It will surely throw itself into the ravine and die." We pulled off into a shallow ditch to wait out the drama.

My companion was off and running again, although the horse had a very long lead and might soon be out of sight. Suddenly a young woman appeared at a bend in the road ahead, and, sizing up the situation quickly, she walked slowly into the path of the terrified animal. She began speaking. The horse slowed for just a second, long enough for her to lunge for the reins. She clung to the still-skittish animal and was dragged for a few yards. Then it was all over. The horse stopped and let her stroke its head.

"You see," my Bhutanese companion explained, "that horse was cared for by a woman in his village. So when he heard the voice of a girl, he felt safe." The son took the reins and led the panting but footsure animal almost straight up the steep canyon beside the road, and fastened it to a tree out of sight of traffic, where it would be left to rest. He told us that the horse had never been out of its village on anything but a dirt trail; this was its first trip to town along the highway. The driver of the noisy bus had blasted his horn at an already wary animal on a road cut into a rocky hillside with no spare land left for refuge on either side. If a second bus jockey had come along, the horse might have chosen to plunge to its death. Fortunately, traffic is still light in Bhutan's farther reaches.

For the devout Buddhist, shouldering the burden of responsibility for animals can sometimes take tragicomic turns. In Nepal, where Hinduism and Buddhism coexist and sometimes overlap, Buddhists run from temple to temple in Kathmandu on certain Hindu festival days to pray for the souls of goats or other animals served up for ritual slaughter. In Bhutan, where Buddhists believe they can eat meat but not butcher animals, a farmer will bring fresh yak flesh to market but never admit to killing the yak. He will say that the yak, a surefooted, high-altitude animal, fell off a rock or met some other unlikely accident. Strips of meat are cured in the winter—sun-dried on the ground or air-dried on clotheslines—to make a delicacy appreciated everywhere in Bhutan. But I never saw a butcher shop. The only animal I saw butchered, in the privacy of someone's home, was a pig being cut up for the winter larder at the headquarters of a joint Bhutanese-European agriculture project. The pig, however, has very low status.

A seller's coyness about the origins of meat or the circumstances surrounding the death of the animal whose parts are for sale pose special problems for someone like Kelzang Tenzin, who struggled for years to make a modest success of the first European-style demi-haute-cuisine restaurant on a back alley in Thimphu, the Bhutanese capital. Optimistically, he called his bistro The Rendezvous, but it never quite lived up to its name. It was shrouded in gloom and empty last time I saw it, shortly before it closed, and its owner moved on to try his luck at the golf course café. Kelzang Tenzin trained as a chef at Holiday Inns in Hong Kong and Singapore and came back to Bhutan in the late 1980s determined to open a kitchen of international standards that would both educate Bhutanese and attract affluent foreigners from the offices of international development agencies and the handful of tourist hotels. He acknowledged when I met him over coffee that he was more or less done in early into the experiment by the absence of culinary herbs—and, more important, high-quality meat. Without good ingredients, his recipes were not very useful.

"Cooking in Bhutan has never been an important thing in life," he said. "People eat at home, and they eat simply. Religion has a lot to do with it. Because killing animals is not acceptable, a lot of our meat comes from India. It is of very poor quality, because animals there are not fed well and they are slaughtered too old, by primitive slaughtering methods. People in Bhutan don't want to catch fish, either, so I can't concentrate on that. We have very good, excellent rainbow trout, but I can't get enough of it. People don't want jobs that take life."

The annals of Bhutanese development economics are replete with tales of Buddhist intransigence in the face of new ideas that might affect the well-being of animals. Silk production will never reach the quantity or quality of neighboring countries, despairing officials say, because the Bhutanese will not throw cocoons with still-living silkworms into boiling water. In the town of Jakar, in Bumthang district, two young men from southern Bhutan, where Hinduism predominates, were tending a demonstration bee-keeping project when I dropped in one day. The royal government is urging farmers to produce honey for extra household income. Most Buddhist Bhutanese balk, saying that making honey kills bees. You can see them lying around on the grass, dead as can be, right in front of the hive, they insist. So many tiny souls at risk.

"We try to tell the northern Bhutanese people that the bees are not killed by our method," said Teknath Chamlagai, who introduced himself as a beekeeper-technician, educated in Alberta, Canada. The experimental bee station, resting on a small patch of clover meadow no more than a dip in a hillside, has developed special hives with multiple trays for extracting honey without the necessity of smoking out the bees. But skepticism still greets the explanation that worker bees self-destruct of their own volition and have not somehow given their lives to the honeypot. "These people don't want any bees to die in any way for the honey," Teknath said with a shake of his head.

In story and symbol, animals and birds enrich the lives of Bhutanese in many ways. Local artists decorate houses and shops with stylized paintings of deer, yak, snow lions, and, of course, dragons. At the center of Tibetan Buddhist paintings of the Wheel of Life are a rooster, snake, and boar—symbols of the three cardinal faults of passion, hatred, and delusion. In the Dragon Kingdom, it is somehow not surprising that the national animal is a sort of half-mythical beast called the takin. A takin, unique to high Himalayan reaches, has a buffalolike head with horns (and a very serious, slightly hangdog face) connected to the body of what could be a sturdy, overgrown furry goat. A few of them live, pathetically, in a fenced enclosure above the Motithang Hotel in Thimphu, but their true home is in the shadows of glaciers, in valleys above twelve thousand feet, where they share steep pastures with musk deer, blue sheep, snow leopards, Himalayan bear, and a number of rare pheasants and other wildfowl.

To the Bhutanese family living as high as thirteen thousand feet or more, all kinds of animals, wild and tame, are omnipresent and often essential in daily life. Domesticated beasts provide all the energy that can be harnessed in hamlets beyond the reach of roads, hydroelectricity, and kerosene-powered generators. Children come of age tending yaks or caring for horses, expanding their knowledge as they work. Father William Mackey, the Canadian Jesuit who has become a Bhutanese citizen and a high-ranking administrator in Bhutan's education department, said he learned decades ago when teaching math to village children that they instinctively understood numerical sets in a way a Western child did not. The knowledge came from tending animals.

"The little boy who takes the cows out, he knows he takes seven cows," the sprightly priest said as he passed around cakes during tea at his Thimphu home. "The foundation of sets, the mathematics of sets, that kid knows, because seven is not seven to him. There may be two cows up there on the hill, three down here in the field—where are the other two? Or four may be brown and three black. The concept of sets that kid knows before he comes to school. Or the little girl who lets out twelve chickens. She needs twelve back when she comes home, so she learns how to count them, six over here, five there, and so on. People on a farm have fantastic knowledge."

Beyond the farmyard, wild animals are omnipresent, blurring the lines that divide human habitation from the realm of other sentient beings, real or mythical, and the world of the spirits who share both spaces. Even in Thimphu, a capital city that is no more than a frontier outpost, bears and panthers prowl. Townspeople tell stories of big mountain cats that snack on chickens and pet dogs, disappearing afterward to sleep off the feast in the trackless surrounding forests. When terrorism began to empty hamlets in southern Bhutan after an ethnic Nepali insurgency took off in the early 1990s, loyal citizens who remained soon complained that wild beasts were returning from the tropical jungles to reclaim the abandoned fields and threaten the families who chose to stay behind. The south has a hot, dense landscape, where not only buffalo but also elephants, tigers, rhinoceros, and deer roam among the mixture of bamboo, chik grass, and temperate-zone trees.

Guests at the Motithang Hotel, on the edge of Thimphu, used to be told to stay indoors at night to avoid the perils of unexpectedly running into wildlife—especially bears or big cats. When my husband and I stayed at the Motithang several years ago, we took the staff's advice. Consequently, the only Himalayan bear we saw was in the drafty lobby, dead and stuffed. Wearing a ferocious snarl, it reared up on its hind legs, its ears wired out at forty-five-degree angles from its massive fur head. But in its forepaws, the poor bear had been humiliated into holding a tray with a red, blue, and green straw basket resting on it. About a dozen pink and white paper flowers on plastic stems with shiny green leaves stuck out stiffly over the basket's edge. The whole effect was ludicrous but sad. Last time I passed by the Motithang to see if there were still takin, the national animal, living in the enclosure up the hill, the lobby was being remodeled for a more sophisticated tourist age. What, I asked myself, will be the fate of the peaceful bear and his bouquet?

Animals portrayed by dancers wearing huge lifelike masks are important components of religious festivals or, increasingly, classical dance performances. In the Stag Dance, which can be performed by monks or laymen or a combination of both, a hunter is brought before the Lord of Death to argue for the best afterlife possible based on his worldly deeds. Unfortunately, his life has included a lot of animal killing, and in the end he is doomed because the fruits of his vocation outweigh his many acts of Buddhist merit. The Lord of Death sentences him to be reincarnated as each of the animals whose life he has taken, and then to experience five hundred deaths in each of those beastly incarnations. In the dance that tells the story, performers wearing heavy stag heads leap and spin with extraordinary strength and vigor. Occasionally, a dancer seems close to collapse as he exits the "stage"—often an open field or courtyard—to be helped by attendants who quickly remove the top-heavy animal mask and relieve the pressure on his head.

Animals and birds also play prominent roles in many moral tales, including the beloved fable of the Four Friends. In the Bhutanese version of this story, a bird, a rabbit, a monkey, and an elephant combine their talents to provide themselves a perennial supply of delicious fruit. The bird found and planted a seed, which was watered by the rabbit, fertilized by the monkey, and guarded by the elephant. When the tree grew and blossomed, the four again worked as a team to pick the fruit that soon appeared. The elephant stood by the trunk, and the rabbit, monkey, and bird climbed on its back to build a tower to the high branches where the best fruit grew. The Four Friends are painted frequently on the walls of temples as well as homes and shops.

At Simtokha Dzong, a seventeenth-century monastery and school, Sangay Wangchuck of the Central Monastic Secretariat paused before a large rendition of the familiar Four Friends parable and placed the tale in a theological perspective. A novice monk of about six or seven stood nearby, rapt (and runny-nosed) as the discourse progressed. As he watched us, his red robe slipped from his small shoulder, revealing a sweatshirt that said, in one of those grab-bag attempts at English so common to Asian bazaars, "High Casual Step It." It was oddly appropriate to the four creatures standing one atop another's back, all eyes on the ripening fruit.

"These are the four brothers, the four very, very good friends; best friends," Sangay Wangchuck was explaining. "So the bird is the Buddha, the rabbit is his closest attendant. He has two main disciples. The monkey is Shariputra, and the elephant is the Maudgalyayana." I nodded, convinced anew that I would never master the basics of a religion where Buddha always turns up where you least expect him, and in a new context. Shariputra, hailed for his wisdom, and Maudgalyayana, who had paranormal powers, were Buddha's chief disciples during his lifetime, I later learned from John Snelling's *Buddhist Handbook.* "Buddhists believe that if you have this one picture," Sangay Wangchuck went on, "then you pacify all the negatives and have better friendship." That part I understood.

I wonder: is it sheer coincidence that the Bremen Town Musicians of German folklore—the donkey, dog, cat, and rooster who scared away brigands—are also four animal friends, or, more precisely, three animals and a bird?

In Mongar, a mountain town of cascading bougainvillea, more beautiful than any overcrowded hill station in India, Dasho Lhakpa Dorji, the dzongda, told stories over dinner about local farmers' efforts to strike a balance among crops, animals, and religion. Several years ago, he said, farmers on the steep hillsides where every available bit of land that could be plowed had been planted found that they and their domesticated animals were vulnerable to wolves. Putting aside theology in the face of an economic crisis, the mountain people had begun killing any wolf identified as a predator. That is usually permissible in Bhutan if the culling takes place on one's own property.

"Well, then they found that with the number of wolves reduced, the wild boars were taking over," the dzongda said. "Wolves had been keeping the wild boar population down. Now we have to think about what can be done—to stop killing wolves, or limit the boars."

Killing boars isn't the answer here or anywhere else, advised Khenpo Phuntsok Tashi, a religious scribe, in an article in *Kuensel*. "In our belief, killing boars only causes them to multiply, assisted by local nature goddesses," he said. This path leads only to more destruction from a vengeful species, he warned. Better to protect the crops, the khenpo said. "If you want to protect your feet against thorns, you cannot cover the whole landscape with leather. It is easier and wiser to put a small piece of leather under your feet!"

It is that homeless dog population, however, that will truly test the limits of theology as Bhutan develops. Already, dogs take a lot of abuse, getting kicked and stoned regularly enough to make them wary of humans, Buddhism notwithstanding. But there is enough ambivalence on the issue of dog control to ensure a continuing supply of strays in the near future. Most wayfarers who inevitably arrive in Paro or Thimphu late in the day discover the dog problem unexpectedly in the middle of the night, just after drifting into a peaceful sleep in the pure mountain air.

Twilight does not linger in the high Himalayan valleys. The sun drops quickly behind the hills and peaks, taking the pleasant daytime temperature with it. As the thermometer's mercury plunges, life moves indoors and the kind of peace that dwarfs humanity in these gigantic natural settings descends on villages and towns. White and yellow pools of light from naked bulbs draw families around small stoves where rice is ready to be ladled into basket-plates, thick hot tea simmers, and children begin to doze. In Thimphu's central square, the busy jeep-taxis, parked backs to the wall, eager to spring out for a fare during daylight hours, collect the last of the marketgoers and vanish with the night. That's when the dogs take over.

Feral Tibetan apsos and former pets of foreign pedigree, local pye-dogs of every size and hue, silken longhairs of unidentifiable breeds, and battle-scarred mutts from South Asia's infinite store of mangy mongrels—out of the shadows and rain gutters and construction sites they come; up from the Changlimithang archery field and royal basketball court, past the shuttered Yangchenma bookshop, down the hill through the labyrinth of lanes behind the Swiss Bakery. After sniffing their way around the square at a trot, they arrange themselves in ones and twos on the stoops of darkened shops and offices, nose to paws, and go to sleep. No longer on the lookout for stone-throwing citizens, they yawn and scratch and snuggle, looking like piles of fur left out to air. This is temporary.

Some time later, prompted by some secret, primordial signal, the half-wild dogs, as if uneasy in human civilization, begin to bark and howl. A piercing chorus of yaps and hoots shatters the heavy silence. In the distant, dark recesses of the narrow Thimphu Valley and from the driveways and byways of the nearer sheltering hills, dotted with houses, other dogs respond, rending the peace with fearsome announcements. And then it is over. But they have made their point. The square, the town, the valley, and the night belong to them.

Whether the dogs bark or howl, and where, is not without meaning.

"Bhutanese believe domestic animals can give us signs," Dasho Rinzin Gyetsen, the dzongda of Tashigang, told me in a conversation over tea one evening in the garden gazebo of a guesthouse overlooking his spectacularly situated dzong, more than twelve hundred feet above a narrow river valley. For reasons that would elude most people, the guesthouse management had contrived to block out the panoramic view afforded by the hexagonal pavilion by hanging cheap lace curtains on all the windows. "A horse that won't go forward can be a warning," the dasho said, as a respectful waiter hovered with a teapot. "And the dog howling in the night—see which way he points. If he points at a certain house, the devil has entered that house and claimed a soul. The person may not die right away, but his soul has been taken."

Apart from their function as messengers of doom, the dogs, of course, could be rabid—enough of them, at least, to worry health officers. Children are getting bitten, an epidemiologist said mournfully. "Very often. Yes. Very often. The dogs should be put down. Yes. Yes. There are thousands and thousands of them. More every day. There is a hue and cry. Yes. Yes. But we Bhutanese are Buddhists. The people would never stand for this. The dogs, too, have a right to live. Most Bhutanese people believe this."

One evening, from my cold little room at the Druk Hotel, overlooking Thimphu's main square, I got a demonstration of what he meant. Watching the town settle down for the night, I noticed a ritual I had missed before. Around the corner from the pavement where a scooter repairman worked all day in the sun in front of his shop, a chubby woman, a warm woolly sweater pulled over her kira, was heading resolutely into the center of town, a battered aluminum cooking pot under her arm. At the edge of the square, she bent down and poured a pile of cooked rice on the pavement, scraping the pot with her wooden spoon, alerting the hounds. Minutes later, from a grocery shop nearby, a few slices of stale bread sailed out to the street, to be gratefully received by a yellow-white mongrel too late for the rice. All around town, the mangy dogs were being fed. The process is repeated all over the country every day, frustrating would-be reformers.

Some dzongdas, using their considerable powers over the lives of the districts they govern, have devised novel ways to curb the proliferation of dogs while stopping short of killing them and inflaming public opinion. It's a struggle, said Pem Dorji, the dzongda of Bumthang.

"Last year, I tried to get rid of the dogs, but the people were against everything I wanted to do," he said as we toured the countryside around Jakar. "Finally, I collected live dogs. People got a reward for bringing them in. I put three hundred dogs on trucks and took them over the mountains to Lingmithang." That's a distance of more than seventy-five miles, over two high passses—one of them, Thumsing La, at 12,465 feet, the highest road pass in Bhutan. The dzongda was bowled over by what happened next. "After two months, the dogs came back," he said incredulously. "They crossed the Thumsing La and they came back!

"This year I had another idea," he said. "What we are trying to do now is make the dogs sterile. I got my veterinary officer to castrate them, and then we cut off their tails to show what dogs have been operated on." From what I could see, the tails were still ahead of the no-tails, but it was early in the game and Pem Dorji is not a man who accepts defeat.

In some districts, Bhutanese have apparently been persuaded to agree to the killing of potentially rabid animals or other strays with lethal injections of chemicals shot from dart guns. In effect, some animals are being overdosed with tranquilizers. Dasho Lhakpa Dorji—now dzongda of Mongar, and best known by his nickname, Jack—recalled how as district officer in Paro several years ago he had struck a deal with the manager of the Olathang Hotel, a tourist stopover in a woodland setting that had also become a haven for cats. Three large felines in particular had been behaving offensively.

"The Olathang wanted to get rid of these three cats that were doing what cats do wherever they wanted to do it, messing up the hotel," he said. "So we called in the shooter for the cats, and I got rid of a lot of dogs at the same time." It wasn't clear whether the shooter in question used tranquilizers or bullets—Bhutanese can be cagey about this—but in any case Jack's triumph was short-lived. "It was much better for a while. But before long, somebody sent down a truckload of stray dogs from Thimphu," he said, laughing at the absurdity of truckloads of mongrels moving from town to town as supplies rose and fell.

All Bhutanese administrators know the perils of offending Buddhist sensibilities when dealing with unwanted animals. Nevertheless, not long ago in Shemgang, in south-central Bhutan, somebody decided on a drastic and probably misguided strategy. Pieces of meat were left around town laced with strychnine. More than one hundred dogs died, but in agony, according to a letter to the editor of *Kuensel* from a foreigner in town, who reported that some animals took up to five hours to die. "In this period, the dogs vomited, went into convulsions, got drowsy, and repeated the cycle." Cats also were poisoned, along with birds that pecked at the vomit of the doomed dogs. In all, it was a most un-Bhutanese event.

"If you are born among the animals, you don't have the chance to understand the truth, and you suffer," said Dasho Rigzin Dorji. But that does not give those in human form the right to use lethal measures when there is imbalance or disorder among speechless, uncomprehending beasts. "If you kill something, you are reborn among hell-beings," he said. "So therefore, breaking the vows as a Buddhist is a serious crime. Then for many eons, there is no chance of Buddhahood."

Chapter 12

AUM RINZI'S
WORLD

"IN THE OLD DAYS before they built the motor road, travel by horse was much more fun," said Aum Rinzi, a septuagenarian who was once a member of the royal court. "There was a lot more pomp to it all," she recalls, as she sits surrounded by old photographs from the days when India was under the British Raj and the Bhutanese were a little-known, exotic people living in a Himalayan kingdom at the juncture of heaven and earth. The Bhutan of her childhood and young adulthood has not entirely vanished, she says, but those who traverse the kingdom now need sharp eyes and a scaled-down sense of urgency to appreciate the old life. We need to tarry more in the splendor of magnificent temples and the peace of gentle meadows.

On trips from west to east and north to south, I thought of Aum Rinzi often and tried to imagine what she had seen, or would see now, along the new roads that weren't there until late in her life. These few roads, merely narrow ribbons of tarmac barely denting a wild landscape of dark forests and bottomless gorges, nonetheless have too quickly become the parameters of contemporary life, preempting many choices for visitors of what to see or where to go. But the few highways do make travel viable in Bhutan for those whose time is limited to something short of a grand expedition, so there is no point in being Luddite about them.

When British political agents, attached first to the East India Company and later to the colonial government of India, toured a wary Bhutan in the eighteenth and nineteenth centuries, they and their extensive entourages of military aides, doctors, ecological specimen collectors, watercolorists, and occasional spouses traveled a rough road, when there was a road at all. They trudged along perilous narrow trails over passes as high as seventeen thousand feet and suffered altitude sickness, snow blindness, and a catalogue of fevers. They swung on rope-and-bamboo bridges over ravines hundreds of feet deep, slid along glaciers, and watched pack animals, provisions, and porters plunge over cliff faces. Mules died from eating poisonous plants.

In 1909, when John Claude White wrote the introduction to *Sikkim and Bhutan*—one of the best books ever written on the region, despite its author's arrogant, even insufferable, attitude toward many of the locals—he explained that he was devoting a good deal of space to the history and culture of the Bhutanese to counter the negative impressions left by his predecessors. He quoted this dismissive bureaucratic summary of Bhutan from the preface to an 1894 British gazetteer: "No one wishes to explore that tangle of jungle-clad and fever-stricken hills, infested with leeches and the pipsa fly, and offering no compensating advantage to the most enterprising pioneer. Adventure looks beyond Bhutan. Science passes it by as a region not sufficiently characteristic to merit special exploration."

This dyspeptic and uncharitable colonial scribe would hardly have anticipated that a century later, time and the experiences of his successors would prove him wrong on all counts. In the hundred years that have passed, Bhutan has become more, not less, of an attraction. Because it has preserved its jungle-clad hills and forested mountains while other Himalayan regions have stripped and eroded theirs, this small kingdom is a wonderland for environmentalists. Many epidemic diseases have been conquered or controlled, though leeches still flourish (and abdominal and lung infections are still killers of children, the weak, and the elderly in remote villages). For the adventurer, mountain peaks remain unscaled, and sometimes also unnamed. Ecologists and naturalists come to marvel at nature and wildlife: groves of tree-tall rhododendrons, butterflies of amazing size and coloration, exotic birds flying free, and endangered animals found in few other habitats.

Culturally, you are there the moment the plane touches down on land that might otherwise be rice fields. There is no town, no airport highway. There is no necessity or requirement, as with travel to Sikkim or Ladakh, to traverse the wholly different, encircling, dominating cultures of Hinduism or Islam to arrive at the gate of this mountain nation. One arrives in Bhutan without excess mental baggage picked up from facilitators: the Kashmiris running the buses and taxis to Leh, the Bengalis and Biharis who deliver you to Sikkim. There is no colonial history or architecture to get in the way of what is Bhutanese. Except for the small airport, and lately a few new hotels, the Paro Valley wouldn't have looked much different decades ago to Aum Rinzi, or to White half a century earlier.

When White went to Bhutan as political officer for the first time, in the spring of 1905, it had been decades since the last British agent, Ashley Eden, had visited the hermetic country—and he had been roundly humiliated by the Bhutanese in subtle and unsubtle ways. London had to maintain a relationship with Bhutan because of its location on the tricky northern rim of British India, where a Himalayan version of the Great Game was played by Tibetans, Chinese, Russians, and assorted other parties. For generations, the Bhutanese made the job of diplomacy as difficult as possible for foreigners, a story gracefully and authoritatively told by Peter Collister in *Bhutan and the British*. But attitudes on both sides had changed significantly by 1904, when Ugyen Wangchuck (then Tongsa penlop and later the first king) decided to cooperate with the British against the Tibetans, and so a year later White and his party, complete with pipes and drums "and the usual following of chupprassies and servants," were struggling across the snowy passes from Sikkim through Tibet's Chumbi Valley toward a lavish Bhutanese welcome. "The arrangements were so good they augured well for the future welfare of our mission," White wrote. He had come to present Ugyen Wangchuck with the title and insignia of a Knight Companion of the Indian Empire, and to explore ways to further improve ties between the Bhutanese and British.

Visitors arriving nearly a century later no longer enter Bhutan over mountain passes from Tibet, which the Chinese, Bhutanese, and Indians have declared off limits to foreigners for a variety of strategic and diplomatic reasons. But tourists do land not far from where White first tarried for a few days of rest after his arduous trek from Sikkim, and where he was assigned a comfortable tent and given "tea, oranges and fruit for our refreshment." From there he went to Tashichodzong, in what is now Thimphu, the national capital. Most tourists start with the same itinerary, and as they proceed from one "night halt" to the next across the country, they measure their journey in dzongs: Punakha, Wangdi-phrodang, Tongsa, Jakar, Tashigang. The distinctive silhouettes of these fortress-monasteries are still the major landmarks of the kingdom. Their architecture is unique: the high, thick walls may slope inward as they rise, as they do in the palaces and monasteries of Tibet and Ladakh, but Bhutanese buildings, more or less perennially under repair, are now probably the richest of any in craftsmanship inside and out. Only the new gompas of Kathmandu would rival them in artisanship, though not in the value of their antiquities or the timeless magnificence of their sturdy half-timbered walls and chambers.

The small British BAE-146 aircraft—there are a total of two of them (both blessed by lamas) that compose Druk Air, the national carrier—slip almost noiselessly between forested hills as they approach the airstrip at Paro, probably the longest straight stretch of paved surface in Bhutan (if you don't count the mysterious runway the Indian military built for itself in the middle of nowhere off the road to Kanglung in eastern Bhutan). To someone sitting on the lawn of the Olathang Hotel in Paro, the appearance of the small plane in the afternoon sky is always a little star-tling and incongruous, as if it had wandered in from some other universe and was looking for a place to rest. For those trying hard to avoid a clichéd allusion to the tale of Shangri-la, the experience of landing in Paro is pretty much irresistibly evocative of James Hilton's fictional ac-count of a landing (but without the crash) in that hidden valley in Tibet. Like British expeditions of old, arriving foreigners are still met by a guide if not a welcoming party. The Bhutanese see their guide-escort service as partly a manifestation of their traditional hospitality to the outsiders they have decided to admit, and partly a way to keep foreigners under what in other, less friendly countries would be called surveillance.

The journey from the Paro airport to anywhere else begins with a brief but ethereal passage between rows of willows along a rushing stream. The narrow lane meets the main road at a ramshackle collection of shops that the newcomer frequently mistakes for Paro town. Unless you have asked to stop over or spend the night in Paro (coming or going from Bhutan), you will not see it, or its magnificent dzong and museum. The broad Paro Valley is noted for its rich farmlands and its appropriately better-than-average houses. Although most homes in Bhutan share the same half-timbered architectural style, the houses in Paro are often grander and are almost always distinguished by windows of three tiers (instead of the usual two) in height. To understand this arrangement, imagine a large picture window perhaps six by eight feet, divided into nine smaller windows, stacked three to a row. Each small window is framed in Bhutanese style, rectangular except for a trefoil pattern at the top, rather like an elaborate Moorish arch. The outer wallspace of a house devoted to windows generally shrinks in proportion to the distance traveled from Paro, though there are all kinds of exceptions. Relatively spacious windows can be found on the better houses of Bumthang, half a country away. And once on a morning walk along a hillside above Thimphu, the center of wealth and influence, I saw a traditional window rendered in *trompe l'oeil* on the side of a very small cottage where, perhaps, the budget didn't extend to wood and glass. Outside the major towns, most Bhutanese do not have glass. Windows are not covered, except by shutters or sliding wood panels that close from the inside at night and during cold or wet weather.

Whatever the dimensions or number of internal components of a real Bhutanese window, it is always handcrafted by woodcarvers working on the ground before it is lifted into the wood-frame, rammed-earth, or stone-walled house. The tiered windows are carved of a pleasing golden timber from a local hardwood tree. The frames may remain unfinished, to weather as the seasons change, or may be painted in intricate patterns and folk-art symbols, most with religious significance.

One winter afternoon on the road from Paro to Thimphu, I stopped with a retired government official of Aum Rinzi's generation to watch two local painters decorating the window frames and nearly every other piece of exposed wood on a new two-story home. The lower level of the house was, as is customary, reserved for farm equipment, animals, and crop storage and was left mostly unadorned. But the half-timbered upper story had become a limitless canvas for the artists, two young men bundled in scarves against the wind that blew over the plank on which they sat, which had been suspended on what amounted to a swing fastened to the roof. They had a small carton of assorted paints in cans and bottles, from which they both worked. The colors they used were traditional and locally made from plants, earth, and minerals. These natural paints, slightly muted in tone, have a longer life than brighter synthetics, I was told in Tongsa, where the dzongda showed me the evidence on two contrasting walls of the dzong. The store-bought paint like that used everywhere else in the Himalayas had faded in a generation; the traditional paint had not lost its colors in a century. The subdued old hues certainly have a more pleasing appearance, not only in the decorative arts but also in woven fabrics.

The painters working on the roadside house had begun by tinting all the wooden trim either a muted gray-blue or terra-cotta: blue for the wall timbering, terra-cotta for the window frames and a foot-tall base-board that delineated the upper story from the one below. On the painted wood, the artists then added bright lotuses or other stylized flowers, geometric designs, chains of conch shells and clouds, vases sym-bolizing repositories of Buddhist doctrine, and rows of white dots. All were combinations of four basic colors: the gray-blue and terra-cotta of the base paint, along with white and mustard gold. Only occasionally, a spot of green was employed or a pale blue was added for contrast. In this house, the windows had eight panels, set in two rows of four frames each. Each small frame was about two feet high and a foot wide. Using only their homemade paints, the folk artists had skillfully transformed each frame, with its trefoil top, into a miniature arch lined with gold, resting on columns, and generously capped with flowers. The eight arched inner frames were then enclosed by an outer frame trimmed in a contrasting pattern. Above the windows, where plaster walls met the overhanging roof, the end of each exposed crossbeam had also been individually decorated, as was the space between them. Thus a band of colorful shapes encircled the house at roof level. Set against the white-wash of the walls, however, this ornamentation, though intense, is never garish, perhaps because of the repetition of colors and shapes and the artists' refined sense of balance in design. Every symbol or pattern seemed right for the surface or space on which it was painted.

Apart from the traditional architecture, there are other enticements in Paro. Instead of turning off the airport road toward Chhuzom—literally the crossroads of Bhutan, where the north-south road meets the east-west highway—the traveler can detour instead through Paro town and on to Drukyel Dzong. Paro may not be very picturesque, but it illus-trates the extreme recentness of the kingdom's commercial develop-ment. Although visitors to Paro nearly a century ago remarked that there were as many as thirty houses, there was no business quarter, and there was none when Aum Rinzi traveled these routes, then trails. Dago Tshering, Bhutan's home minister, remembers walking as a boy from Paro over mountain paths to the new national capital at Thimphu, when modern towns were just beginning to evolve. Most Bhutanese commercial centers have been built since the 1960s, after the construction of roads and the introduction of a cash economy. These towns, still mostly in the shadows of dzongs, function almost entirely as service areas selling fuel and provisions and offering basic health care and education.

The history of the Paro Valley begins with the legendary origins of Buddhism in Bhutan. According to the Bhutanese, it was near here that the Tibetan king Songtsen Gampo built a temple in the seventh century, one of 108 temples intended to pin down the extremities of the giant she-devil who had sprawled maliciously across the Himalayas. (The Bhutanese were nailing down demons with chortens well into the eighteenth century.) The Paro temple may have lured the Guru Rinpoche—the missionary Padmasambhava from the Swat Valley of Pakistan—to this sacred spot a century later. Bhutanese mythology says that when the Guru Rinpoche flew here on the back of his miraculous tiger, he landed at Taktsang, now a cliffside monastery more than 2,500 feet above the valley floor. Eight classes of evil spirits were subdued by the Guru before he went on to perform other stupendous feats elsewhere in the country. By the fifteenth century, the monastery was known across the Himalayas as a place of meditation for great Tibetan saints, including Milarepa. The monastery, fused to the sheer-rock cliff face, remains a very holy spot, barred to tourists, who nonetheless trek and climb hours to a nearby ledge just to get a closer view.

Beyond the approach to Taktsang, the paved road from Paro town comes to an end near Drukyel Dzong, the ruins of a seventeenth-century fortress that burned to a shell in 1951. "Pens," said two little boys who had learned there may be rewards in scampering along with visitors who climb the steep hill to reach the skeletal dzong through a series of walled courtyards where wildflowers grow. This was the first time in several trips that anyone had asked me for anything in Bhutan, and I tried to ignore the request. The path passed a pocket-size monastery, where the chants of monks mingled with the scolding that a woman keeping house for them gave my two little hiking companions as they babbled their way up the trail. For the moment, the pens were forgotten.

Drukyel Dzong, within view of sacred Mount Jhomolhari, once guarded an approach from Tibet, one of four passes into Bhutan available to marauding Tibetan armies as well as to pilgrims and traders moving in both directions in the days, now gone, when the Bhutanese and

Tibetans of Aum Rinzi's generation inhabited one cultural and spiritual world. From the ramparts of the ruined dzong, while the local boys ran here and there collecting flowers they now knew I seemed to like, I looked down to the road below, where a few horses were tethered outside a lazy trading post. It is not hard to imagine a scene of much more activity not many years ago when pack animals might have been forming up for an excursion. We can only mourn the rupture of daily human contact between Bhutan and Tibet.

A Bhutanese geography book for children of junior high school age—one of a series of innovative new texts that base learning on local themes and experiences—includes reminiscences of the Tibetan trade drawn from the memory of a retired *thrimpon,* or magistrate, Dasho Reddy. As a young man living in an age of barter, he and his companions traveled regularly from Paro to Phari, in eastern Tibet, to sell varieties of roasted or fried grains that are mixed with tea or other drinks in Himalayan homes, along with wood products from forested Bhutan that were scarce on large areas of the windblown Tibetan plateau. Tibetan and Bhutanese products could also be traded for manufactured goods along the border with India. This is Thrimpon Reddy's story:

"We used to carry rice, *seap, zauw, kaapchhi* [roasted grains], dried fruits, and even wooden handles for axes, knives and spades. In return we used get brown salt, wool, silk, tea, and soda. Until the mid-1940s, salt was brought from Tibet. We used to bring the salt from Phari for sale in places like Phuntsholing, Pasakha, Dagana, and Samchi in exchange for cotton clothes, utensils, sugar, and tobacco. We used horses, particularly mules, to carry the loads to Phari. This was a hard five-day journey from Paro when we traveled with horses and luggage. Journeys had to be made during the dry seasons of spring and autumn. I think the worst thing, and most difficult part of the journey, used to be our fear of *amdos,* the Tibetan highwaymen. This seemed to happen around the 1920s onward for some reasons which I do not know. So we had to travel in groups for our protection. Traveling alone and without the support of able companions was out of the question."

Bhutanese and Tibetans, once linked by monastic orders and trading caravans, are today divided by geopolitics into two antagonistic spheres. After Beijing began to suppress Tibetan nationalism and dilute Tibet's ethnic composition and its Tantric Buddhist culture following the 1959 rebellion against Communist Chinese rule, and after China's attacks on

India in 1962, Bhutan had little option but to cast its lot with New Delhi, whose army regards these hills as part of its own frontier. To do otherwise would have put Bhutanese independence in jeopardy. Thus, open borders and overland journeys to the great Tibetan temples at Lhasa, Ralung, or elsewhere are only memories among elderly Bhutanese and those Tibetan exiles who fled here before the borders closed.

"In olden days, many Bhutanese people used to go to Tibet for higher education," Rinpoche Mynar Trilku told me. The rinpoche, who was born in Tibet but fled the year the Dalai Lama went into exile, is now the curator of Bhutan's National Museum. "Many of the most learned Bhutanese monks we have here, who are called as *gyshye*—which means professor or doctor of divinity—took all their degrees and studies in Tibet." Because of the tradition of sending monks to Tibetan monastic institutions, the Bhutanese clergy never established major centers of learning or religious publication in their own country. That is not to say that Bhutanese monasteries did not produce great scholars or commentators, the rinpoche hastened to add. It's only that the pinnacle of Tibet was so high, its lights so bright, and its influence so wide that all others stood in its shadow.

Still, the dzong named Drukyel—"Victory of the Druk People"—is a reminder that life next door to Tibet had its downs as well as its better moments. Historical records say that the fortress was built by Ngawang Namgyal, the seventeenth-century unifier of Bhutan, to celebrate the 1644 defeat of a Tibetan army apparently bent on taking Paro, about fifteen miles away, one of more than half a dozen Tibetan attacks over several decades. About the same time that Drukyel Dzong was being constructed, another large fortress was going up in Paro, the Rinpung Dzong. This solid, square fortress-monastery, though periodically ravaged by fire over the years, remains the capital of Paro district and the site of one of Bhutan's best-known religious-folk festivals of music and dance, the Paro Tshechu, held each spring. The fortress, which most people call Paro Dzong, has all the local history. The dzong's old watchtower, Ta Dzong, several miles up the hill above the fortress, houses the National Museum.

I was in one of the museum's upper galleries, sneaking another look at Bhutan's brief but wildly eccentric postal history—stamps in honor of Walt Disney, mushrooms, and a classic Rolls-Royce—when Rinpoche Mynar Trilku came along to answer some of my questions about more serious exhibits of thangkas, images, and objects used in worship. Some of the items displayed are so sacred that all visitors to the museum must circumambulate the galleries in a clockwise direction, as if all the rooms were temples. The rinpoche, who was wearing a giant plastic wristwatch with a bright orange face, is a genial monk with a ready smile who radiates enthusiasm when he talks about his collection. His lively discourse brings the chilly and dimly lit galleries to life and gives them meaning. Though a scholar of renown, he revels in the thought that in Bhutan the past is not confined to artifacts and academics but is still alive and all around us.

"I think that in many of the European countries a museum is where you go to see something of the past—unless it is a modern art museum," he said. "Normally you try to learn there what people have forgotten. But here this is a living museum. On auspicious days, we have lots of local visitors. They are coming to the museum not really to see the collection. They come here to take the blessings from the images. As a result you see that in two galleries we always burn the butter lamp and bring the waters, and put incense and everything, which sometimes may be against the conservation rules. International conservation rules don't allow that because of the precious thangkas."

Bhutan resists demands from grant-giving foreigners that its museum be sanitized. The rinpoche has taken his persuasive case for keeping this a living museum to the doors of international art experts raised on more orthodox galleries, places where people would not feel at home as they do here padding around with prayer beads, mumbling mantras. He scents victory.

"Recently when I have attended some of the conservation meetings, they note it may not be really bad to do what we do. They are now saying: Suppose an image in a monastery for three-four hundred years has been exposed to that kind of heat with the butter lamps, that kind of smoke. If you take it out and keep it in a museum without this environment surrounding it, the decay of that piece may be worse."

From the rinpoche's viewpoint, a visit to this museum may be educational but should never be merely an intellectual exercise. The intricate and colorful torma offerings, the amulets, the robes, the vessels of copper, the stuffed wild animals, the images of bodhisattvas, all objects (except maybe the stamps and the antique armory), speak of the daily intermingling of life and belief. "Here all can see what kind of offerings we make, how the images are placed, what are the venerations," the rinpoche said. "And all of this is real—no reproductions."

The first time I came to Paro, late on a spring afternoon, fresh from the mania of Kathmandu, I stumbled into another kind of unexpected encounter with the continuity and authenticity of Bhutanese life. The occasion was an archery contest on a field near the sixteenth-century Druk Choeding temple. Archery, Bhutan's national sport, is also a ritual with roots in a warrior past. The archers, whose powerful bows shoot arrows to targets nearly four hundred feet away with a speed that makes following the line of flight almost impossible, celebrate each score with a brief slow-motion dance accompanied by incantations and howls drawn up from a timeless past. The effect is electrifying and chilling in its other-worldliness. So much so that it took a few extra minutes to notice that some of the archers were using hi-tech American-made Hoyt bows. The bows, and argyle knee socks from New York or London to wear with a gentleman's gho, are among the country's most highly prized imports.

The trip from Paro to Thimphu, everyone's jumping-off point and provisioning place for a road tour of Bhutan, takes less than two hours. But the short journey is a primer for what is to come. As the Paro Valley narrows, the eye catches small temples or monasteries identified by a wide red band painted high on the outer whitewashed walls. There are farmers at work in their fields near farmhouses not only decorated in the distinctive colors that enliven window frames but also adorned with folk paintings on the walls. Folk artists have a pretty standard repertory of themes: real and mythological animals, some of them characters in fables, and phalluses. It is not unusual to see a large erect penis or, better, two, one painted on each side of the door, gently adorned by the artists' rendition of floating ribbons and sometimes flowers. Wooden phallus shapes accompanied by daggers dangle from the eaves of homes; an erect clay phallus may protrude over a doorway, draped in a silken *thaka,* a gauzy white scarf. These serve not as fertility symbols, as I was once told erroneously by a guide reluctant in his modernity to discuss superstitious throwbacks, but as guardians and protectors of the home.

Long before Chhuzom, the road begins to snake through a gorge, clinging to hillsides or teetering along the edges of cliffs. It will get much, much worse, but not until after Thimphu, when fear and nausea begin to compete ferociously for attention in the consciousness of many a tourist. It doesn't help that most four-wheel-drive vehicles in Bhutan run on diesel fuel and reconditioned engines. Straining on steep gradients, the motor pours clouds of acrid black smoke through ventilator ducts into passengers' faces and clothes. One begins to appreciate Aum Rinzi's revulsion for the age of motor travel.

Racketing cars and trucks are quickly coming to symbolize what Bhutan gave up in tranquillity when highway construction began not so long ago. It may seem strange to us, but in many developing countries there is a real debate about the cultural destruction caused by roadbuilding, which often speeds up unwanted urbanization as farm folk flock to town. On the other hand, there are advantages. People who would surely have died of disease or injury can be brought to hospitals if they are reasonably near a roadhead. Mobile medical teams bearing vaccines and antibiotics can reach isolated hamlets in a shorter time. Families living at subsistence level can improve their lives by raising crops to bring to market and sell for cash to buy small luxuries or different foods to diversify and improve their diets. In Bhutan, whole hillsides are being turned into orchards because harvests can be loaded on the bus or jeep for quick transport to Thimphu or Phuntsholing. A bumper fruit or vegetable harvest might mean new clothes for the children, a radio, or a gas-cylinder stove.

Few Bhutanese—not even Aum Rinzi, who is closer to her extended family by car than she has ever been—would want to roll back the highways. In fact, everyone wants a road. The king and the planning chief spend a lot of time explaining why every hamlet cannot have one in a country where the cost per mile to build roads is astronomical. Once, the king ran out of patience during an audience when the hundredth request for a road was made by a rural villager, someone traveling with him told me. "His Majesty just suddenly lost his shirt, and cried out, 'Okay, break for lunch!'" he said. "He cooled off during the meal, but after eating, the people came right back and asked for the same thing."

The unregulated explosion of private vehicles on Bhutan's narrow, twisting roads is undeniably subtracting from the joy and adding to the hazards of travel in a country where the airstrip at Paro is one of only a few flat surfaces. Bhutanese guides are especially proud of a stretch of the east-west highway called the Yadi bends, a dizzying series of hairpin turns that zigzag down a mountainside of airy, long-needled conifers about twenty miles from Mongar on the road to Tashigang in eastern Bhutan. Because the filmy trees and unusual topography make it possible to see the whole collection of Yadi bends from the top of the slope, they are a major tourist attraction. Locals say they made the *Guinness Book of Records*. That begs the question of why all of Bhutan was not entered in the competition.

I hadn't given the downside of roads much thought until I met Aum Rinzi at her farmstead near Mendegong, only a few hours' drive from Thimphu at the top of a rocky dirt track not really meant for cars. Although her family had a home in Thimphu, she said she was happiest in the country, where her heart and head overflowed with memories. Her lively mind ranged over past and present, sifting and analyzing and balancing the limits of the feudal society into which she was born against the excesses of the life she saw evolving around her. She was not judgmental, but she was very wise. Her life was a reminder that in this extraordinary country there are people whose experiences span eras, not just generations.

Aum Rinzi had lived through epochal change. But she had always chosen to hold on to that which she saw no reason to discard in haste. She had enjoyed a privileged life, and owned the substantial house and farmland she shared with her late husband's second wife. She slept on a simple pallet bed and worshipped at the small temple she had built adjoining her home; it was probably her largest extravagance, and she showed it off with great pride. As we stood there by her family altar, a bird flew in from the garden and began to flap around in panic, banging into walls and unfamiliar panes of glass. When I opened a narrow window on the temple's outer porch and helped the bird escape, Aum Rinzi turned to me with a smile somewhere between amused and beatific and said, "You will gain merit for that."

Aum Rinzi—*aum* means grandmother—speaks thoughtfully but not without passion at what has been lost as well as gained by three decades of rapid development. As a young woman not yet out of her teens, she became a companion and lady-in-waiting to a Bhutanese queen and later the wife of a government minister.

But privilege in Bhutan was a relative thing in the days of Aum Rinzi's youth. That was a time of greater equality among Bhutanese, says King Jigme Singye Wangchuck. "I remember my father saying when I was a small boy that in the old days—although there was a lot of hardship and suffering that we faced due to the policy of complete isolation—one of the main reasons Bhutanese were united, were happy, were contented, although we were poor, was because all of us were equally poor," he said. "I think that is very true."

Aum Rinzi's reminiscences of travel are full of happy times on the road, when no one was in a hurry, there were no noxious cars and buses, and everyone, farmer or lord, moved from home to home or temple to temple or palace to palace at a human pace, sharing the foot tracks and horse trails that wound through the mountains and valleys. "First of all, in those days it was inconceivable that people would go back and forth as much as they do now," Aum Rinzi said, as her granddaughter, Doma Tshering, a foreign service officer educated at Macalester College, did the translating. "Just to travel around one's home meant a journey on horseback. So for the most part, people tended to remain around the house, tending to the work. Of course, we didn't have vehicles of any kind. We didn't even think of that in those days. We had no reason to go out much. We used to have a lot of land, so we were pretty much self-sufficient. We didn't have to buy any commodities. We didn't even have to buy butter for the butter tea and lamps, because we kept cows. To a certain extent it is the same now for me in Mendegong. We grow all our own vegetables and rice. So in that way, life hasn't changed so much for many of us.

"But nowadays, wherever you go, people are always in a rush," she said. "They hop in their car, and off they go. They hop out, and it's over. In the old days, you started off with people loading luggage on horses. Then the children were loaded. Finally we all rode off. As we went, we looked for a nice field whenever we wanted to stop. Wherever we chose, the servants would start a fire and we would break for tea. Then we would move along again, gradually. In the evenings, when we got to a nice rest spot, someone would put up tents for the night. The servants and the women would start singing songs and dancing, and we would all sit there and enjoy the evening."

One serendipitous evening in Bumthang, I was invited to such an entertainment, and was able to glimpse the world Aum Rinzi described. The dzongda, Pem Dorji, had summoned all his district officials to a conference, and the day ended around a huge bonfire built against the chill of a dark mountain night. Huge vats of food were prepared: curried stews, dumplings, red rice, and salads. Beer flowed. All the while, young people danced story-dances, some mischievous or even a little wicked in theme. Not infrequently, the tale was of men being outwitted by women—or at least that's what they told me. We all sat in a semicircle around the fire and watched. The atmosphere was warm and convivial, sometimes uproarious, but never too loud to disturb the little children dozing at the edges of the gathering. Aum Rinzi was right: there is nothing to equal this spontaneous celebration among generous people.

In 1934, when Aum Rinzi was barely twenty, she made the journey of a lifetime, to Calcutta, as part of the entourage of King Jigme Wangchuck and his queen, Ashi Phumtsho Choegron. King Jigme, the grandfather of the present ruler and the second hereditary monarch of Bhutan—he reigned from 1926 until 1952—had been invited as the official guest of the British colonial government in India. It is fascinating to hear Aum Rinzi talk about that trip, and then read a description of the same visit written by Margaret Williamson, the wife of Frederick Williamson, the British political agent for Bhutan and the official responsible for arranging the visit.

"This was the first trip I made anywhere," Aum Rinzi said, preparing a betel chew from ingredients she kept in a plastic container. "We all went to see the foreigner, the Lord Sahib. From Bumthang, where we were staying, we went to the Indian border by horse. There someone had sent us automobiles to take us to a train for Calcutta. I was astounded. We were all afraid to step into the cars. We had about twelve people in His Majesty's entourage, and there were five more with the Royal Grandmother, who also had her cook and servants." Aum Rinzi calls the former queen "Royal Grandmother" because that is her present title in the Bhutanese court.

"I was very shocked when I first got to Calcutta," Aum Rinzi went on, her eyes twinkling as she paused to spit betel juice into something she had stashed in the fold of her kira. "It was as if I were in a dream. I could never imagine that such things existed, that so many people could be there. Calcutta was very clean and orderly. Wherever we went there were all foreigners. Even the shopkeepers were British. We didn't go out very much. It was all too overwhelming. We stayed twenty-five days in Calcutta, and then went to Nepal, where we were for a very long time."

Mrs. Williamson, who recorded her memories of the same event in a 1987 book, *Memoirs of a Political Officer's Wife in Tibet, Sikkim and Bhutan,* could not have known of the Bhutanese apprehensions when she and her husband, whom she called Derrick, set out to receive the royal visitors. With their extraordinary innate aplomb, the Bhutanese hid their fears.

"Derrick and I went down to Jalpaiguri, where the narrow gauge joins the main railway line, to meet the train bringing the royal party from Hashimara," Mrs. Williamson wrote. "And what a spendid sight they were when they arrived! Their Highnesses wore colorful Bhutanese costume, as did the more than 200 retainers who accompanied them, each of whom was armed with a bow and arrow and had a shield slung over his shoulder."

Mrs. Williamson recalls wondering whether the Bhutanese would be nonplussed by the "hooting, speeding traffic, by the milling crowds kept in constant motion by the remorseless drives that activate the modern commercial world, by the sheer profusion of buildings, among the great administrative, business, religious and public edifices." To her delight, the royal visitors "took it all in their stride." As for the armed retainers, they decided to set up an archery competition on the Maidan, Calcutta's Central Park, and had to be dissuaded by their hosts, who feared certain disaster if Bhutanese arrows started flying from warriors' bows. "Graciously, they took down their targets and withdrew," Mrs. Williamson wrote.

As for Aum Rinzi, "I was happy to come home, but also thrilled to have been in India and Nepal," she said. "I was able to come back and say, oh, I've been to these places. It was very exciting for me. In those days, no one really ventured outside Bhutan, even to India." Aum Rinzi later traveled to Tibet, to Sikkim, and even to Delhi, but by then, these jaunts were becoming part of life, if not exactly routine. Nothing lived up to the wonder of the trek to Calcutta. "That trip of mine," she says now, still relishing the memory, "was quite a feat."

Chapter 13

TWO CAPITALS,
TWO ERAS

I

THIMPHU

THE PLANE from Kathmandu was late, and darkness is creeping up the steep valleys along the road from the Paro airport to Thimphu. It is winter and the hills are brown, with russet pompoms of barbary or gorse. The last glow of the sunset illuminates a white chorten, but the houses I recall from other seasons have vanished into black shadows. There is no electricity in these gorges. "Unless there are nine, ten houses, only then the government gives," the driver explains.

We have a flat tire within a few miles of Simtokha Dzong, which heralds the approach of the Thimphu Valley. We pull over by a roadside shop/bar, where a monk is reciting prayers in front of boxes of soap powder, candy in cellophane bags, and strings of homemade cheese cubes. The owner's wife is on the floor of an adjacent room in front of a supply of beer and whiskey bottles, nursing a plump infant. A small metal stove for burning wood gives off some heat. Outside the shop, the owner and a mate are banging back into shape the bumper of a truck that has been seriously sideswiped. In the pitch darkness, though under a brilliant display of stars in the sky, a high school student hiking home to a roadless village in the nearby hills stops to lend us his flashlight. The taxi driver is struggling to change the tire he can't really see with a jack that doesn't seem to be lifting the heavy Land Cruiser off the dust.

The student, Passang Dorji, is garrulous, though ill. He has been sent home from a boarding school for superior students in Punakha, a few hours away by bus, to have a lung infection treated. "After school sports day, I fell sick," he explains. His flashlight (he calls it a "torch," the British term) saves the night. He won't take new batteries from me, though the sale might have been a windfall for the shopkeeper, whose stock of Indian batteries lack date stamps. The prudent purchaser buys more than needed, since a fair number of Indian batteries are recycled—that is, taken back from the trash and repackaged for sale as new. I learned this from friends in Delhi who stomped on dead batteries to foil recyclers.

Passang Dorji does want pen friends, however. He writes his address—C.O. Kinlay (GupDup), P.O. Wangehutaba, Thimphu, Bhutan, Asia—in my notebook. Speaking almost colloquial English, he tells me that he has been learning the language since the equivalent of junior high school. Now in his late teens, he says he wants to "serve the country" when he finishes school. "The country has given so much to me," he says without artifice, still holding his flashlight on the jack and the driver. "I have my schooling, and the hostel to live in is free. When it is over, I think I want to go to the army." Bhutan has a small army, trained by Indian officers and therefore serving as an adjunct of India's border defenses against China. No nation threatens Bhutan militarily, least of all China, now that many border issues have been resolved. But military officers, even in a Buddhist nation, can enjoy assured status and ceremony. In Thailand they get rich and periodically stage coups.

In the dark of the night, the bobbing and weaving of other flashlight beams etch bright lines into the horizon, identifying the trails of people going home to villages where hours of walking—to a job, to fetch water, to work in the fields—are a daily routine. Along the road, the car's headlights shine on thin men bent over as they struggle under bundles of straw or bags of grain. When they reach home, their evening meal is likely to be much like that of the shopkeeper on whose bit of land we changed the tire: a heap of rice, served in a colorful basket or pottery bowl, to be formed into a small ball in the fingers and dipped into a thin stew garnished with hot peppers.

Bhutanese cooking, never advertised as a notable cuisine, was a nice surprise on my first trip to Bhutan. Nothing in Thimphu's Motithang Hotel gave my husband and me much reason to believe that dinner would be the highlight of the day we checked in, after what seemed like a very long trip from Kathmandu. Our room was miserably cold and damp, though it was May. The hall carpet outside our door was soggy; there had been some kind of a pipe rupture somewhere along the line, and puddles had been left in the corridors, apparently on the theory that they would sooner or later dry of their own accord. No one was sure exactly when dinner would be ready. A fair amount of time passed after we took our seats in a cavernous dining room—the Motithang had been an official guest lodge of the royal government, and the dining room was still commandeered now and then for government functions. Then the headwaiter and his assistants began to shuffle out of the kitchen to place hot pots of food into the warmers on the buffet table. The evening picked up.

In dress and bearing, our headwaiter was a character drawn from one of those turn-of-the-century photos of the royal court and its retainers taken by leaders of British Himalayan expeditions. He was a great bear of a man in a stained and faded gho, worn knee socks, and shoes that had seen many miles of mountain hiking. His rough hands seemed unaccustomed to handling the glassware and china, which he put down and lifted with great deliberation, grunting and wheezing at every exertion. He said nothing extraneous, but was attentiveness personified. He brought us cans of Druk fruit juice, the pride of a nascent Bhutanese agro-industry, and bottled water from India. When the moment was upon us, he welcomed us to the buffet with genuine hospitality. As well he might. On the table were heaped mounds of red rice, a tasty Bhutanese variety not found in many other places. On these we piled slender fresh asparagus, lightly sautéed, and a choice of simple but well-seasoned stews and curries. This was long before I knew that some of the finest vegetables, fruits, and grains in Asia were the staples of Thimphu's produce market. The statistics about Bhutan—life expectancy, infant mortality, prevalence of infections, or whatever—never prepare you for the discovery of how well many people can live on the harvests of this underpopulated land.

Because Bhutan spans several climatic bands, all sorts of good things flow into Thimphu: oranges, apples, apricots, many varieties of rice and onions, buckwheat, bushels of roasted grains for steeping alcoholic drinks or mixing into yak-butter tea, homemade soft and dry cheeses, wonderful new potatoes, yams, mushrooms, fiddlehead ferns, young bamboo, cauliflower, cabbages, lettuces, eggplants, squashes, dried river weed, nuts, spices, herbs, root crops I couldn't identify, and, always, lots of chilis. Meat and dried fish, as I learned from cooks, usually come from India.

Eating hot green or red chili peppers straight is a test of growing up in Bhutan. A mother told me little children are proud when they can tuck into a bowl of them without ill effects; the feat is a rite of passage. The unofficial Bhutanese national dish is *ema-datsee,* a stew of chilis and homemade cheese. I knew this the first time I ordered it, but then carelessly let my mind wander and forgot the green things weren't string beans, but only for a blinding, throat-clearing second. The best antidote for this mistake is rice in large mouthfuls. Cooked chili dishes, salads with raw chilis, and chili-laced stews grow on most people after a while, but in small portions. In places where the cooking isn't very good (the Olathang Hotel in Paro springs immediately to mind), chilis can liven up a boring dish.

The source of all good things in Thimphu is the weekend market, now sheltered under open-sided, tin-roofed concrete pavilions near the bus station below the main part of town. It is very close to Changlimithang, the park for sports and festivals. Changlimithang has an auspicious history. On this field in 1885, a climactic battle—a brief but bloody swordfight—ended Bhutan's last civil war and removed the last challenger to Ugyen Wangchuck, the penlop of Tongsa, who twenty-two years later would be crowned king. His enemy, the Thimphu dzongpon, Alu Dorji, was forced to flee to Tibet after the humiliation.

At the crowded market, where produce spills out of baskets and country sacks, there are also real handicrafts (nothing mass-produced) for sale: bamboo ware, blankets, burled-wood bowls from the east, rough-carved spoons and ladles, and woven bags of all kinds. Bushy yak tails, good for dusting and swatting flies, are there, along with Tibetan-style jewelry, amulets, seals, pictures of the Dalai Lama, and the occasional human thighbone for use as a ceremonial trumpet. The market is a social gathering too, as monks, householders, craftspeople, herbal medicine vendors, and farmers from outlying regions get together to gossip and exchange opinions.

Thimphu, its market, its shops and restaurants, its business houses and hotels, is the new Bhutan. The town did not really exist until King Jigme Dorji Wangchuck, third ruler of the Wangchuck dynasty, decided to rebuild the dzong in the 1960s and establish a permanent new town in its shadow. Until then, Bhutan had been governed from dzongs alone, where the two traditional institutions of Himalayan Buddhist nations, the monastic orders and the royal government, coexisted.

Secular town life is something Aum Rinzi has watched develop, and she is skeptical. She sees self-reliance dwindling with the growth of service industries, and she takes refuge on her productive farmland in the hills near the road to Punakha, the old capital, where the dzong is still the center of life. The location of her Mendegong farm, somewhere between modern and medieval Bhutan, is coincidentally symbolic.

With urban growth and tourism has come a hotel boom in Thimphu, and visitors can be choosier about where they want to stay. After one experience with the Motithang Hotel, which is too isolated for anyone who wants to get a sense of daily life in Thimphu, I moved downtown next time to the Druk Hotel, a commercial establishment right on Thimphu's main square and within walking distance of nearly everything a visitor wants to do. Then the Druk's owners started to renovate the place. When the door handle of my newly refurbished room popped off, leaving me locked inside, it seemed time to move on from there also. The Druk, with a Bhutanese owner but Indian management, had some other drawbacks. For one thing, the dining room was cleaned by an Indian sweeper of indescribable scruffiness, grotesquely out of place in Bhutan, where institutionalized indignity is extremely rare. Wearing an undershirt and a *lungi* layered with filth, he would appear not before breakfast was served, but during the meal. With a short broom in one hand and a greasy gray rag in the other, he would proceed around the dining room, brushing up clouds of dust as he moved his pile of rubbish across the grimy carpet.

One morning, when my stomach wasn't quite up to his performance, I sat by a window to look out over the street below. But between the hotel and the opposite side of the road, there was another disturbing sight. A group of scavengers, also probably outcaste Indians, were huddled around a trash fire sharing with a stray dog bits of food they had found somewhere. It is ironic that those Bhutanese who never travel outside their country and know of India only as the regional superpower and the lord of a viceroy-sized embassy in Thimphu should see Indian citizens reduced to living on the streets of this minuscule mountain capital, eating scraps. Sometimes Indian scavengers, women with young children, could also be seen combing through open sewers for usable trash. That practice will end, however, if Thimphu's administration follows through on its plan to clean up the town (with the help of European sanitation engineers and solid-waste managers) and keep it free of the plastic bags and the other detritus of a burgeoning consumer society that have ruined the streetscapes and public squares of Kathmandu.

In the early 1990s, when privately owned hotels began to proliferate, I eventually settled on the Yu-Druk, a spacious hillside lodge overlooking Thimphu from the west. It was a longish walk into town, though downhill, and a fairly energetic climb back. But from my breezy room at the front of the hotel, with its wide rooftop porch over the floor below, Thimphu displayed a hidden beauty, especially during a misty dawn or a full-moon night, when the landmark spire of the Memorial Chorten stood out on the horizon as the town slumbered under golden streetlights among the black hills. The Yu-Druk, an amalgam of two large houses with a private temple on the upper floor of one, has a gang of eager young men and women on its staff who are always around and cheerful, making the place feel like a well-run home. The young men were on the lookout for reading material; my Indian magazines, bought in Kathmandu, and the novels I would normally have discarded after long flights from Europe or the United States were snapped up for reading during long afternoons when guests were out and there was only the telephone to attend to. Often, they played tapes of Bhutanese folk music on their modest boom box behind the bar, which was stocked mostly with bottled water and a few odd liquor bottles down to dregs. The only guest I ever saw try to order drinks at the bar was an Australian. All over the house we could hear the bottles in the adjacent cupboard clanking as a frantic young man tried to find something his guest, in an honest-to-God bush hat, would accept.

Most of the buildings in Thimphu, a town cupped in a deep valley between steeply rising slopes, are not very attractive. Although the facades of shops and most homes hew faithfully to the national architectural style of half-timbering and Buddhist folk-art trim around compound windows, there is a Potemkin quality to a lot of it. The really appealing, though poorer and simpler, towns are far away from Thimphu. There, designs painted on houses and shops are richer and express the true devotional, moral, or even superstitious purposes they were intended to fulfill.

Despite its growth as a commercial center, Thimphu's main attraction is Tashichodzong, the seat of royal government. Its five massive red pagoda-roofed, gold-topped towers—one in each corner of the rectangular white fortress and one rising above them in the central courtyard—are a majestic sight when seen from higher up the Thimphu Valley on the way toward a royal palace at Dechencholing, or from a hill on the road to Motithang. Tashichodzong, housing the king's court, the ministries of royal government, and, for half the year, the office of the head abbot, the je khenpo, is many times older than Thimphu town. Bhutanese historians say that the dzong was built on the site of a monastery erected in the thirteenth century. Certainly a fortress stood here along the Wang Chhu (often called the Thimphu Chhu) in one form or another since the seventeenth century. In succeeding centuries it was rebuilt or restored from time to time after fires, wars, and natural disasters. The last renovation took place in the 1960s when the dzong became the national capital.

In recent years, the gracefully proportioned dzong resting in meadows and groves of lacy trees along the narrow stream has lost some of its once-sweeping pastoral views. Government offices, the golf course, a new High Court, and a conference hall have moved into the neighborhood. But within the precincts of the dzong, an older order still reigns, as government officials and supplicants in formal scarves of rank or office move briskly around the inner courtyards and climb the steep monastic wooden stairs to offices above.

A few especially vivid impressions remain of life in the dzong. One is of a tailor seated among ceremonial brocades on the floor of the former National Assembly hall; he had moved his sewing to a window to catch the afternoon sun, which lent a glow to his needle and the colorful hangings being repaired in his old man's hands. Another abiding picture is of young clerks and office assistants rushing to the calls of ministers, pulling aside the heavy cloth panels that serve as doors and scurrying, heads lowered, into the presence of superiors. An order received, junior officers back away respectfully, with a great deal of head-nodding, to execute requests. In summer, the climate of a thick-walled fortress is mercifully cool. In winter, Bhutanese rugs and woven blankets may warm the chairs and sofas, but electric fires and hot tea are needed by the humans unaccustomed to the rigors of monastic life who work and visit there.

As Thimphu town has grown, it has added some unusual royal institutions that offer primers on traditional Buddhist arts and are increasingly providing the authentic craftspeople sought by other Himalayan communities where culture has been diluted or lost. Next to the Handicraft Emporium there is a studio-school for creating classic thangkas of painted panels mounted on brocade. Hanging in Buddhist temples and homes everywhere in the Himalayas, thangkas bear the likenesses of familiar saints, among them the Guru Rinpoche, and manifestations of Lord Buddha and of demigods or representations of the Wheel of Life. Farther afield, there is the National Library, with its silk-bound books, and near it the National Art School, where children from primary level upward are taught painting, sculpture, carving, and manuscript calligraphy, along with English.

After a couple of visits to this school, I came to understand how disciplined and restrictive the Buddhist canon can be in the arts, where all workmanship is sacred. Our vaunted free expression or artistic license would not be encouraged or even tolerated by Bhutanese masters. At the art school, little boys sat in rows on the floor of spartan rooms modeling identical images of the Buddha, or copying the same scripts or mandalas from finger-worn old models. A public school teacher later told me that children in secular schools, where the rules are different, are often reluctant to improvise, so stylized is their visual art world. Rewards do not come from taking liberties with the images of saints or the Lord Buddha in his many forms.

At the National Art School, I also noticed that all the pupils seemed to be poorly dressed, and I asked if they came from disadvantaged families. The faculty member showing me around looked embarrassed at the question, and seemed to evade it. When we stepped outside, my translator said that yes, the boys were poor, but the teachers didn't want to say so in front of them. Most had been brought from distant villages, where they had shown an aptitude for artisanship, and to which they would return to glorify the local architecture. They were being taught to take pride in themselves and their heritage, I was told. No one wanted to make them feel inferior because of their relatively lowly birth. In Thimphu there were temptations enough to lure boys away from traditional crafts and into what they might imagine to be more exciting, lucrative trades and pastimes. The school was trying to hold the line.

Like most visitors with time to spend in Thimphu, I walked a lot, because the town is small, two or three longish streets fed by back alleys and footpaths into the hills. The altitude hovers around 7,500 to 8,000 feet, not high enough to cause problems for the reasonably fit. The main thoroughfare, with no hills to climb, is Norzim Lam, where dozens of shops sell a mix of local products like handwoven textiles, food grains, and religious objects and imported goods such as clothes, processed foods, and other household items from India or China.

Everyone in town is conversant with the shops' specialities. When I asked a monk where to find the beautifully engraved slates that some-times adorn a temple wall, I thought I heard him reply: "Go to Number 32, next to the passion shop." Passion? Could there be a pornographic video store in the heart of town? When I arrived at Sangay's Store Number 32, I saw the clothing shop next door and realized he had meant "fashion." Interchanging the English sounds of *p* and *f* is a common practice in several South and Southeast Asian places I have spent time in. A housekeeper in Bangkok was forever talking about how badly a high-living driver treated his pregnant "wipe." In Kathmandu, I was intro-duced to someone who had opened a factory making Tibetan "carfets."

Thimphu, with its new golf course and a string of recently opened bistros to serve the new moneyed middle class and such foreigners as may pass through or live here briefly, is beginning to develop a restau-rant culture of relative sophisticaton, at least for those who can afford it. Until very recently, the smart set was limited to dining in hotels, at a financially shaky café or two, or at home. For lunch, there was the Swiss Bakery, a unique social institution in the heart of town. The owner of the place really is, or was, Swiss. He is among a very small number of foreigners granted the privilege of staying on in Bhutan and becoming citizens. He married here, and all his family now seem to lend a hand in running the rustic café with its wooden benches and tables and a few struggling strands of philodendron. The baked goods, freshly prepared (or reheated in a microwave oven), are comfortingly simple, leaning toward sandwiches and cakes, served with pots of good coffee or tea.

Most people seem to come to the Swiss Bakery not only to eat but also to meet other members of the Bhutanese fast class (including the cabin crews from Druk Air, still an elite in a country with only two small airplanes) and the expatriates who come to share news from home and abroad. One day, it was mail call for a group of blond outsiders, who immersed themselves in letters that had arrived by pouch from some northern European city. On other days, the foreigners seemed more intent on sizing each other up, especially if a stranger appeared. Competition has begun to surface among development organizations, and turf matters.

The Bhutanese do not wish to be lectured about what they need or don't need, and they skirt the edge of judging some well-meaning foreigners a little too self-righteous and hectoring. This was an unspoken undercurrent in several conversations I had with government officials about human rights and the treatment of Nepali-speaking rebels in the troubled south. The issue, which had crystallized debate about Eastern and Western ways, had also provoked some unusual criticism of Christians among usually tolerant Bhutanese Buddhists. To at least some Bhutanese (and many other Asians), human rights activists seemed the product of a didactic Judeo-Christian West, a description more often intended to be cultural rather than religious. Furthermore, in Bhutan, where conversions to Christianity are not permitted, many people are aware that Christian missionaries working in refugee camps in Nepal were early champions of southern Bhutanese rebels who fled there with florid and overheated accounts of abuse, and that these foreigners had pressed American diplomats in Kathmandu to accept the rebels' version of events without visiting Bhutan to see for themselves.

I was struck by a government official's remark about the gap between Asian flexibility and Western moral absolutism when he talked about the joy of dealing with Sadako Ogata, the United Nations high commissioner for refugees, who is Japanese. All over Asia, even in the rough-and-tumble Indian subcontinent, this theme is repeated, and it is troubling for those outsiders who want to steer a reasonable course between an understanding of other cultures and a belief that certain basic human rights are a universal concept that cannot be conveniently watered down, especially by governments, in the name of civilizational differences. To hear Buddhists argue the case for intolerance is especially unsettling.

For the tourist who passes briefly through Thimphu, staying well away from the smoldering political and cultural issues, this is the town where itineraries are fixed, cars rented, and guides assigned. It is the place to provision oneself with fat candles and matches for electricity-less nights, a few groceries for ad hoc picnics, and bottled water. Thimphu is also where visitors not on prepaid trips stock up on ngultrum, the Bhutanese currency. This transaction, regrettably, requires a trip to the Bank of Bhutan. For that, most people have to set aside at least an hour, though on a recent trip I managed to accomplish a currency exchange in forty-five minutes by going in just before the staff lunch break, when service suddenly speeds up.

The Bank of Bhutan is a barn, where cashiers are kept in stalls and pens and the rest of us are left to graze in the anteroom while waiting interminably for a simple traveler's check to be cashed. For anyone familiar with the subcontinent, it doesn't take long to figure out the problem: Indians have trained the staff and seem to hold pivotal positions, seated at battered tables initialing transactions. From the look of the chaos they have created, I would guess that these tutors come from the State Bank of India, any branch. It goes something like this:

I enter the bank and line up at the foreign-currency window. Two women are chatting, their backs to us customers. Eleven minutes pass. I hand over three checks, being careful to countersign them in front of the sari-clad clerk who pretends not to be looking. She pulls out several ledgers and begins to enter elaborate transaction records. She goes away. Nearly fifteen minutes go by. She returns, adjusting her sari, and gives me back the checks. She says I haven't signed them exactly the way I signed my passport (in another color ink, nearly seven years ago, on a desk, not a high counter). I sign them again, and again on the back. She goes away once more. This time I win the brass ring, or rather the brass disk with a number, which entitles me to fight my way to another cage at the opposite side of the barren hall where an unmistakably Indian Sikh is in charge of handing out the cash. Meanwhile, a veritable basket of papers with my applications for currency are circling innumerable desks for initials. Forty minutes into the adventure, my number comes up, and I push my way toward the Punjabi turban in the wire enclosure, all but hidden behind supplicants two or three deep. In under an hour, I have my money and am out of the bank. If Southeast Asians can train Bhutanese broadcasters and airline cabin crews, surely it would be possible to get a Singaporean or Thai to create user-friendly banks. Well, at least I had what I needed to leave for a trip through the other Bhutan.

"VINOD," said a voice from somewhere over the front fender of a battered Land Cruiser parked in front of the Yu-Druk Hotel. This was the driver introducing himself as he tinkered with the motor. It was not long after dawn, but nearly an hour later than I had hoped to leave for Bumthang, a full day's drive into central Bhutan. Not much reassurance was forthcoming from the nervous protocol officer assigned to accompany me across Bhutan because of his skill with all its languages (though I was given the option of traveling alone for the first time on this trip in 1992). "The car wouldn't start," he explained as we prepared to head into a country with no service stations for a hundred miles. Vinod, who had just introduced himself, was under five feet tall and looked all of fifteen years old. He was an Indian from Kalimpong. With tourism on the upswing, Bhutan was running out of homegrown drivers, and the private car-rental companies had gone prospecting for help in the hill stations of West Bengal. At least the terrain was similar, I reasoned, as Vinod jumped into the driver's seat, his short legs stretching to reach the floor pedals. On the dashboard reposed a Hindu god and a more or less indescribable ornament of blinking red lights.

As we climbed away from Thimphu, with the outline of Simtokha Dzong darkly visible through the morning mist, we caught up with a large, lumbering dump truck loaded with monks. It was, by wonderful chance, the autumn morning when the je khenpo and his monastic following began their annual move to the old capital of Punakha, where winter is less harsh. I had always imagined the decamping to be a dignified procession of holy men with their books and sacred paraphernalia. Who would expect a convoy of Indian-made dump trucks, festooned with garish decorations and "OK Tata" slogans, piled high with trunks, bundles, drums, horns, monks, and novices? There were vans, too, packed to the limit with lamas.

Everyone seemed to be in high spirits. At Dochhu La, the first of the high passes on the road to Tashigang, we stopped to admire an unusually clear view of the high Himalayan peaks along the border of Tibet. There is, apart from the view, a certain spiritual peace at Dochhu La, perhaps because the pass is sheltered by forests and dominated by a chorten, a mani wall, and thickets of prayer flags flapping gently against a natural backdrop of startling beauty. That morning, a row of migrating monks stood at the edge of a clearing, facing the snow-covered peaks of Masangang, Tsendagang, Terigang, Jejegangphugang, Kangphugang, Zongaphugang, and maybe Gankar Punsum—all more than 22,000 feet high. I was transfixed, and hesitant to intrude on what seemed to be a moment of reflection and meditation. It wasn't. The monks were making a pit stop to relieve themselves of morning tea, and they laughed uproariously as they turned toward us, adjusting their robes, amused at having been caught in the act by a foreigner. Half a dozen of them, seeing my camera, lined up to have their pictures taken beside a late-model car parked on the grass; its occupants had apparently gone to the small rest house nearby for morning coffee. The monks asked for copies of the picture to be sent to Punakha, to the slight annoyance of the protocol officer, who interrupted to say that I needn't bother; if I sent the snapshots to him he would pass them on. I hope he did.

II

PUNAKHA

IF BOOMING THIMPHU is what Bhutan is becoming, Punakha represents much of what it was. Punakha, with a labyrinthine dzong of remarkable proportions, the more so because it rises suddenly from flat ground near the confluence of two small rivers, was the country's capital for several centuries and is still the preferred venue for important royal ceremonies. The climate here is gentle and the altitude, about 4,400 feet, low for Bhutan. In the area north of the dzong, where the motorable road ends and the narrow track begins its steep climb toward the high Himalayan districts of Laya and Lunana, semitropical plants make their last stand. Punakha, on a side road off the main Thimphu-Tashigang highway, rests in a kind of cul-de-sac for those on wheels and thus escapes what passes for heavy traffic in Bhutan. There is not much of a town here, and most of what there is, across a footbridge from the dzong, is very new and very utilitarian: a branch bank, a health center, a school, and a scattering of houses and shops.

Almost any time of year, but most of all when the je khenpo is in residence in the winter months from November to April, there are monks all over Punakha Dzong, spilling into the shady courtyard below the grand staircase that leads into the fortress and lingering outside the walls. Punakha Dzong is stiff with lineage. The Guru Rinpoche was said to have had a vision in the eighth century that something great would be built here by a fellow named Namgyal. Or so it was said after the Shabdrung Ngawang Namgyal came along in the seventeenth century. The Shabdrung was reported to have been apprised of this vision in a vision of his own as he camped by the confluence of the Po Chhu and Mo Chhu. A glorious dzong was duly erected. The Shabdrung's embalmed body is entombed in one of its inner temples, the Machey Lhakhang.

What little there is of the present in Punakha vanishes in the dzong. It was a balmy spring day when I first got inside, armed with the government permit that was intended to open forbidden holy places to me. Doma Tshering and I plunged into the dark, dank corridors of the massive monastery in search of someone in charge who would see to it that we didn't get evicted or cause some kind of unseemly uproar by our presence. My companion was a very attractive young woman, elegantly dressed. Not the sort of person likely to turn up in the medieval squalor of some of the corners we passed. Looking for a minor abbot or anyone in authority, we raced along toward inner and more inner sanctums, barely glancing at the altars, paintings, statues, and unexplained niches whose images blurred. At last we reached a sunny, open inner courtyard where restoration work was underway in a great monastic assembly hall and, several floors higher, in the private quarters of the je khenpo. Both had been damaged by fire years earlier. Rebuilding was taking time because all of the work was being done by craftsmen using only traditional methods and tools.

Doma and I were looking for the man in charge of restoration. Someone directed us to a spot just outside the walls, and we set off again along stone corridors. After a false start into the fetid corner inhabited by novices, we found a fine old ramp leading down a tunnel to ground level. Wide enough for a large cart, it must have been built so that supplies could be more easily wheeled or carried to the upper chambers. Minutes later we were back in daylight and in the prefab office of an engineer. The devastated quarters of the dzong now being replaced, he said, had been built before 1753. In front of his office, stretching across a meadow, an army of craftsmen were at work among piles of fragrant wood identified as hemlock, blue pine, and "key-press," which I assumed was cypress.

After the customary tea and a brief lecture illustrated by a scale model of the dzong in the engineer's office, we wandered out into the work area. The workforce was a mix of local carpenters and less skilled laborers from all of Bhutan's administrative districts, who had been requisitioned under the national shared-labor system. They were given free lodging and a small amount of money for subsistence. Several told us with obvious sincerity that it was an honor to be here working on such a treasure as Punakha Dzong, and that they were pleased to volunteer. The carpenters, barefoot and often seated cross-legged on the ground, were fashioning huge ceiling beams with interlocking joints to connect with vertical posts without the use of nails. Where necessary, large wooden pegs were used to hold planks or beams in place. The men worked with simple instruments. No electric tools were anywhere in sight. There must have been scenes much like this around the great cathedrals of Europe as they were built over years by craftsmen camped at their feet.

Under a roof to one side of the bustling meadow at Punakha, woodcarvers were creating the ornamented window frames and interior detail. As they labored, they could see the outer walls of the great dzong rising six stories high in front of them, with some of their handiwork already in place on the upper floors. New bay windows, magnificently large and extravagantly carved, were ranged high along the third and fourth stories like the latticed balconies of a Mogul palace. Below that level, as in past centuries, the old white fortress walls (stained pinkish from the red earth of the worksite) were left solid and unbroken except for a few much smaller, utilitarian windows to let in light.

The carpenters and woodcarvers at Punakha were Buddhist, of course, but they had also taken care to respect the local spirits that lived in a grove near the foot of the dzong, land on which they worked and slept. They had built an altar of rocks and red clay at the base of a tree. On it they had placed various carefully chosen stones, many of them sedimentary rocks with colored layers of gray, black, and sometimes red. At the front of the squarish altar top, on a protruding stone, rested a kind of stick figure of dried reeds and bamboo. A foot or so behind it, plants suitable for offerings had been stuck in a block of clay. Altogether, it was a small but powerfully arresting shrine, its primitive construction a reminder that something older than the monumental, sophisticated Buddhist edifice that overshadowed it had a claim to the spirituality of this place.

Chapter 14

TO TASHIGANG

SOONER OR LATER there comes the time when we all have to take the road to Tashigang. There is no other route to Bhutan's easternmost large town except this narrow highway the Bhutanese call the Lateral Road, and no way to cover the 350 miles from Thimphu except by car (or horseback or on foot). Nearly all the great dzongs and temples lie along or near this road, which follows valleys and gorges across the inner Himalayas, where most Bhutanese live and farm whatever land can be terraced, plowed, and planted. Everybody—tourists, pilgrims, government officials, and farmers with produce to sell or goods to buy in Thimphu or the southern border town of Phuntsholing, the gateway to India—uses the Lateral Road. I got to picturing it as something akin to a fragment of the Bayeux tapestries or a medieval woodcut describing events great or small in two-dimensional, linear progression: car following truck following bus meeting yak, with occasional buildings or natural landmarks sketched above or below the main story line. Here is a man dragging home long bamboo poles suspended from his head and back like the long tail of a peacock. Here is a caravan of traders with strong Bhutanese ponies bearing huge baskets. Here is a weaver, working in her dooryard. Here are the prayer wheels spinning in front of shops. And so on.

With the luxury of time to spare, this trip should be made in Aum Rinzi style, with ample stops to absorb life and refresh the traveler. Otherwise, one's eyes get riveted on the terrifying road, and precipices are all you remember, or dream about at night. In an underpopulated country, there are almost no impediments to choosing a place for lunch, a walk, a nap, or an al fresco bathroom stop. A foreign woman in Thimphu told me she took to wearing an ankle-length kira for the privacy and convenience it gave her on long trips. "You don't have to wear anything under it," she explained.

The inner Himalayas, mountain ranges that run north to south, through deep, dark valleys and high passes, are forested spurs of the greater Himalayas. Their permanently frozen peaks stretch in an east-west direction along the border with Tibet. The inner Himalayas are an environmental wonderland for the traveler because the prolific vegetation, bird life, and animals vary as the twisting road rises and falls and rises again from fertile woodlands to subalpine meadows and back down into vine-tangled glens sprayed by waterfalls. More than 60 percent of Bhutan is forested, and much of it is virgin. With the help of the World Bank, the country was the first to set up a trust fund to protect its environment in perpetuity, citing its Buddhist commitment to nature and wildlife. There is no similar environment on this scale left anywhere else in the region. But this terrain has to be savored slowly, and Aum Rinzi would advise that right from the start, you rein in the driver assigned to your car, who wants to be able to boast at the other end about how fast he made the trip.

Although the hillsides around Dochhu La, an hour or so from Thimphu, display the richness of Bhutan's forests and, in the spring, its glorious tree-high rhododendrons, it is not until well after Wangdiphrodang that the road disappears into real uninhabited wilderness. As I approached Wangdi with Vinod, who had been a model of restraint since Dochhu La, he suddenly reverted to a display of motor showmanship, which entails driving recklessly through populated areas, scattering pedestrians and animals, and careening to within inches of market stalls. This behavior, if not caused, as in Thailand, by the consumption of tonic stimulants that blunt judgment and perception, can probably be explained as a subconscious or maybe conscious effort to demonstrate who has the power of life and death, or the great distinction of knowing how to drive—and a car to go with it. In Wangdiphrodang, it seemed particularly irrational for a young man from faraway Kalimpong, clearly not a Bhutanese by dress, language, or physical appearance, to be barreling through a busy bazaar in a military garrison town, where he stood to be mobbed if he struck a local resident. Hostility toward people from the Indian border areas runs deep among the mountain Drukpas, who see the roots of all the country's ethnic distress planted in the lowlands, whence come also greed, corruption, violence, drugs, and disease.

Maybe Vinod just wanted to get out of Wangdiphrodang. A lot of people feel that way, though not at the outset of a visit. The approach to the town along the road from Thimphu is lovely. A river of pale blue-green flows between sloping hillsides where villages cluster on productive farmland. On the left, a ridge rises as the road nears the dzong, giving Wangdiphrodang fortress and town an imposing elevation above the surrounding fields. After a police post at the junction of the road south to Chirang, the east-west highway crosses the Puna Tshang Chhu on a newish bridge and begins a switchback climb to the Wangdi bazaar. Wangdiphrodang had a fine, centuries-old, traditional Bhutanese bridge until the 1960s, when it washed away in a flood. Some of the iron chain from that bridge is at the National Museum in Paro. The old roofed bridge had carved slate reliefs in panels along the sides of the span, similar to the exceptional slate portraits of famous holy men, carved and delicately painted, still in place in the outer wall of the seventeenth-century temple at Simtokha Dzong, all but hidden behind a row of prayer wheels.

Legends compete to tell the story of how Wangdiphrodang Dzong came to be where it is, although most agree the fortress was built in the 1630s under the direction of the busy Shabdrung Ngawang Namgyel. Either a local deity, Yeshi Gompo, or the fierce god Mahakala appeared to the Shabdrung and told him to construct a dzong on either the ridge with the shape of a sleeping elephant or the place where ravens fly off in four directions, depending on which story you are told. Alternatively, the Shabdrung may have named the spot for a little boy he saw playing in the river's snow-white sand. Various accounts translate the name Wangdiphrodang in different ways, depending on the version of the town's founding one believes, a reminder of the tenuousness of historical truth in a land of legend.

Wangdi always seems like the perfect place to take a break and enjoy the view over the aquamarine river and spacious (for Bhutan) fields before moving on toward the dark forested roads and passes that lead into the Black Mountains. This is when the disappointment sets in. The town has but one small guesthouse, welcoming but exceptionally unappealing. If there is running water that day, it may flow out of control and you have to wade through it to the toilet. Electricity is scarce, as are candles. The staff is usually willing to rustle up coffee or tea, to be served in a dismal, windowless hall or (if that's pitch-dark) on a claustrophobic enclosed porch abuzz with flies if it's fly season. Dragging a chair out into the front garden to enjoy its commanding view seems to be regarded locally as an indicator of insanity, though this aberrant behavior is tolerated. A few steps from the garden gate is the town center, famous for its gas pump. The village is a ramshackle affair whose wooden lean-to shops resist all efforts to perceive them as quaint.

Beyond Wangdi, however, the scenery is again fine. The road east, blacktopped only in the mid-1980s, spirals out of a large valley, winding around and finally above substantial two-story farmhouses standing in terraced fields. In winter, at isolated farmhouses, the gently sloping rooftops made of loose wooden shingles anchored with rocks occasionally wear a mantle of bright red, as baskets of chilis are spread out neatly to dry in the sun.

After Wangdiphrodang, there is one detour to be made before crossing the mountains that divide western Bhutan from the central and eastern parts of the country, geographically and linguistically. A few miles after the hamlet of Nobding, a side road turns off to Gantey, climbing into a forest of oak, magnolia, and giant rhododendron. In April and May, the trip to Gantey is a drive through a natural botanical garden splashed with color. In this forest, as in so many other wild places in Bhutan, nature evolves and passes through cycles of life and death in full view of passersby. Trees die, fall, and decay, to be claimed by ferns, mosses, fungi, and sometime orchids, clinging in profusion to disintegrating trunks left untouched by villagers, who are forbidden to pillage or scavenge in protected forests—and who in this area are in any case few and far between. "To cut a fresh tree we consider a sin," an administrator told me, "because a tree also has life." The woodland floor is deep in a damp compost of leaves and twigs, through which new trees rise, nourished, to look for light.

The side road ends on the rim of the Phobjika Valley, a serene open space of perfect natural proportions in a perfect enclosure of hills. Here one can picture the genteel tea parties or night halts of Aum Rinzi's youthful travels. In the spring, this high valley (over nine thousand feet in altitude) is a bowl of emerald fields; in winter, a dun-colored haven for black-necked cranes, one of the few safe places left for them in Asia. A scattering of farmhouses and flocks of prayer flags rest on the valley floor. Overseeing all this from its perch on a hill at the valley's northern edge is the Gantey Gompa, the largest Nyingmapa monastery in Bhutan. According to Bhutanese legend, Gantey was built in the seventeenth century by a grandson of the saint Pema Lingpa. The monastery invites pilgrimage, standing as it does at the end of a narrow lane that wends through a cluster of houses and up a gentle incline to the gompa walls, where novices roughhouse in the grass and dogs snooze under trees.

A royal government permit allowing me to enter monasteries closed to foreigners, a document that wasn't always honored by abbots, passed muster with a senior monk at Gantey. The abbot, he told us, was halfway through a three-year meditation at a retreat on a nearby hill. The monastery had a somnolent air. A few more novices were messing around in the first courtyard we entered. The monk said that boys came here to study at the age of ten; their childish restlessness seemed to be tolerated most places. Everywhere boys seemed to be racketing around monastic compounds, often in rubber flip-flops. They don't always pay attention during prayers, and nothing in a temple moves faster than a novice at the end of worship or a ceremony.

The monk in charge at Gantey, who was seized from time to time by a racking cough, didn't want to talk very much about the origin and significance of the religious objects and symbolic decorations that filled one temple after another in the monastery, except to say that he thought some of the paintings were "about two thousand years old" and that restoring them was forbidden. He nonchalantly pointed out the urns holding the remains of reincarnates of an important early abbot. But he became animated when we came to a set of big old trunks, handworked with brass finishings. In those, he said, were Gantey's temple festival costumes and the animal masks worn by the monks.

He said that children were taught to pay close attention to the animal dances so that they would be prepared for the variety of beings they might meet in succeeding lives. He drew us to a painting that illustrated the many intermediary deities of varying dispositions and powers a pilgrim encounters en route to heaven. In one corner of the mural were small white figures still awaiting a decision on their fate, poor writhing souls. He looked at them with pity.

It was spring when I first saw the Phobjika Valley—not with Vinod, but on an earlier occasion, with a cheerful Bhutanese driver who plucked rhododendron blooms and tucked them under the windshield wipers to beautify the journey. This seems to be a seasonal custom, since to the Bhutanese rhododendrons are just another wildflower, with plenty to go around. The day was balmy, so we stopped for a picnic of boiled potatoes, eggs, bread, and cheese on a grassy slope with Gantey to one side and the Phobjika Valley in front of us. No sounds of modernity penetrated this place; it was a brief taste of life in Aum Rinzi's era. At least until Michael Bloomen's sputtering jeep came along.

Michael Bloomen is an artist. To be more specific, he is an art teacher in England who works hard to save for periodic trips to Bhutan, where, like his predecessors on British expeditions of old, he is systematically sketching and painting the country's people and regions. Systematically is the hope, anyway. On this trip, the good-natured artist had seen just about everything go wrong, or at least not according to plan. A skilled trekker and climber, Bloomen had intended on this long-awaited visit to cross the roadless subalpine belt from Laya to Lunana, a grueling march at the best of times. The whole expedition collapsed when his porters and pack animals suddenly went home to do other work. That scotched not only the Lunana trek but the hope of walking down to Jakar, in Bumthang, along an old Tibetan trade route from the north. So he retraced his steps to Thimphu and set out along the Lateral Road for Bumthang to salvage what he could of his solo expedition. That's when his four-wheel-drive vehicle developed coughs and wheezes.

He was philosophical. "But this is what we *expect*," he said that night at dinner in Tongsa. "This is why we *come here!*" His reworked schedule had already proved serendipitous. He had holed up in towns unknown to foreigners, and had been rescued from one by a very high-ranking army officer, who told him fascinating tales of Bhutanese high life. In Gantey he had seen bright yellow rhododendron blooms for the first time, and was enthralled. He had made some fine sketches of chortens and other small landmarks along the way. Able to see something interesting wherever he became marooned on this unplanned expedition, he was content to stay in Tongsa while a search party tried to scrounge up a more reliable car or fix the one he had been assigned.

There were fewer than half a dozen foreigners sharing dinner in Tongsa's small hotel that night, and we were all fascinated by Bloomen's accounts of his earlier visits to Bhutan. The company was, as always, pleasant, because this remote and rugged country has developed a small fraternity of devoted followers drawn back again and again despite the expense and the inevitable hardships. Almost never have I heard tourists complain in Bhutan, even at the end of very difficult days. Bhutan charms and entraps its guests with simple and honest hospitality.

Taking good care of travelers is a traditional priority, particularly if the guest is someone who commands special respect. On various trips, I stopped to admire the natural rest quarters villages had erected along the road for King Jigme Singye Wangchuck, his peripatetic uncle Prince Namgyal, or other important people. Typically, a dense fence is woven of sweet-smelling evergreen (sometimes arborvitae) supported by bamboo or wood poles to create an enclosure that becomes a private garden or a roofless room. There may be a short maze leading to a completely hidden latrine. Occasionally, there will be more than one chamber with evergreen walls, allowing a meal to be prepared and served away from the main rest area. When a ceremony or a sporting competition of some kind is due to take place in larger towns, the Bhutanese erect large white fairy-tale tents festooned with colorful drawings of dragons.

Tongsa is a memorable town for several reasons, not the least of which is its spectacular setting. A traveler from Thimphu approaches Tongsa through the Black Mountains and over the Pele La, a 10,800-foot pass where the vegetation is mostly grass and scrub. On my recent trip, Vinod, the protocol officer, and I had stopped on the Pele La for a picnic lunch on the first day of our Thimphu-Tashigang jaunt. Above the pass stood a satellite dish, part of Bhutan's new hi-tech communications network. Near it, local people had staked prayer flags, perhaps to catch the breeze on the open slope as much as to preserve the sanctity of the spot. I happened to be looking in that direction when a yak herder materialized without a sound from over the crest of the hill behind us. Drawing his wooden bowl from his gho, he accepted some tea, showing interest in the Yu-Druk's sandwiches too. Soon he had joined us for a meal, chatting to the protocol officer, Ugyen Wangchuck, namesake but no relation of the first king. The herder said he had been told that one of his yaks had got into a fight with an animal from another herd and had been killed. He had climbed up the mountain to take a look at the situation, which was not yet resolved; it wasn't clear why.

Lunch over, he thanked us and resumed his task. We headed on to Tongsa over a notorious patch of road given to landslides and rock showers. Paving occasionally collapses into abysses formed in sharp corners where waterfalls pound the shallow road surface and torrents land on small concrete bridges from on high. Repairs are made by Bhutanese citizens giving time to the state under a volunteer work system known as *wulah*. Each family is now required to contribute two weeks of labor, ideally that of the strongest member of the household. Only it doesn't turn out that way. There are certain predictable exemptions; civil servants, for example, don't break rocks. And families have taken to sending along women, some of them barely teenagers, to spare others for tasks on the farm. Workers, children included, are bivouacked like gypsies, covered in dust or the soot of fires under melting tar, as they huddle in lean-tos on the edges of chasms. My companion-interpreter always made sure that we gave any excess food we had to these workers.

Not long after the road from Pele La regains its composure on the descent to Tongsa, it passes the Chendebji Chorten, a landmark to travelers who know they have now entered eastern Bhutan. The eighteenth-century chorten, its bulk built in the rounded Nepali style with eyes looking in four directions from the square base of the stylized point near the top, was constructed to hold down a demon that had been bothering the people in this valley. All is peaceful here now, with the silence of the place broken only by the wind in the prayer flags and the gurgling of a stream running through a gorge. Less than twenty miles (but as much as an hour's driving time) later, Tongsa Dzong bursts dramatically into view at a bend in the road—though it will take nearly another hour to reach its gates across the Mangde Valley. The dzong commands a ridge backed by higher mountains but overlooking the deep, wide valley at its feet. At the point that this classic dzong can be seen to best advantage, the roadbuilders have constructed one of the country's few official lookout points, where it seems criminal not to stop for a photo.

Tongsa's origins are relatively recent, so its history is refreshingly straightforward. In 1541, Lam Ngagi Wangchuck, a Drukpa monk of Tibetan royal lineage, came down from Ralung in eastern Tibet and stopped to meditate on the ridge above where the dzong now stands. He established a small temple, around which a village sprang up. In the next century, the Shabdrung Ngawang Namgyal ordered a fortress built here. It grew and grew into a huge complex several city blocks long, strung along a spur overlooking the Mangde Chhu. Though its formal name is Chhokkor Rabtentse, everyone calls it Tongsa Dzong.

"The dzong was once astride the main road that came up here over a bridge down by the river," Dasho Phub Dorji, the Tongsa dzongda, said as he greeted us at a massive wooden gate to the fortress. "There was then a western gate and an eastern gate, and everyone had to pass through the dzong until about 1960. These gates were for the security of the dzong, so just before dark somebody would close, and open again in the morning. Anyone who wanted to continue on the road had to be here before sunset, from west to east or east to west." He added that the dzong might seem very large from outside "but inside it is very narrow."

We walked from courtyard to courtyard and level to level of the old dzong. It was more than a workout. Bhutanese are accustomed to running up and down monastic ladder-stairs (and at high altitudes). After a while, even a foreigner catches on, though, and the climbs do not seem so vertiginous. We went from sanctuary to sanctuary in the monastic section of the fortress, away from the administrator's offices. The dzongda pointed out the urns with the ashes of learned monks.

"We don't know how old some of these are," he said. "Unfortunately in our system so far no one has kept the records. One reason is that in olden days, they didn't register and record anything. People did not feel the necessity to mark time." The Dasho said there were three hundred monks in residence at Tongsa, including one hundred novices. There were also some nuns, but they did not stay in the dzong. By tradition, women never do. There are only a few hundred Buddhist nuns in all of Bhutan, and they play a peripheral role, as everywhere in the Himalayas, outnumbered as they are by thousands of monks in state monasteries or privately supported temples.

The dzongda was marveling at how the monks were able to master the sacred books by memory, without necessarily understanding all they read, as we entered a bare wooden hall where a group of about twenty novices were learning a lesson in self-discipline and silence. Most of the boys seemed to be about ten or twelve years old, and they were having a hard time being serious. With their scrubbed faces bathed in the sunlight that poured into the dark room through its only window, the boys looked angelic, but the sparkle in their eyes gave them away. Each time the elderly monk in charge turned his back, the boys—standing in rows, palms clasped together—would fidget and giggle. One or two of them elbowed or tickled the boy next in line, setting off a round of muffled jostling and suppressed tittering. The dzongda laughed.

We moved on to another temple to the cawing of crows and the rising drone of a prayer. People from the nearby town had brought oil for lamps and some other offerings to mark a special occasion at that particular shrine. "According to our religion, we say, if you donate something to poor people, give help to the needy, and if you are good in this world, if your mind is clear, then when you are reborn you go up," the dzongda remarked as we headed for his office for tea and cookies. "If you are bad, you go down to the animals."

Dasho Phub Dorji said that as dzongda of Tongsa he played no part in the monastic activities of the dzong, which were directed by the chief monk, who in turn reported to the central monastic body. "But as a public administrator, I'm very much involved in development activities in this district: engineering projects, education, the agricultural extension centers, health, and so on," he said. "At the village level, though, religion plays a greater part than administration, because the people have the faith that everything comes from religion. Therefore we have a program of integrating monks officially in development. If the monk knows something about health or other things, then in the village he may be of more help than a layman. If we say you have to wash your clothes every month or something like that, people may not listen. But if the monk says . . ."

When we met, Dasho Phub Dorji, who was educated entirely in Bhutan, had been giving thought to the problem of reintegrating into village life young Bhutanese who had been abroad and who would probably be initially unwilling to return to a rural existence thereafter. He was trying to convince the educated young that with a cash economy taking root, there would be opportunities in the countryside to help turn a subsistence economy based on barter into a lucrative one using market forces to create disposable incomes. "Somebody who is studying in U.S.A. or Australia, naturally he might not like to go back to the village, where there is no social life," the dzongda said. "But gradually, he can know the situation. Today the farmer, if he keeps sheep, needs someone to look after the sheep. If he keeps cows, someone has to look after the cows. Somebody has to work in the fields." Better farming, he said, would need better management. This would, in turn, create more jobs in the countryside, especially in Bhutan, where the steep terrain makes mechanical farming impossible in most areas. "No matter how much money you make, you will always need manpower," the dzongda said. "And in our villages, the whole life has changed. I was a student in the 1950s, when we had a subsistence life. Now villagers have some communications, health coverage, community schools. The lifestyle is very different."

Not long after five the next morning, I went for a hike up the hill behind the Sherubling Tourist Lodge, the fourteen-room hotel where most foreigners stay. Because it was very early, I had a chance on my way out to snoop around the unattended reception desk near the door. I saw that Tongsa had thirty telephone lines, six of them to the dzongkhag administration offices, two to the thrimpon's law court, one for monks, and most of the rest for branch offices of the central government. There was a phone book, too: it consisted of one mimeographed page of two-digit numbers.

Outside the reception hall, the driveway of the lodge bordered on a hill with sweeping views of Tongsa Dzong and its watchtower, the *ta-dzong*, higher up the mountain. As I began to climb the hill behind the hotel, I was soon joined by the usual pack of curious dogs, and a free-ranging horse. A few minutes later, I passed a veterinary substation, relieved that there might be a supply of rabies vaccine. Before long, it was apparent that I was headed into a schoolyard, where the track seemed to dead-end. The path was stony, and miserably littered for so beautiful a site. I inventoried one Maggi seasoning packet, two unmatched tennis shoes, numerous candy wrappers, an Indian newspaper, rusting tin cans, and the ubiquitous plastic bottles. At the top of the rise was Tongsa Junior High School, a boarding establishment. Boarding schools (all of them free) are inevitable in a country as difficult to traverse as Bhutan. I could hear the students splashing and shrieking at their morning baths, and it seemed too early to interrupt, so I retreated to the lodge until the school day began, and then returned.

The headmaster, Chewang Dukpa, was alive with enthusiasm as he ordered aides to run off in several directions to prepare the classes for a visitor. As we marched from room to room, I knew I had lost control of the day. But the exercise was worth it. At Tongsa, teachers were giving an old twist to new ideas. I heard children learning to sing folk songs in English. One went like this:

Someone's in the kitchen with Karma.
Someone's in the kitchen I know, oh, oh, oh.
Someone's in the kitchen with Karma,
Strumming on the old banjo.

I was given a copy of the newly minted *Tongsa Junior High School Magazine,* in which there were stories and poems written by pupils in both English and Dzongkha. Some had folk themes, or were attempts to reproduce parables in which animals demonstrated lessons applicable to human life and behavior. Some were touchingly human moments recorded with the candor of children. One little boy wrote of his loveless life since the death of his mother. Another child, Kuenga Wangmo, a girl in seventh grade, gave away her homesickness in a poem called "A Message for My Parents Far Away." Echoing a verse that sounded vaguely familiar, she wrote:

Oh, soft-blowing wind from the North,
Wait and hear a message from a daughter
To her parents far, far away.
Tell them that their daughter is well
With her beloved friends and elders.

Oh, fast-flowing water from the high mountains,
Wait and hear a message from a daughter
To her parents far, far away.
Tell them that their daughter is studying hard
To face the forthcoming exams.

Oh, fast-flying robin from the West,
Do wait and carry a message from a daughter
To her parents far, far away.
Tell them that their daughter is eagerly waiting
To meet her parents once again.

Down in Tongsa town, a bumpy trip from the hilltop school and the tourist lodge, we ran into Mani Dorji and his pony Tshering outside a provisions store. Tongsa is an engaging village, a strip of basic shops and rudimentary restaurants with a nice collection of folk-art paintings on what would otherwise be mundane commercial walls. Mani Dorji and Tshering had been in town loading up on essential supplies for his village, some days' walk into the higher reaches of the valley. Tshering the pony (really a small horse) was relaxed as his master loaded him with grain sacks and other commodities that would have to suffice for several months, since a trip to town was long and arduous. Tshering was a veteran.

Two days later, Vinod, my interpreter, and I finally neared Tashigang, after what was for them a very leisurely trip with overnight stops in Bumthang and Mongar. "I've driven from Tashigang to Thimphu in one straight trip," my interpreter boasted. I wasn't fazed, particularly since we had hit snow and ice on the highest passes along the road, the Ura La and Thumsing La—just about the time when Vinod allowed that this was his first trip to the east. This news would have been a little less unnerving if we weren't destined to take the same route back to Thimphu when our eastern jaunt ended.

Tashigang, everyone said, would be fun. And it was. It is a big town by rural Bhutanese standards, and the commercial center for the most heavily populated (that is, several hundred thousand people) part of Bhutan. Tashigang's main street was colorful, with shops trimmed in bold blue paint outside and overflowing with goods inside. There was the buzz of a frontier trading post, and the streets were enlivened by groups of nomads from the eastern reaches of Merak-Taksang who wore clothes made of hides and felt caps with protruding tails all around that acted like little gutters, forcing rain to run off away from their heads. There were passable eateries and bars that did a good business, judging from the uncoordinated lurchings of some folks on the streets. Yet here in the east lived people who were proud of being much more pious than their western Bhutanese counterparts.

This is one part of Bhutan where deforestation is a problem. The hillsides above Tashigang Dzong were bone-dry and stripped of trees, a by-product of too much land-clearing for farming. But apart from that, the prevalence from Mongar to the eastern border of bamboo-and-thatch construction and the flowers I had learned to associate with Southeast Asia softened the atmosphere. A view of bougainvillea made my spartan guesthouse room in Tashigang easier to live with. Never mind that taking a (cold) shower meant being careful not to fall into the squat toilet that shared the drain on the floor of what was quite literally a water closet in a cubbyhole off my bedroom. At least I had the WC to myself. I had to go to town to buy a towel, since my traveling model was drying on the rail fence outside. But this was a good excuse for wandering around the local shops, where all kinds of garish Indian towels were sold, along with the machine-made imported fabrics that were undercutting weavers in a region known for its fine loom work. From Tashigang there is a road south to the Indian state of Assam; some Bhutanese traders could speak Assamese, they said, so frequent were their trips.

There was no electricity at night in our little guesthouse, but that's when my fat candles from Thimphu came in handy. I lit two of them the first evening and broke out *Rabbit at Rest,* a book by a fellow Pennsylvanian that I had been meaning to read for several years. Here, I thought, I finally have all the time in the world to complete John Updike's Rabbit cycle while getting back in touch with that other civilization I had temporarily left behind as I voyaged through Himalayan Buddhism. After several hundred miles on the road and a lot of temples, a change of mental imagery was in order.

But as I turned the pages, lo and behold, there was Harry Angstrom talking about the Dalai Lama.

Chapter 15

ONE SUNDAY
IN BUMTHANG

FAR FROM the tropical torpor of Lumbini, and a world away from the desert-dry caves and ruins of what was once Buddhist Afghanistan and Pakistan, there is one perfect valley, temperate in climate and holy in atmosphere, where a traveler through Himalayan Buddhism can put down all the baggage of the voyage and begin to sort the images and souvenirs. In Bumthang, many strings begin to come together. Here our old friend the Guru Rinpoche seems never to have left this earth, so vivid are his manifestations. The entertainments of Aum Rinzi's youth live on in folk dances around a fire when travelers get together for a meal. Here monastic communities, some very small, seem to have been living and practicing a faith unchanged in centuries. It would be easy to believe that in dark monastery chapels, founders of the orders still walk among the relics.

Perhaps most important are the people of today who live in the midst of all this antiquity and theology. Richard Gombrich, introducing *The World of Buddhism,* reminds us that "spread by traders and protected by kings, through most of its history Buddhism has flourished among peasants." Bumthang is a valley of farmers and herders. But there is more to the people of Bumthang than occupation. Men and women of character, adaptable and self-confident, the Bhutanese of Bumthang have been propelled into a great experiment. With a little help from outsiders, they are upgrading their standard of living in some important material ways, while being encouraged to protect and burnish all that is traditional. If grassroots Himalayan Buddhism can modernize here without a cultural price, there can be hope in many other valleys beyond those of Bhutan.

For centuries, travelers have been writing about the special qualities of Bumthang, perhaps no one so floridly as the fourteenth-century lama Longchen Ramjampa. He was moved to call Bumthang a grove of the gods, a paradise, a home for heroes and demigoddesses, "a lotus in bloom." The Bhutanese Special Commission on Cultural Affairs quoted the lama liberally in its laudatory pamphlet *Bumthang: A Cultural Nest of Bhutan*. He found the views marvelous everywhere his gaze wandered in the valley. "It appears to be enclosed by a fencing of gems. The snow-capped hills and mountains are symmetrically arranged, the fertile valleys and plains are wide and extensive, the forests are lush, smooth and green. Flowers, fruits and medicinal herbs abound, and the climate is equitable," the longchen noted. He also discovered that in Bumthang "blessings are near and it is easier to practice dharma without inertia and to achieve *siddhi*," or magical Tantric powers. Just looking at the impression of the Guru Rinpoche's body on the rocks at Kurjey "is sufficient for one to attain liberation."

As for the people, Longchen Ramjampa classified them as "mild-natured, peace-loving, well-behaved, law-abiding and rather more good-looking than the others." Most contemporary visitors are inclined to agree. If Bhutan had not been shut off from the world when the sixties generation and later the dabblers in New Age mysticism went looking for Nirvana, Bumthang might have been overrun and suffered, in miniature, the fate of Kathmandu. In Thimphu, the Bhutanese are alert to the danger even now, since a road through the valley reduces travel time to only a day from the international airport at Paro. But the capable people of Bumthang don't seem to worry too much. They can handle just about anything. Just look at Tshering Hamo.

Tshering Hamo is in my bathroom at Bumthang's Wangdicholing Guesthouse, scrubbing noisily and furiously on an old bracelet from the eastern town of Radi. It was one of two offered to me in Tashigang by a waiter who told me that the grimy, chunky silver bands he pulled from the folds of his gho belonged to an old widower forced to sell his late wife's jewelry to raise cash to light butter lamps in her memory. I wanted to believe this sweet, sad story and go on thinking that the quick-buck philosophy had not yet been introduced this far east. Eager to see what lay hidden under the patina of grime, I fantasized that in Bumthang, where I would be the next day, I could find some silver polish that had strayed over the mountains in the sack of a trader from India or China. Lurching and skidding back across the icy mountain passes from Tashigang to Bumthang, I dwelt on the hope of spending the long evening by the fire polishing my treasures.

At Wangdicholing, Tshering Hamo scoffed at my silver-polish plan, as did the shopkeepers in Bumthang's main market town, Jakar. One of them giggled behind her hands as she watched my silly attempts to act out my need. Finally a boy of about twelve, left in charge of a small general store crammed with, among other things, prayer flags, candles, plastic flowers, rope, buckets, laundry detergent, towels, incense, ballpoint pens, school exercise books, locks, wheat flour, candy, and what looked like dung cakes but could have been tea bricks, helpfully sold me a seventeen-rupee (less than fifty-cent) toothbrush from India that he thought might dislodge the generously encrusted village dirt, adding without conviction that I could wait to try the brass polish he heard they sold in Thimphu.

Tshering, taking charge, scorned the toothbrush idea, too. She took immediately to the bracelet. "My granny grandmama left me one like," she said, splashing lye-laced soapsuds around the bathroom sink and walls as she attacked the hapless jewelry with a scrubbing brush meant for the floor. "I know how to clean. Leave to me." When she finished, one large red stone had been unmasked as a finely cut piece of bicycle reflector and one of the smaller turquoises looked suspiciously like a fragment of aquamarine bathroom tile. Another, apparently real, turquoise was imbedded in unidentifiable goo, and there was a space where there should have been a coral. But the silver had begun to shine, and she was pleased.

Tshering looked after the rooms at the guesthouse, a collection of about a dozen cottages built in what was once the front garden of a royal residence, the Wangdicholing Palace. Bumthang, the seat of at least half a dozen important temples and the birthplace of the saint Pema Lingpa, whom the Bhutanese regard as an ancestor of the royal family, was also where Bhutan's first king, Ugyen Wangchuck, was born. Thus the royal family (and therefore the civil service) has always had close ties to Bumthang, which has duly benefited. In this valley, the spirit and the state come together.

The old royal lodge, a deteriorating masterpiece of traditional architecture that was the scene of many courtly spectacles, still stands behind the tourist lodge, but is rarely used. When King Jigme Singye Wangchuck comes to Bumthang these days, he stays at a modest newer bungalow in a secluded grove about a mile upstream on the same bank of the Bumthang Chhu. The king clearly prefers rustic settings and natural building materials—he had cement steps removed from the front veranda of the new residence and replaced with timber. In the bungalow, his bedroom is spartan but spacious, dominated by a large woodstove and, naturally, a king-size carved wooden bed, imported from India. The king's four stunning queens sleep almost summer-camp-style in a much smaller room all but filled by their four simple single beds. A caretaker accompanying the dzongda of Bumthang on an inspection tour of the bungalow smiled affectionately as he ran his hand lightly over the tiny pitmarks in the bare wooden floor made by Their Majesties' stiletto-heeled shoes. If you're a wellborn Bhutanese woman, wearing high heels with a kira has become essential, it seems, no matter how rustic the setting, rocky the terrain, or precipitous the temple stairs.

Wangdicholing Guesthouse, where many foreign visitors to Bhutan stay, is separated from the old royal palace by a stone wall where noisy crows perch to scream at nothing in particular. Lazy dogs indifferent to the persistent cawing snooze in the sun on ledges around a caretaker's cottage, preparing for the night's howling sessions and dogfights. But on the bright Sunday morning that my bracelets were getting the lye treatment, about the only sound outdoors was the guttural sputtering of a hot-water heater boiling over on the back wall of my cabin, trying to keep up with Tshering Hamo.

To describe Tshering as merely the chambermaid of this establishment would be selling her short. Round-faced, beautifully rosy-cheeked, and solidly built, like most of the women of rural Bhutan, she was also the guesthouse porter, shouldering huge loads of camping gear and suitcases that would crush a pony. British political agents who first penetrated Bhutan several centuries ago, while recording in their diaries radically different judgments on the women's comeliness or lack of it, were on the whole impressed by the physical strength of the Bhutanese of both sexes. These mountain women with their uniformly cropped thick black hair framing their weathered faces are strong, tireless, and shrewd. A British military engineer in Ladakh came to the same conclusion there, recalling in 1846 how the women carried his tent over the mountains after whimpering male coolies had complained about its weight.

Tshering could sometimes be found winging stones at stray hounds, washing dishes in the hotel kitchen, bartending, delivering room-service orders around the compound, or waiting on tables in the paneled lodge with a huge woodstove that serves as restaurant and social center. (Formal entertainment was limited, however, mostly to old Bhutan tourism videos, with jumpy pictures and scratchy sounds played on a television set whose veil-like cover was lifted only in the evening hours.) No one ever saw the guesthouse manager work as hard as Tshering, when he worked at all.

Tshering could also build a mean fire. It was firewood that first brought us into friendly small talk. She professed to be pleased that I knew good kindling when I saw it and that I was conversant about flues and drafts after years of experience with an ornery woodstove in Pennsylvania. After a while, she was bringing me choice logs dry enough to ignite, compact enough to push through the small round opening of the stove in my room, but fat enough to smolder all night—the difference at Wangdicholing between reasonable comfort and subquilt hibernation in the winter months.

The heater used here and elsewhere in Bhutan is called a *bukhari,* a reminder of its Central Asian origins. In essence, a bukhari is a large tin can on spindly feet with a hole in the top, over which there is a cover that fits only when the two whimsically handcrafted circumferences on the stove and its lid can be made to coincide. Sometimes they never do, and the whole contraption becomes a riot of uncontrollable drafts. At Wangdicholing, a hot bukhari on its small slab of concrete is the only source of warmth in a wood-floored, wood-paneled room devoid of fire extinguishers, unless you count the bathroom bucket. But then, much of forested Bhutan and its half-timbered architecture classify as firetraps. It is a rare monastery or dzong that has not burned to the ground at least once or twice in its history. The monks will point proudly to the distinction of having escaped the inferno when they can make that claim.

Tshering was not very impressed with my cautious paper-and-sticks method of starting a fire in the stove. She had a lot of bukharis to light at Wangdicholing, morning and evening, and she didn't want to waste time on niceties. With compact movements of her broad, capable hands, their skin chapped crimson and cracked from work and exposure, she would stuff the little stove to its capacity with wood, then lace the pile lavishly with kerosene from a Druk Marmalade jar. To that volatile combination she quickly applied a wad of flaming toilet paper. Even before the roar had subsided, she would sweep out into the evening darkness to thaw the next freezing foreigner.

After a few years of dealing with tourists, most of them paying more than two hundred dollars a day for the privilege of staying in what was akin to an unheated motel room whose economically cut curtains didn't always extend to the full width of the drafty windows, Tshering had begun to take the measure of the outside world from her Bumthang vantage point. Other young Bhutanese of her generation were being sent abroad for training in tourism; she learned on the job, toting trays and receiving complaints. She got accustomed to (but never could explain) the harrumphs of guests who returned to find their door keys not in the guesthouse reception office, which was usually locked anyway, but sticking smartly out of the padlocks on their room doors. Until very recently, Bhutanese never locked their houses, even in towns; why should guests? The mealtime whims of tourists didn't make sense, either. "I bring six-o'clock breakfast; he says I want seven," she groused one day after apologizing when I got tea instead of coffee for the third consecutive morning. "At night he says eight o'clock next day; next morning at six forty-five he says where is toast, tea. Fire is out."

The occasion for this outburst was the impending arrival of a German tour group, whose list of demands and special orders had preceded them across the Black Mountains. Wangdicholing was being cleaned from one end to the other with Teutonic thoroughness by a staff that had worked out what each nationality expected of a hotel. Malingering guests had been evicted or forced to double up so that the staff would be spared having to tell the arriving Germans they were staying somewhere else. Somewhere else in Bumthang can be a bleak experience best symbolized by outdoor latrines and cold-water washes, if not tents hastily pitched in meadows to the astonishment of cows. This Sunday, the grounds had been scoured for minute bits of trash, and a general stoning of stray dogs had cleared the yard of animal life.

Nonetheless, by midday the situation had started to deteriorate. The guesthouse was out of bottled water, a sad-faced waiter announced, noting that "Americans drank it all." It was just as well he didn't catch the brief return of the most despised of all the outcast dogs—a pretty, long-haired, reddish mongrel whose appearance among the pack of regular kitchen-door beggars inexplicably provoked the staff into a special frenzy of shooing. Dogs everywhere in Bhutan recognize an insistent "Ssh! Ssh! Ssh!" not as an order to be quiet but as an invitation to get lost. This pariah dog, in the ultimate get-even gesture, sniffed its way to the benches arranged in a small square under a warm noonday sun on the lawn outside the dining room and chose a strategic spot, just easy enough to miss but certain to be stepped on, in which to deposit a generous pile of feces.

The water-guzzling Americans being evicted from rooms in the face of a German advance that Sunday were the kind of tourists Bhutanese consider most fascinating. There were twelve of them in this group, and they had come to study Bhutanese Buddhism. It was their great good fortune that Robert Thurman, the Tibetan scholar and head of Columbia University's religion department, had joined the trip as mentor. A Buddhist, he was also on a journey of discovery, making his first trip to Bhutan after a lifetime of studying Tibet and Tantric Buddhism. A few others in the group considered themselves Buddhists but had never experienced life in a Buddhist environment as pervasive as this, particularly in rural settings where religion is marked by unexamined ritualism and unself-conscious practice.

The theological core of Buddhism was embellished here long ago with the enthusiastic worship of unorthodox spirits and legendary local saints, a bewildering prospect for the Western intellectual whose understanding of the religion is more spiritual or cerebral. Predictably, some of the Americans had brought their metaphorical hair shirts to don when bemoaning the lack of spiritualism in the materialistic West—only to run into uncomprehending young Bhutanese who had had enough of material renunciation and wanted nothing more than the chance to wallow in consumerism. As if to illustrate the point, one of them stole an American pilgrim's Walkman.

Older Bhutanese, even when critical of the corrupting influence of foreign guests, are often the most appreciative of outsiders who come to learn and share. Aum Rinzi told me that she is cheered by even the half-understood or intrinsically therapeutic Buddhism of mainstream America and Europe. "I don't think our religion will ever fade; that is impossible," she said. "It can only grow and prosper, because nowadays you'll find followers in Western countries. I am very interested to see that wherever in the Buddhist world there is a sermon being preached by a famous lama, Westerners go there and listen. Some have taken religious robes. They know that only ignorant people—fools—will ignore our beliefs."

From Tshering Hamo's point of view, the Americans at Wangdicholing that weekend were distinguished in more practical ways. At dawn, the California writer Sam Keen, one of the leaders of the group, would go out and select and chop his own firewood. He had some tips for the hotel on how to better utilize the woodstoves. In fact, he recommended that they should be replaced with more efficient and environmentally sound American models. Tshering had not known that some Americans heated their homes this way. Sam—author of the best-seller *Fire in the Belly* and a recognized founder of a post-feminist male self-esteem movement, who had been described all around town as rich and famous—seemed an unlikely candidate for a bukhari. He soon told us that he heated a thirty-two-foot West Coast living room with wood. In talking about this, Tshering and I didn't get into the question of the size or price of Sam's bukhari—or of the necessity of chimneys in places like northern California. Most rural Bhutanese houses don't have them. The smoke just collects in rooms, stinging eyes and polluting lungs, until it can find its way out a window or through the roof of an upper story, blackening the whitewashed outside wall as it goes.

Coincidentally, that same week Bumthang (in its role-model role) had been playing host to a group of women from around the country who were being taught to build and operate smokeless cooking stoves. Camped out in a fallow field a mile or so from town, the women, from unmarried teenagers to middle-aged householders, were digging clay from the earth, packing and pounding it into molds made of boards, and scooping out tunnels for air to circulate and exit cleanly through an exhaust system made of tin sheeting.

Wood burns slowly in these clay stoves, saving fuel while radiating heat from earthen constructions that can be built (or replaced) at a very low cost almost anywhere in the country. The women, a couple dozen of them who were expected to pass on their knowledge of this economical and health-enhancing technology to their neighbors after returning home, lived together as students in dormitory-style tents, attended study sessions in another tent heated by a homemade barrel stove filled with smoldering sawdust, bathed in a pool warmed by hot stones, and ate in the sun near a mess tent where tea always bubbled and rice steamed.

Chatting with visitors as they worked beside rows of finished stoves that would be broken up and recycled into the earth when the course ended, the women said they had not met resistance from husbands or fathers when they were chosen for training that would take them far from home for several weeks. But the presence of so many attractive women camped out in a meadow in his bailiwick gave the dzongda of Bumthang, Pem Dorji, some cause for concern. So he let it be known around town that the campsite was off limits to curious and predatory local men. Bhutanese are not puritanical about sexual relations, and physical relationships are easily formed and broken, with or without marriage. The dzongda had devised a policy that balanced his responsibilities with the realities of youth.

"I put up a notice that says, 'No Men,'" he said. "And I came down here and told the girls if you see any man apart from the instructor on the site, you can catch him, beat him up, tie him down, and bring him to me for punishment. I'll put him in jail.

"But on the other hand," he added, "if you go to the Sunday market and see a boy you like, and your minds click and your bodies click and you become pregnant—well, that's your problem."

That crisp and sunny Sunday in Bumthang had begun with meditation for the Americans. Gathered in the Wangdicholing Guesthouse's largest suite, its curtains drawn and a warming fire in a rather more substantial bukhari (the fire courtesy of Sam), the Americans, with eyes closed and legs akimbo, were at work trying to see inside their souls from outside themselves. Members of the heterogeneous group—a psychologist, writers, a retired businessman, and at least one Wall Street financier among them—had more or less auditioned by essay for an expensive trip that promised to immerse and instruct them while trundling them across more than three hundred miles of Bhutanese wilderness. Like many Americans encountered in the Himalayas and India, at least a few of these travelers seemed to be looking for themselves as much as for that elusive, superior Eastern sense of priorities we seem to think leads to contentment and fulfillment. Indeed, part of the tour was devoted to seminar sessions in which they were asked to tell their life stories with brutal honesty and candor—"their hungry hells as well as better times," explained Brent Olson of Inner Asia Expeditions of San Francisco, who organized the esoteric trip and came along to direct the logistics. Brent, who had been making several visits a year to Bhutan for nearly a decade, was obviously the arbiter and soother of ruffled feelings among his high-sensitivity charges. But then, almost anyone could have trouble coping all at once with high-altitude mountain terrain, intense introspection, and mind-draining meditation, punctuated by cold nights and hot chilis.

Some of the Americans had brought a supply of dried soup in packets to guard against intestinal tragedies while traversing the unknown culinary landscape. The instant-food packet is now widely recognized in Asia as the universal hallmark mostly of Japanese tourists, who are capable of traversing whole countries without having to order anything more in local restaurants than giant thermoses of boiling water. Newly affluent and often devout Japanese are coming to Bhutan, as they are now visiting Nepal, Burma, Sri Lanka, and India, on pilgrimages to Buddhism's holiest and earliest landmarks. An unknown number of them apparently move around these less developed nations (relatively luxurious Sri Lanka excepted) sleeping on nothing other than their own peripatetic sheets and quilts, which they hang out to air in the morning sun. In Burma several years ago, a group of nervous Japanese sat down to dinner at a table near mine in the Strand Hotel's pre-renovation dining room and ordered only bowls and cups with their hot water. They produced from their airline carry-on bags many envelopes of dried noodles, broths, crackers, seasonings, cookies, and tea bags. But then, unlike the smug among us, they probably didn't have to spend a night on some cold bathroom floor after eating sliced mangoes apparently laced with invisible tap water.

The Americans in Bumthang that Sunday had sped away from Thimphu a few days earlier in their tourist vans to follow the roller-coaster Lateral Road, the country's only east-west highway, across Bhutan to Tashigang for an important monastery festival. Bumthang was as far as they got. Carsickness had felled nearly half their number; others seemed to be in justifiable shock from the toilets at Gantey, the first overnight stop. The majority, not wanting to spend all their time on this serpentine road, had no trouble deciding to vote for mercy and succumb to the embrace of this valley of pastures, gentle slopes, evergreen forests, and a rushing stream. Temples, monasteries, and natural sites of intense holiness promised real-time seminars. Cloaked in the approval of Her Majesty the Queen Mother, who supported Sam Keen's plan to film the trip (and Bhutan) for American television, they could enter forbidden recesses of Bhutanese worship. There was no better place to crash than Bumthang.

Bumthang can comfortably draw outsiders in small numbers into its remarkable daily life—market town, destination of pilgrims, center of agricultural experimentation—without making a single major concession to foreign guests that would alter the quality of the place. The word is getting around, however, that Bumthang offers almost everything a visitor comes to Bhutan to experience and enjoy, including gentle terrain for treks that are more like walks through a medieval landscape of hamlets and monasteries. Just arriving in Bumthang is a pleasure.

When the road from Tongsa descends from the Yutong La and drifts into the Chumey Valley—one of four usually wide (for Bhutan) open spaces that together form the district of Bumthang—the soft beauty of the landscape is enhanced by the traveler's relief that tortuous roads and dark mountain gorges have been left behind and that the way ahead is enveloped in broad, sunny fields of buckwheat and potatoes. Twig fences that line the road sprout shoots; wildflowers of gold and white color fallow land where animals graze on thick green grass. Small farming settlements of only six or seven houses shelter sturdy temples and monasteries. Zugney village, a town of weavers, claims a seventh-century Tibetan temple. At Domkhar, an old palace is being transformed into a Buddhist center. This is all only a preview of what is to come in the heart of Bumthang, just beyond another (but not too difficult) mountain pass, the 9,515-foot Kiki La. There lies the Chokhor Valley and Jakar, the district's largest commercial center and base for exploring the region. The last two Bumthang valleys, Tang and Ura, both wilder and steeper, home more to yaks than cows, are farther to the east.

Jakar itself is doomed. The town—one street and a roundish empty space that everyone treats as a traffic circle, steering carefully around its circumference—is no more than a collection of a few dozen wooden shacks and more substantial two-story buildings that house general-merchandise shops, a branch bank, a struggling handicrafts store, and numerous teashops or "hotels," which are really restaurants of sorts serving the cross-country travelers for whom Bumthang is an important stop. Off to one side, a jump across a narrow brook, is a Sunday marketplace, where traders lay out for sale dried fish from Assam, tropical produce from southern Bhutan, parkas from China, and Indian-made running shoes. The flaw is that all the activity in Jakar is concentrated between two bridges—one over a tributary brook, the other spanning the river—that define a flood plain along the tumbling, swift stream of the Bumthang Chhu. Dasho Pem Dorji, the dzongda of Bumthang, plans to tear it all down and rebuild on higher ground.

The dasho always means what he says. For several years he has been on a sanitation crusade in Bumthang, and he enforces it with a reign of terror. He stalks the byways of Jakar and the villages of the surrounding hills and valleys, paying unannounced visits to hidden corners of backyards in search of stashed trash. Children flee noiselessly but speedily at his approach. Grabbing whatever stick is at hand, he attacks discarded tires, paper scraps, and plastic bags, ordering grown men into the street to pick up the mess publicly. Fines are liberally awarded on the spot.

"The fear is there, and they have to do it," he said as we bounced along in his Land Cruiser one day. "Once they learn, I remove all the punishments. One and a half years back I was disliked," he acknowledged, leaving the rest of us to wonder how he judged his popularity at this point. "Of course, I went maybe a bit too far, beating up about four people. But later they realized that having a clean environment around their own households was for their own good. Most of the villagers, you know, walk barefoot. That worm that enters through the foot could be wiped out, so the cleanup is a preventive measure. Second thing, if they have a clean stove, eye problems will be solved. If you have clean drinking water, then all the diseases like diarrhea, dysentery, cholera can be prevented. Similarly, if you have a healthy body, then for so much development and field work you want to do, there can be good participation.

"You see a lot of smokes coming up from the villages?" he asked, sweeping his arm triumphantly over the surrounding mountains. "They're burning up their dirt!"

The dasho, an agriculture expert of some standing, says he became an apostle of sanitation in a Christian boarding school in the Indian hill station of Kalimpong, where Scottish missionaries made all the boys clean their own rooms and bathrooms. The relationship between cleanliness and progress (if not godliness) was seared into his soul by those austere Presbyterians of Dr. Graham's Homes, the school where many Bhutanese boys have been educated over the past three-quarters of a century. The legacy of J. A. Graham, who had been a tutor of Bhutan's second king and was founder of the school, is imprinted across the Himalayas in small pockets of order. Graduates now in their thirties and forties also account for a significant part of the Himalayan intellectual and literary elite.

Dasho Pem Dorji says he was impressed by the equality and sense of responsibility he learned in Kalimpong, a town that more than a century ago was Bhutanese. When he heard recently that the more affluent shopkeepers of Jakar were thinking of hiring Indian outcaste "sweepers" to do their cleaning for them, as Thimphu property owners do, he forbade the practice before it began in Bumthang. Instead, he placed green bins labeled "Use Me" around shops and in settlements, and ordered that the townspeople start learning to pick up their own rubbish. A blizzard of edicts flowed from his feudal sword.

"You want to sell sweets?" he asked rhetorically. "If the people who come to your shop throw sweet papers, it is your duty to pick them up and tell them, put rubbish in the Use Me box. Every week, I've asked the district engineer to dig eight-by-eight-foot temporary pits where they will throw the rubbish from the Use Me bins, and they will burn it. Every Sunday I will inspect. If they don't clean up, the first punishment is a one-hundred-ngultrum [about four dollars] fine. The second punishment is one week of sweeping the town. The third punishment is carrying three weeks of stone to the dzong without payment. This has to be done to teach people, you dirty, you clean. If your dzongda can clean his own bathroom, you can clean your own rubbish. So this is the thing I am trying to teach. I hope to succeed in a year."

Later in the safety of a cluttered shop, the proprietor, who had been sitting on a stool watching the dasho cut a swath through someone's shed, allowed that the dzongda had made a difference to the quality of life—or anyway, the cleanliness of gutters and the narrow earthen streets he had ordered paved with stone for drainage. "The people are all scared of him," she said. "But after he goes? They'll go back to the old ways." She shrugged and grinned. But she wiped the counter and tidied up some sacks just in case. Her small daughter streaked past with a surprised puppy about to be thrown out the door.

This Sunday in Bumthang, it was the turn of the dzongda's deputy, the *dzongrab,* Khandu Tshering, to make the weekly inspection tour. We dropped in on the Sunday market. Stallholders rushed forward to present their best *domas,* betel chews, to the dzongrab, an elegant older gentleman in a spotless black gho and silken knee socks whose air of reserve and deliberation served as a perfect foil to the manic style of the dzongda. The dzongrab may have commanded more respect than fear, but a lot of subtle, even furtive, tidying up was going on all around him nonetheless. On the way back to Wangdicholing, with the dzongrab at the wheel, we inadvertently hit a dog headed toward the dzong but did it no evident harm.

Dzongrab Khandu Tshering cares a lot about sanitation, too, he said as he sat for a while in the Wangdicholing Guesthouse garden answering questions from me and from Kate Wyatt, a psychologist in the American seminar group, who was eager to know whether life in Buddhist Bhutan had its built-in buffers against psychological strain and mental illness. The dzongrab did not disappoint her. He said that stress and psychological problems were not a major concern among the Bhutanese, who often turn to a lama for help in the kind of personal crisis that would send an urbanized Westerner to a psychiatrist or analyst. In Thimphu, I had heard of a young man educated in Australia who on his return was unable to reconcile himself to Bhutanese family life and worship. He had gone to a lama for advice. Together, he and the lama were negotiating their way through Buddhism to help the young man understand what his ancestors' faith could still offer a science graduate who had ceased to believe in the myths and rituals on which he was raised.

"In many ways, maybe a lama can help head off mental problems," the dzongrab said. But he had reservations about jumping to the conclusion that Buddhism can unfailingly provide balm for troubled minds. "It is entirely dependent on the individual who is mentally in trouble. When he goes to lama, lama will from different angles try to make him understand by telling all the good things about religion. Some can change their minds and outlook after listening to the holy lamas. Some will not. We are not all the same."

Dzongrab Khandu Tshering—a tall man with a strong, high-cheekboned, tanned and weathered face that would become an ancient warrior—was introduced to me as a former "royal compounder" and a repository of information on the history of medicine in Bhutan. He began his career in the 1950s as a master of traditional remedies before Bhutan had Western-style doctors or any significant interchange with the outside world. He had been witness to a medical revolution.

"A compounder is just like a pharmacist," he explained in his quiet, methodical manner. "He made some diagnoses and gave medicine, because at that time there was not a qualified doctor in the country. A few Bhutanese were beginning to be trained abroad as doctors, but in the meantime, the government established dispensaries in all the districts to look after the ill people. Three of us were taught first locally in Bhutan and India. After three years, we three were sent for further training in a mission hospital in Kalimpong. We were there for two and a half more years. Local diagnosis and treatment we learned from there. After finishing the course, we came back, and I joined in Tongsa district in 1957 as district in charge. I was in Tongsa as dispensary in charge for twelve years. After that I was posted to the old Thimphu General Hospital, just near the dzong, where I was training officer and head compounder. In 1972, during the coronation time, the new general hospital in Thimphu was opened, and again I was appointed as administrative officer." A few years later, he was moved out of health and into general administration, reaching the highest levels of royal government service.

"Now I don't have any time to concentrate on the medical system. But sometimes, when I go to villages on tour, I explain to the public personal hygiene, cleaning up and that sort of thing," the dzongrab said. "The health of the people is far better now than earlier. In the ancient time, there was VD; now there is no VD at all. In the ancient time, there was a lot of this tuberculosis. Now there is very little tuberculosis; it has been controlled a lot. There was a lot of goiter. Now we have very few because we have iodized."

Family planning has been more difficult, even in this progressive district. "Those who have understood the benefits are coming forward themselves," he said. "But the main thing is that most of the Bhutanese are religious-minded people and believe that religion says, if you do family planning it is one of the great sins. The people keep this in mind. So most of them don't want to undergo family planning. So now we, from all the different angles—from administrative side, from medical side—we're trying to convince them that three, four is okay, but more than four is very difficult to maintain. They can't give the education properly to their children, the clothing, everything. It is a great problem."

Bumthang has a model hospital that, like smaller clinics elsewhere, is designed to bridge quite literally new and older forms of medicine. The building has two wings: one for traditional methods of healing and one for Westernized care. Patients are encouraged to move across the sheltered walkway between the traditional and modern wings depending on their instincts and the nature of their illnesses or injuries. In Bumthang, the dzongrab said, efforts are also being made to wean people away from a reliance on lamas in times of illness. Throughout Bhutan, where most villages have basic health units but hospitals are few and widely scattered, precious hours can be lost when a sick person first goes or is taken to a monastery or temple to undergo healing rituals.

"If there is some evil, some spiritual problem, the lama can do something by worship of the god, doing some *puja* or something like that, something traditional," the dzongrab said. "But it is also very necessary to use hospitals. The local people, most of them rely on religion first, then on medicine. Now we have been trying to convince them whenever they feel unwell—something cold, hot, something like that—then and there they must attend a medical person. We try to explain this to them. And on the lamas' side, also, we have a program. We try to use them as media. All the lamas go on invitation to villages frequently. So the government thought, maybe also we can use the lamas as messengers, so that they can also motivate the people to go to the hospital when they find someone sick. So we are using the lamas like the women's associations and the posters as motivators for progress."

Because Bumthang has as easy a relationship with foreigners as it has with new ideas, it is an especially good candidate for experimental development projects. One of the first to succeed here was the Swiss Dairy, built by the Swiss development agency, Helvetas. The agency also gave Bumthang one of its most eccentric and beloved citizens, Fritz Maurer, who came to help and stayed to marry a Bhutanese woman and raise a family in an alpine setting not unlike that of a high Swiss valley. Not satisfied with milk alone, Maurer has branched into a line of delicatessen products produced in a processing plant in a hamlet across the Bumthang Chhu from Jakar and sold in a small shop next door that doubles as a bar and tearoom.

His gho casually askew, workworn, and soiled in the tradition of the Bhutanese countryside, Maurer walks briskly through the small cheese factory and drink-bottling plant that has made Bumthang the gourmet capital of the country. Words like "factory" and "plant" need some elaboration in the Bumthang context. The Fauchons of Bhutan is a large shed with a perennially puddled concrete floor around the sloshing bottle washers and rumbling brewery vats that make juices and alcoholic drinks from local produce. But open a heavy door to the cheese works and you are led to a cool, dry, dark room to stand in the presence of world-class Emmentaler, Gruyère, or maybe Gorgonzola, depending on what kind the cheesemaster is concentrating on that week.

"Have some, and tell me what you think," Maurer says, slicing through a Gorgonzola wheel and extracting a creamy slice of pungent cheese. "We're still working on this; I'm not sure it's right yet." We go next door to the small outlet-shop-cum-café for biscuits, juice, and coffee to round out the feast. The cheese is superb. No wonder this unusual local product is sold out as soon as a batch is ready for marketing. News that a new shipment of cheese or apple juice or honey from Bumthang has arrived in Thimphu, more than a hundred miles away, can cause a stampede to Shop Number Seven, the exclusive purveyor in the Bhutanese capital for the specialties of Bumthang. All over the country, people taste-test some new alcoholic concoction to emerge from Bumthang's vats: herbal brandy, for example, or an unusual fruit wine.

The little shop-café next to the cheese works, where Bhutanese and foreigners vie for Maurer's specialties, seems to be striving for an ambience to match its international reputation. While waiting one day for the dzongda to return from one of his impromptu sanitation inspections, I took an inventory of the decor. To the sound of monks chanting in the next room, the storekeeper's family temple, I counted more than twenty photographs of Switzerland pasted to the walls of the two-table café, along with a picture of a South Indian temple, two Sylvester Stallone posters, a picture of a Druk Air BAE-146, and another of Kai Tak Airport in Hong Kong. Most intriguing was a glossy portrait of a kitten wedged in a gigantic hamburger roll, with layers of cheese, lettuce, and tomatoes on its furry head. An inscription read, in full: "You cannot omelettes without breaking eggs."

I asked Fritz Maurer once if he ever misses Switzerland. He didn't seem to think the question meant much. "I go back now and then," he said. "But I am happy here. And I could live anywhere, I think—except in a hot tropical place." He had been to Bangkok, which he fled.

Heiko Dekena, a German horticulturist who came to Bhutan more recently to help the Bhutanese develop a seed industry, was more effusive when I went to visit his National Seed and Plant Production Program's experimental farm just before dusk on a long, lazy Sunday in Bumthang. Dekena, a crisply tailored, no-nonsense administrator, had spent decades in the developing world, mostly in Africa and Asia, and this would be his last assignment before retirement, he explained. Hardened by years of working in environments of violence and corruption, he was unprepared for Bhutan. After a wonderfully productive year in the country, he was ready to stay a decade. Coolly scientific when talking about his seed-producing plants, he suddenly became passionate on the subject of Bhutan and the Bhutanese.

"I feel for this country with my whole heart," he said, as we drove up a trackless hillside, fording crystal streams to reach the seed fields. "I love Bhutan so much, like I have never fallen in love with any other place. This is one of the advantages of my work here. It makes life for us very easy. I have no problems at all. I find so much understanding and intelligence. If I want to explain something, I really have interested listeners. I have never felt it so easy to come close to the people."

As the sun was sinking, Heiko Dekena and I returned to the Bhutanese house he and his wife, Cristel, have furnished and decorated with the work of local craftspeople. He reminded me it was the first Sunday in Advent, and there was a homemade *Apfelkuchen* for the occasion, along with coffee and a bowlful of whipped fresh local cream. Around a handsome table in that cozy room glowing with golden wood paneling, we might have been in Bavaria, or a small town in Switzerland, *Schlagsahne* and all.

It was not only comfort that the Dekenas had found here in Bumthang, but also trust and friendship. The adaptable Bhutanese meet outsiders as equals and work as colleagues, giving or taking advice as the moment requires. There is great integrity and wisdom here, Dekena said, as he walked through the barnyard of his high-altitude experimental farm sloping down from a hilltop over nine thousand feet above the Bumthang Valley. Expensive imported farm machinery is left undisturbed in isolated, unlocked sheds. Dekena said he could leave a million dollars on the table in his office and it would not be touched. In return, he says, he tries to understand without criticizing the farming methods of the rural Bhutanese, who he believes are depleting the land and degrading seed stock by overworking small plots in traditional ways.

"I can't call it primitive, because there is nothing on earth that is primitive," he said. "It's just a different way of life, a different way of working. When people have lived here for such a long period, then we have to accept that. But on the other side, we are here to improve something. It's not a question of being critical. It's more or less asking whether if something is going on on the right side maybe it is also possible to do it on the left side, and so on. Just to give the idea."

From what Dekena has seen and experienced in Bumthang, he believes that Bhutan stands a good chance of developing its small economy without losing its spiritual culture or destroying the rural social fabric—or the village farming system—because it came into the foreign-aid game late, after many other countries had made serious mistakes. He applauds the determination of the royal government to make its own decisions, not to be whipsawed by powerful international agencies with prepackaged programs and agendas of their own, often concocted in cultural vacuums continents away.

He is so convinced of Bhutan's potential for success that he has decided if Germany will not see his seed program through several planting and harvesting cycles, he will ask Bhutan to allow him to stay as a private citizen-expert. He made this point in an audience with King Jigme Singye Wangchuck, an event he describes as "a great honor." In that thirty-minute conversation, he said, "I committed myself to His Majesty."

And so a modern seed-producing farm with European technology flowers on a hill not far from the holy spot where the Guru Rinpoche's walking stick took root and produced a miraculous tree. There is room in Bumthang's heart—and maybe Bhutan's—for both. For many Bhutanese, this is critical to their survival and maybe to their brand of mountain-grown Buddhism. There is an unspoken sense that somewhere a place must be saved for the Buddha's next appearance on earth.

"From this place, since early times," records the Special Commission on Cultural Affairs, "arose kings and ministers, scholars and saints. Here were built marvelous, sacred temples. This glorious tradition will remain alive: such illustrious personages and such magnificent structures for worship will continue to appear in Bumthang, which is destined to be the seat of the future Buddha Maitreya"—the Buddha-to-come.

AN AFTERTHOUGHT

ONE AFTERNOON in Kathmandu, I sat down for a while to draw on the wisdom of His Holiness Ngawang Tenzing Zangbo, the abbot of Tengboche monastery, which rests in the lap of Mount Everest. I asked him how much it mattered whether or not the last Himalayan Buddhist kingdom, Bhutan, survived.

"As far as the survival of the Bhutanese is concerned," he answered, "I believe this: We must work everywhere to save our religion and culture, not in Bhutan alone. Ladakh, Sikkim, Bhutan, Nepal—everywhere in the Himalayas."

The rinpoche fears the effects of materialistic success on Buddhism; for him, hewing to Buddhist purity is central to the salvation process. But he also said that all Himalayan Buddhists and those who value their teachings should ponder the hubris of Tibet, where he studied.

"In Tibet they thought that Tibet was the only one, and that this would last for all time. Tibet had everything, and kept everything to itself. When that went, everything went.

"Now we know that our religion must be preserved everywhere. Only that way can we also save Bhutan."

A GLOSSARY
OF COMMON WORDS

bukhari Bhutanese metal woodstove
chhu river
chogyal king in Tibet or Sikkim
chorten; stupa; chaitya religious monument, square or dome-shaped in a variety
  of sizes, often containing relics of a holy man or religious scripts and objects
dasho nonhereditary title conferred on high officials in Bhutan
dewan Indian adviser to chogyal of Sikkim, functioning as prime minister
druk dragon; thunder or thunder dragon
Druk Gyalpo king of Bhutan or the Drukpas; translated ceremonially as Precious
  Ruler of the Dragon People
Druk Yul Kingdom of the Thunder Dragon; Bhutan
dzong Himalayan monastery-fortress; in Bhutan, headquarters of a dzonkhag
dzongda; dzongdag district administrator in Bhutan
dzongpon administrator of semiautonomous subregion in Bhutan
dzongrab deputy district administrator in Bhutan
dzonkhag administrative district in Bhutan
gho national dress for men in Bhutan
gomchen lay religious leader in Bhutanese villages
gompa monastery
je khenpo Buddhist head abbot in Bhutan
kabne scarf showing rank in Bhutan
khenpo Buddhist abbot
kira national dress for women in Bhutan
la mountain pass
lam road or street
lama religious teacher who may or may not be a monk
lhakhang temple
ngultrum Bhutanese monetary unit, worth about 3.3 cents

penlop regional governor in Bhutan

rinpoche religious teacher or scholar

sadhu Hindu mendicant holy man

terton discoverer or revealer of Buddhist treasures or writings

thangka religious painting mounted on a silk or brocaded scroll

thrimpon magistrate in Bhutan

torma flour-and-butter cake left as a temple offering

tshechu religious festival held in a dzong

tsho lake or other body of water

tulku a reincarnate lama

BIBLIOGRAPHY

Adamson, Hilary, and Isobel Shaw. *A Traveller's Guide to Pakistan*. Islamabad: Asian Study Group, 1981.

Ali, Salim. *Field Guide to the Birds of the Eastern Himalayas*. Delhi: Oxford University Press, 1986.

Aris, Michael. *Sources for the History of Bhutan*. Vienna: Arbeitskreis für Tibetische und Buddhistische Studien, 1986.

Aris, Michael. *Bhutan: The Early History of a Himalayan Kingdom*. Warminster, England: Aris & Phillips, 1979.

Aris, Michael. *Views of Medieval Bhutan: The Diary and Drawings of Samuel Davis 1783*. London: Serindia Publications; Washington: Smithsonian Institution Press, no date.

Bechert, Heinz, and Richard Gombrich, eds. *The World of Buddhism*. London: Thames & Hudson, 1984.

Beckwith, Christopher I. *The Tibetan Empire in Central Asia*. Princeton: Princeton University Press, 1993.

Collister, Peter. *Bhutan and the British*. London: Serindia Publications, 1987.

Das, Nirmala. *The Dragon Country*. New Delhi: Orient Longman, 1974.

Das, Sarat Chandra. *Journey to Lhasa and Central Tibet*. New Delhi: Bibliotheca Himalayica, Manjusri Publishing House, 1970.

Datta-Ray, Sunanda K. *Smash and Grab: The Annexation of Sikkim*. New Delhi: Vikas Publishing House, 1984.

David-Neel, Alexandra. *Magic and Mystery in Tibet*. Calcutta: Rupa and Co., 1989.

Dilgo Khyentse Rinpoche. *The Excellent Path to Enlightenment of Jamyang Khyentse Wangpo*. Boulder, Colo.: Nalanda Translation Committee, 1987.

Donden, Yeshi. *Health Through Balance*. Ithaca, N.Y.: Snow Lion Publications, 1986.

Evans-Wentz, W. Y., ed. *Tibet's Great Yogi Milarepa*. London: Oxford University Press, 1928.

Fisher, James F. *Sherpas: Reflections on Change in Himalayan Nepal*. New Delhi: Oxford University Press, 1990.

Foning, A. R. *Lepcha My Vanishing Tribe.* Bangalore: Sterling Publishers, 1987.

Getty, Alice. *The Gods of Northern Buddhism, Their History and Iconography.* New York: Dover Publications, 1988. Reprint of a 1928 Clarendon Press edition, published in Oxford.

Guenther, Herbert V., and Chogyam Trungpa. *The Dawn of Tantra.* Boston: Shambhala Publications, 1975.

Harvey, Andrew. *A Journey in Ladakh.* Boston: Houghton Mifflin, 1983.

Hasrat, Bikrama Jit. *History of Bhutan: Land of the Peaceful Dragon.* Thimphu: Royal Government of Bhutan, 1980.

Himal magazine, Vol. 6, No. 5. "Whither the Tsampa Eaters? Confused Identities in the Tibetan Borderlands." Kathmandu: Himal Association, 1993. An issue devoted almost entirely to articles on the Tibetan-speaking ethnic groups of Nepal and how they relate to other Tibetan peoples.

Hopkins, Jeffrey, ed. and trans. *Tantric Practice in Nyingma: Instructions by Khetsun Sangpo Rinbochay.* London: Rider, 1982.

Hopkins, Jeffrey. *The Tantric Distinction: An Introduction to Tibetan Buddhism.* London: Wisdom Publications, 1984.

Kapur, Kusum. *Tales from Dragon Country.* New Delhi: Mosaic Books, 1991.

Karan, P. P. *Bhutan: Environment, Culture and Development Strategy.* New Delhi: Intellectual Publishing House, 1990.

Marshall, Sir John, *A Guide to Taxila.* Cambridge: University Press (for the Department of Archeology of Pakistan), 1960.

Mierow, Dorothy, and Tirtha Bahadur Shrestha. *Himalayan Flowers and Trees.* Kathmandu: Sahayogi Press, 1978.

Norberg-Hodge, Helena. *Ancient Futures: Learning from Ladakh.* San Francisco: Sierra Club Books, 1991.

Parmanand. *The Politics of Bhutan: Retrospect and Prospect.* Delhi: Pragati Publications, 1992.

Pedron, Yeshi, and Jeremy Russell, eds. *Cho Yang, Year of Tibet Edition.* New Delhi: Council of Religious and Cultural Affairs of H.H. the Dalai Lama, 1991.

Pommaret, Françoise. *An Illustrated Guide to Bhutan.* Hong Kong: Guidebook Company, 1990.

Rawson, Philip. *The Art of Tantra.* New York: Oxford University Press, 1978.

Rawson, Philip. *Sacred Tibet.* London: Thames & Hudson, 1991.

Rizvi, Janet. *Ladakh: Crossroads of High Asia.* New Delhi: Oxford University Press, 1989.

Rockhill, William Woodville. *The Land of the Lamas.* London: Longmans, Green, 1891.

Ronaldshay, Lord. *Himalayan Bhutan, Sikhim and Tibet.* New Delhi: Ess Ess Publications, 1977.

Rose, Leo. *The Politics of Bhutan.* Ithaca, N.Y.: Cornell University Press, 1977.

Royal Government of Bhutan. *A Geography of Bhutan.* Volumes for Class VI, VII, and VIII. Thimphu: Department of Education, 1991–92.

Royal Government of Bhutan. *A History of Bhutan.* Volumes for Class VI, VII, and VIII. Thimphu: Department of Education, 1990–92.

Shearer, Alistair. *Buddha: The Intelligent Heart.* London: Thames & Hudson, 1992.

Sherubtse College, Bhutan. *Bhutan and Its Natural Resources.* New Delhi: Vikas, 1991.

Snellgrove, David L. *Himalayan Pilgrimage.* Boston: Shambhala, 1989.

Snellgrove, David L. *Indo-Tibetan Buddhism: Indian Buddhists and Their Tibetan Successors.* London: Serindia Publications, 1987.

Snellgrove, David L., and Tadeusz Skorupski. *The Cultural Heritage of Ladakh*. Vol. 1. *Central Ladakh*. New Delhi: Vikas, 1977.

Snelling, John. *The Buddhist Handbook*. Rochester, Vt.: Inner Traditions, 1991.

Tenzin Gyatso, the Fourteenth Dalai Lama, et al. *Tree of Life: Buddhism and the Protection of Nature*. Geneva: Buddhist Perception of Nature, 1987.

Thapa, Manjushree. *Mustang Bhot in Fragments*. Kathmandu: Himal Books, 1992.

Thondup, Tulku Rinpoche. *Buddhist Civilization in Tibet*. New York: Routledge & Kegan Paul, 1987.

Upasak, C. S. *History of Buddhism in Afghanistan*. Varanasi: Central Institute of Higher Tibetan Studies, 1990.

White, John Claude. *Sikkim and Bhutan*. New Delhi: Cosmos Publications, 1984.

Williamson, Margaret D. *Memoirs of a Political Officer's Wife in Tibet, Sikkim and Bhutan*. London: Wisdom Publications, 1987.

ACKNOWLEDGMENTS

MANY PEOPLE in the Himalayas helped and inspired me in the writing of this book, and an exhaustive list would be impossible to compile, since countless men and women and lots of children whose names I never knew—monks, novices, students, householders, shopkeepers, artisans, practitioners of traditional medicine, and farmers among them—all contributed something to my impressions and understanding, if only in fleeting encounters. In Bhutan, the last country in the world where Himalayan Buddhism and a Tibetan-based language have official status, a number of government officials, initially wary of journalists, gave hours of their time in conversations about their country and its policies. Two of them, Foreign Minister Dawa Tsering and Home Minister Dago Tshering, also apparently smoothed the way for lengthy interviews with His Majesty, King Jigme Singye Wangchuck. Dzongdas, governors of the country's geopolitical districts, were unfailingly hospitable and made it possible for me to spend many hours in monasteries and temples normally closed to foreigners. In particular, I would like to thank Dasho Lhakpa Dorji, Dasho Pem Dorji, Dasho Phub Dorji, and Dasho Rinzin Gyetsin.

Sonam Tobgay, chief justice of the Bhutanese High Court, not only explained the functioning of a unique justice system that starts with the teachings of the Lord Buddha but also introduced me to a rich secular folklore. In matters of religion and culture, I owe much to Sangay Wangchuck, now director of Bhutan's National Library, and to Dasho

Rigzin Dorji of the Special Commission on Cultural Affairs. Sadly, Rigzin Dorji, a man of great verve and spirit, died as I was writing this book. Kinley Dorji, editor of *Kuensel* and the person who knows more than just about anyone about the stories and trends behind the news, has been both a source of information and the object of admiration as he steadily builds his newspaper into an independent voice in all of the nation's three official languages. During my years of reporting from Delhi, I was helped in understanding Tibetan Buddhism and its organizations in exile by His Holiness the Dalai Lama and his staff, especially Tashi Wangdi.

In New York, Ambassador Ugyen Tshering, head of Bhutan's United Nations mission, gave me many useful tips about the Bhutanese, and also helped me arrange trips to the country as an independent researcher with considerable freedom to travel. Robert A. F. Thurman, a Buddhist and scholar who at this writing is Jey Tsong Khapa Professor of Indo-Tibetan Studies at Columbia University, was willing to answer questions and give encouragement, although I certainly would not qualify as a student of Tibetology. Leo Rose of the University of California at Berkeley, a lifelong scholar of the mountain kingdoms and the author of several valuable books, provided me with introductions to Nepali experts, including Purna Harsha Bajracharya, a Newari Buddhist from a long lineage of scholars and the former head of Nepal's Archaeology Department. Purna Harsha was among those who initiated the excavations at Buddha's birthplace in Lumbini. In Kathmandu I was also helped by Charles Ramble, a British anthropologist and Tibetologist who has amassed a store of knowledge about the daily lives and prospects of Himalayan Buddhist communities, and by Kesang Tseten, a writer born in Tibet, who had many useful ideas and suggestions to share. Thanks also to Kanak Mani Dixit, founder and editor of *Himal,* for creating a magazine that—however controversial—is setting the agenda for intellectual debate across the region.

Everyone who travels in the Buddhist Himalayas owes an enormous debt to a small number of fine Western scholars who have devoted their lives to the difficult work of sorting legend from historical fact in a region replete with mysteries. David L. Snellgrove and Michael Aris are two on whose discoveries and analyses I relied most. Françoise Pommaret, a French expert in Tibetan Buddhism and author of the only cultural guide to Bhutan, was generous with her knowledge of the Himalayan kingdoms accumulated over years of travel and living in the region. I still have the rough family tree of Bhutan's Wangchuck dynasty that she sketched on the back of some scrap paper during an evening we spent in the restaurant of the Tushita Guesthouse in Kathmandu. Her *Illustrated Guide to Bhutan,* academically researched yet attuned to village life, filled an unusually wide gap in a country with few explanatory publications. With its glossaries and sensible standardizations of Bhutanese spellings, it became an encyclopedia.

In Ladakh, Helena Norberg-Hodge provided insights from more than a decade of work in a former kingdom trying to retain its identity. Several prominent Sikkimese, including some connected to the last chogyal and his family, spoke candidly to me about the sad history of that realm. They do not want to be identified, but they know who they are.

On a personal level, I owe thanks to Steven Powers, a family friend who at a still-youthful age has trekked over large areas of Nepal, Bhutan, Ladakh, and Sikkim in his years in the Himalayas. In Kathmandu, he provided many books I would not have found myself, along with names and phone numbers of people to meet, from rinpoches to some of the businessmen who are Buddhism's patrons. As always, I would never have been able to write this book without the encouragement and critical interest of my husband, David Wigg, who dissuaded me more than once from abandoning the project.

Finally, thanks go to Jonathan Segal, vice president and senior editor at Alfred A. Knopf, who was willing to take a chance on the esoteric idea of the Himalayan Buddhist world and its endangered civilization.

B.C.

INDEX